THE UNIVERSITY OF NEVADA, LAS VEGAS

The University of Nevada, Las Vegas

A HISTORY

Eugene P. Moehring

FOREWORD BY Carol C. Harter

UNIVERSITY OF NEVADA PRESS RENO AND LAS VEGAS

University of Nevada Press, Reno, Nevada 89557 USA
Copyright © 2007 by University of Nevada Press
All rights reserved
Manufactured in China
Design by Kathleen Szawiola

Library of Congress Cataloging-in-Publication Data

Moehring, Eugene P.
The University of Nevada, Las Vegas : a history /
Eugene P. Moehring ; foreword by Carol C. Harter.
    p.   cm.
Includes bibliographical references and index.
ISBN 978-0-87417-709-1 (hardcover : alk. paper)
1. University of Nevada, Las Vegas—History. I. Title.
LD3745.M64 2007
378.793'135—dc22   2007003381

FIRST PRINTING

16 15 14 13 12 11 10 09 08 07
5 4 3 2 1

Frontispiece: Aerial photograph of UNLV looking south,
ca. 1985. Special Collections, UNLV Libraries 0062-1007

For Maude Frazier, whose dream
and dedication to her students began it all.

"Our dreams are coming true, and from a small beginning, a
great campus will develop here"

—Maude Frazier at the groundbreaking ceremony
for Archie C. Grant Hall, May 11, 1958

CONTENTS

ILLUSTRATIONS

MAPS

A s UNLV prepares to embark on its historic 50th Anniversary Celebration, it is fitting that we commemorate this occasion with the publication of this book—*The University of Nevada, Las Vegas: A History*. I was pleased that UNLV professor Eugene Moehring agreed to take on the monumental task of assembling the stories, photographs, and historical documents associated with the university's rich fifty-year history.

As I read Dr. Moehring's text, I was struck over and over again with how apt our "rebel" name really is. From its very inception as little more than a collection of courses taught as an extension of UNR, UNLV—its faculty, staff, student leadership, and its enormously supportive community—has been fighting geopolitics for the entire history of the institution.

So much of what has been accomplished at UNLV is because of the "pioneering spirit" of those who came before us. What this book makes so clear is that UNLV has always relied on "the kindness of strangers" and the private sector to develop and advance its agenda.

Indeed, looking back—from Nevada Southern's early days in the mid-1950s to the university of today—it has always been clear that, given the rapid growth

PRESIDENT CAROL HARTER IN HER OFFICE. UNLV OFFICE OF
PUBLIC AFFAIRS IMAGE NO. D63600-24

of Las Vegas and the continued diversification of the economy, much of what
UNLV has accomplished in its fifty-years history has been dependent upon the
support of the very people the university serves.

Each decade in the university's development has produced academic
visionaries and benefactors without whom we would be a markedly inferior
university today. Every president has raised private funds that were the *sine qua
non* for that period's development, and each administration has helped move
the university forward in many important ways. We all stand on the shoulders
of those who toiled before us—committed to raising the level of excellence at
UNLV by partnering with community members and business leaders, because
we all know that there will not be enough state funding to create the premier

metropolitan research university that we are all striving to create here in southern Nevada.

The university's rich history is replete with stories of people who have seen the needs and have given unselfishly of personal, intellectual, and financial resources over many years. And the university's extended family—including alumni, community members, faculty, and staff—is proving to be increasingly generous in its commitments.

The publishing of this book as part of the 50th Anniversary demonstrates, in a very tangible way, the generosity, commitment, and vision that the Las Vegas community has had for its hometown institution. For some, you will recall the early days when "Tumbleweed Tech" was a mere two or three buildings on the dusty outskirts of town. For others, it is your recent memories of today's university, located in the heart of a bustling urban environment, that is dramatically and positively affecting the human community.

UNLV is indeed young—almost frontier-like in countless ways. But unlike the centuries it has taken to develop many prestigious eastern universities, UNLV's rapid rise in sophistication and entrepreneurship has far outpaced the slower development of major universities in other parts of the country. The development of pioneering programs and innovative research areas that reflect and serve the desert Southwest exemplifies the synergy between our "rebel" nature and our growing and dynamic Las Vegas community.

We are an institution of overachievers who have accomplished great things in the past fifty years and who plan to overachieve even more splendidly in the years to come. Future leaders of this university and community will, from this day forward—just as those before us—struggle to find the path to excellence and preeminence.

Carol C. Harter

In the fall of 2003 Carol Harter was UNLV's president, and she asked me to write a full-length history of the institution that would trace the school's development from its earliest days to the 50th anniversary of the campus in 2007. During the research process it became clear that from James Dickinson to the present, leadership has been critical to the school's advancement. Presidential chapters therefore occupy a good portion of the book, because all of these leaders helped the school progress to the next level. Supporting this effort were not only the faculty and the larger metropolitan community but also scores of influential donors. I also wanted to emphasize the importance of students and student athletes in the school's history. Indeed, during the first two decades, when Nevada Southern was most vulnerable, the students played a significant role in making sure that state officials neither neglected nor marginalized the school.

Despite the many photographs, this is not a coffee table book. I have made every effort to provide an informative account of the people and events that shaped the school's history. While the prose is celebratory in tone throughout—after all, this volume commemorates the campus's 50th birthday—I have not shied away from analysis at appropriate points in the text. However, in the book's few controversial sections, I have merely attempted to explain the positions of the protagonists so that readers can draw their own conclusions.

A brief note about the campus's early name is in order. Although the school was officially called the University of Nevada, Southern Regional Division, virtually everyone in town, including the regents, popularly referred to it as "Nevada Southern." The mid-1950s class schedules used that name, as did the students in their newspaper even before the Maryland Parkway campus opened in 1957. There are also several quotations in the text that contain that name. So, for reasons of clarity, I will refer to the school as Nevada Southern until it becomes the University of Nevada, Las Vegas in 1969.

Space does not permit detailed administrative histories of university offices and other bureaucratic structures. The same is true for colleges and departments. The administration will ask the colleges to prepare exhibits and texts chronicling their development as part of the 50th Anniversary Celebration. Departments should also consider preparing accounts of their notable faculty, especially the many wonderful teachers who are fondly remembered by majors and graduates. The faculty senate could serve as a model; in 2004 longtime senate secretary Donna Kelly began preparing a substantial history of that institution.

Similarly, tracing the development of student life on campus will require the efforts of multiple groups. Because of space constraints and other considerations, my chapter primarily emphasizes the period 1951–75. During these years, students faced the twin challenges of establishing organizations to create a sense of community and fighting to develop their school into something more than the junior college that many Reno administrators envisioned. The civil rights movement and Vietnam protests only intensified campus activism. The period after 1975, while more quiescent, holds just as many memories for the students who attended UNLV in those years. The same is true for the rough-and-tumble history of CSUN politics, which I simply do not have the space to cover. I hope that UNLV's 50th Anniversary Celebration will inspire the student government and other groups, such as clubs, associations, religious organizations, and Greek societies, to sponsor written accounts of their histories.

Finally, let me offer two editorial comments. Numerous sections of the text describe details of the campus landscape and various Las Vegas roads and locations that have changed over the years. As a result, there are many places where I use "today" or "now" to signify the current situation, in 2007. In referring, for example, to the 1960s-era science and technology building, I may add the words "today's Lilly Fong Geoscience" where appropriate. Rather than making constant references to 2007 in the text, I prefer that future readers keep in mind the year this book appeared.

And second, since this is a book for the general reader, we have provided endnotes only for quotations. In the presidential chapters especially, most of the quotations come from newspaper sources because UNLV issued a press release, or held a news conference, or the story was significant enough to warrant a column. Most of the information in the book that is not quoted, and therefore not footnoted, came from the non-newspaper sources listed in the bibliographical essay.

I am indebted to many people for their ideas and help in corroborating facts, providing sources, and finding photographs. Robert Davenport, who initially began this project in the early 1990s, was especially generous with his time and knowledge. He not only shared his research findings on the period up to 1968 but also read large sections of the manuscript. Many others lent their expertise in key areas to help improve the manuscript, among them Fred Albrecht, Tony Allen, Judy Belanger, Shelley Berkley, Rev. Jerome Blankinship, Michael Bowers, Teri Brown, Kari Coburn, Jerry Countess, Jerry Crawford, James Deacon, Nasim Dil, Douglas Ferraro, Tom Flagg, John Gallagher, Melanie Greenberg, Andy Grossman, Jeff Halverson, Mike Hamrick, James Hulse, John Irsfeld, JoAnn Jacobs, Gary Jones, Chris Kelly, Donna Kelly, Russell Kost III, Alice Mason, Tony McGilton, David Millman, Diane Muntal, Stephen Nielsen, Les Raschko, Brad Rothermel, Diane Russell, Marla Scher, Jack Schofield, Ron Smith, Marta Sorkin, Gretchen and George Stamos, Dina Titus, Jerome Vallen, and Ed Von Tobel. Former university chancellor Neil Humphrey helped with identifying persons appearing in some of the older photographs.

I especially thank the presidents who read their chapters and advised me about errors and omissions. They are Donald Moyer, Donald Baepler (who also read Roman Zorn's section), Leonard Goodall, Robert Maxson, Kenny Guinn, and Carol Harter. Special thanks go to Joseph "Andy" Fry, Carol Harter, and

Michael Green, who read the entire manuscript and offered useful suggestions. Lucy Klinkhammer of the UNLV Foundation deserves special mention for giving generously of her time to make sure the philanthropy chapter was completely accurate.

I also appreciate the help of the Special Collections staff in UNLV's Lied Library, especially Su Kim Chung, Peter Michel, and Jonnie Kennedy, as well as my student assistant, Yonna Polehn. Kathy War, Geri Kodey, and Aaron Mayes were especially helpful with the selection and processing of suitable photographs. Once again, I benefited greatly from the guidance and encouragement of the University of Nevada Press staff and its director, Joanne O'Hare.

I would also like to acknowledge my colleague and former dean Tom Wright for his help and encouragement through the years. A pioneer NSU professor and founding member of the history department was Tom's father, John Wright, whom I had the honor of replacing following his retirement in 1976.

I especially thank my wonderful wife, Christine Wiatrowski, who not only provided her usual spousal support and tolerance of a husband who does his best writing in the middle of the night but also employed her considerable library skills to locate hard-to-find facts for an endless list of subjects.

Finally, it is impossible within the limited space of this book to acknowledge all of the faculty, staff members, students, and Las Vegans who, through the years, have contributed to making UNLV a great institution. It is an underlying assumption of this work that the school's leaders could not and did not do it alone. It is my intention that this work serve as a tribute to everyone on the campus and in our city, region, and state who helped make UNLV what it is today.

THE UNIVERSITY OF NEVADA, LAS VEGAS

CHAPTER ONE

The Birth of "Nevada Southern"

JAMES DICKINSON

The seeds of UNLV lay in the development of Las Vegas itself. While the construction of Hoover Dam in the 1930s brought the first tourist waves to the once sleepy whistle-stop, World War II launched the process that transformed Las Vegas into a booming metropolis and a destination for visitors from around the world. The horde of soldiers, sailors, and defense workers who nightly thronged Fremont Street's bustling casinos and the slowly emerging strip of resorts on the Los Angeles Highway convinced Las Vegans that gambling would be their small town's salvation. Each new hotel created more jobs, and more jobs meant more population, economic growth, and taxable revenue for the state.

As Las Vegas's 1940 total of 8,422 residents swelled to 24,624 by 1950, it became obvious that demographic changes in southern Nevada could no longer be ignored. The Desert Inn's debut in 1950 followed by the Sahara, Sands, Riviera, Dunes, Hacienda, Tropicana, and Stardust, coupled with the development of Nellis Air Force Base and the Nevada Test Site, only drove the population higher as the decade progressed. Added to this was pressure from Nellis airmen, eager to obtain a college education under the GI Bill of Rights. Negotiations between regens and military authorities broke down when regents insisted that classes be conducted at the base and that civilians be allowed to enroll at no cost to the state. With the cold war intensifying (the Korean War began in June 1950), air force officials objected to having civilians on the base for security reasons. They were also frustrated by Nevada's requirement that degree candidates live on the Reno campus for a year. For these reasons, the air force contracted with the University of Southern California (USC) for degree programs, because that school did not require servicemen to take coursework in Los Angeles and there would be no civilian students on base.

Other forces were also at work to create a college at Las Vegas, including pressure from local Mormons. Following World War II, there had been some informal talk between Las Vegas Mormons and church officials in Utah about establishing a branch of Brigham Young University in Las Vegas to offer a two-year program and serve as a feeder school for

MAUDE FRAZIER, THE FOUNDING FORCE BEHIND NEVADA SOUTHERN. SPECIAL COLLECTIONS, UNLV LIBRARIES 0062-1167

the Provo campus. Regents also had to contend with Clark County teachers, who resented the state's insistence that they attend classes in Reno to become certified and to maintain their qualifications with graduate coursework.

Then there was feisty assemblywoman Maude Frazier, who wanted to see southern Nevada students earn college credit without leaving home. Frazier, a native of Wisconsin, had first come to Nevada in 1906, serving as a teaching principal in Genoa. She later taught in Beatty, Goldfield, Sparks, and a variety of other towns. In 1921 Frazier came to Las Vegas, where she would remain for the rest of her life. Using the young railroad town as her headquarters, Frazier served as the Nevada Department of Education's deputy superintendent of schools for Clark, Esmeralda, Nye, and Lincoln counties. In 1927 she became superintendent of the Las Vegas Union School District. After retiring in 1946, she ran for the state assembly in 1950 and served for the next ten years. Her nearly fifty years of experience with Nevada schools convinced her of the need to fight for more education funding. This same spirit carried over to higher education. Indeed, Frazier not only supported a higher budget for the university in Reno but also dreamed of building a substantial college in Las Vegas for her beloved students.

In 1951, during her first term in the state assembly, Frazier authored a bill allowing local school districts to offer junior college classes in high schools. Although the legislation passed, the state attorney general later ruled that it violated the Nevada Constitution. This forced Frazier to seek another solution. By the early 1950s, all of these forces combined to create the required critical mass of political pressure that forced the board of regents to act. Contributing to the process were university officials who, by the 1940s, had recognized the need for extension courses in distant populated areas of the state.

The official origins of unlv lay in a July 1951 announcement by Dr. Harold Brown, director of the University of Nevada's Extension Program, that several college courses would be offered that fall in Las Vegas. Brown told reporters that twenty Reno faculty representing fifteen academic departments would "tour" the state offering instruction in subjects ranging from music and drama to agriculture and politics. The fee would be $7.50 per course. This small extension program had been roving the state, mostly in the summertime, since the mid-1940s. During the late 1940s, Reno professors had occasionally offered coursework in Las Vegas, but now they were creating a formal, ongoing program in the city with a resident director. Although the *Las Vegas Review-Journal* and other local sources referred to this program in 1951 as a "branch" or as the university's "southern branch," that was just wishful thinking. It was a program only and not an official branch of the university until 1954.

In August, Brown provided more specifics, declaring that the first classes in Las Vegas would begin on September 17 and run until December 10. In a positive yet somewhat deceptive statement, President Malcolm Love insisted that "the university long has been interested in cooperating with the people of Las Vegas to provide an educational program on the college level." He noted that the program was the "result of plans formulated over a number of years." Actually, it resulted from intense lobbying by Frazier and other community leaders. The

University merely acquiesced reluctantly to their demands and made no immediate commitment past the 1951–52 school year.

In his description of the program, Brown noted that it was "intended to fulfill freshman requirements at the University" while students still lived at home in southern Nevada.[1] Over the course of the year, history, English, geography, and many other required courses would be offered. In that first year, there was no hint of graduate coursework for teachers or even sophomore classes. While the schedule hardly compared to what students at the Reno campus could select, the price was right.

The university president appointed a young instructor in Reno's Department of English as the program's first administrator and teacher. According to department chair Robert Gorrell, thirty-four-year-old James R. Dickinson, a promising doctoral student from Stanford who had been in Gorrell's department for only two years, was in danger of not completing his dissertation to fulfill Reno's tenure requirements. By moving Dickinson's position into the extension program, those requirements would be less stringent, Gorrell thought, and the young assistant professor would have more time to finish his degree. Sources conflict about Dickinson's enthusiasm for his new assignment, but once he arrived in Las Vegas with his wife, Marjorie, a music instructor and talented soprano from Florida, Dickinson unquestionably gave the new program his best effort.

In early September, Brown, Gorrell, and Dickinson visited the city to locate classroom space and enroll students. The three recruited several Las Vegas high school teachers to offer French and geography courses along with Dickinson's surveys in English composition and literature. The first major problem was low enrollment. Records indicate that the extension program began that fall with only 12 full-time students, supplemented by 16 part-timers. In that first year Dickinson relied on local newspapers to advertise courses and urge residents to register. In December 1951 the *Las Vegas Review-Journal* announced a January 5 registration deadline for the spring semester's offerings of English 101, 102, and 132, French 102, History 102, and Geography 109 and 261. In addition to being the program's director and only full-time instructor, Dickinson also served as registrar. In this capacity, he invited prospective students to enroll at his office, located in room 103 of "Frazier Hall," part of the auditorium area at Las Vegas High named for the former Las Vegas school superintendent.

As Christmas 1951 approached, Dickinson became increasingly concerned about the lack of enrollment. He had to not only advertise the extension program but also convince a doubting public that the courses were official. To this end, he told the *Review-Journal* in December 1951 that "the residence study program" beginning its second semester at Las Vegas High offered regular university coursework that was fully transferable to the Reno campus, where students would eventually have to go to complete their degree.[2] To convince residents that the courses were official and to please his superiors at the university, Dickinson used the Reno campus's outlines, reading assignments, and even its examinations, at least until 1954.

Later in January, with enrollment still lagging, Dickinson boosted the program further by emphasizing not only the full transferability of local coursework but also the lower cost. He pointed out that local enrollees escaped the student union, physical education, and health service fees that Reno students had to pay, not to mention dormitory room and board. The maximum fees at Las Vegas were only $23 a semester plus textbooks. The final advantage was that all coursework in Las Vegas took place in the evening, unlike at the Reno campus, where most classes met during the day. Surveys indicated that the chief reason why Las Vegas residents did not attend the Reno campus was because their jobs required them to stay in southern Nevada, so Dickinson touted his all-evening program as the ideal way to satisfy freshman course requirements.

The nagging issue of low enrollment posed the major obstacle to convincing the northern-dominated board of regents to renew the Las Vegas program for a second year. By January 25, 1952, only 11 students were enrolled for the spring semester, although Dickinson expressed optimism that the final figure would "double that of last semester."[3] To encourage more registrations, Dickinson used an interview with the *Review-Journal* to point out that veterans wishing to enroll under the GI Bill of Rights of 1944 could do so. After that, veterans were always part of the school's student body.

Still, enrollment grew slowly, almost threatening the program's future. The fall 1951 head count was only 28; in fall 1952, it barely hit 40, and the following year the total increased only to 58, with most of these numbers coming from nonmatriculated part-timers. The regents' decision to continue the program stemmed partly from concerns that if the Las Vegas area continued to grow—and every indicator signaled it would—they could face a significant political backlash if they abolished the classes. In addition, the regents had just hired Minard Stout as the university's new president, and Stout was an "educationist" who championed the idea of extending the university outward to distant communities with required freshman and professional-vocational courses.

In a state like Nevada, then the sixth largest in area, this view was politically expedient. Stout's policies thus reinforced the Las Vegas program. And while the new president had to be convinced that Dickinson was the right person for the job, he stayed with him. After all, the young professor never challenged Stout's authority, and, the president surely reasoned, a good freshman program at Las Vegas would erode support for activists like Frazier and regent Archie Grant, who preferred a separate state college in southern Nevada. So, despite sluggish enrollment in the early 1950s, university officials renewed the Las Vegas program each year and kept Dickinson in charge. A more permanent commitment to Las Vegas came in April 1954, when Stout established a statewide development office headed by Dr. William Wood. On May 8, Wood announced the creation in Las Vegas of a "southern branch" of the university. It was Wood who called it "Nevada Southern" in his correspondence and public meetings, although the official name was the University of Nevada, Southern Regional Division. Despite being a more permanent entity than the year-to-year extension programs of 1951–54, Nevada Southern did not become a regular college, like its counterparts on the Reno campus, until 1957, and it did not become a semi-autonomous university (NSU) until 1965.

Enrollment, while still relatively low, grew enough to justify the more permanent program. In fall 1954 the student count finally jumped to 310, then 361 before hitting a respectable 499 in fall 1955. For some Las Vegans, like Maude Frazier and Archie Grant, these figures were enough to warrant purchasing land for a small campus. But the regents were in no hurry to do that. In the meantime, the number of course offerings expanded, as curricular development and enrollment growth continued. In May 1954 Dickinson received a letter from Wood announcing that he and the dean of students (and future head of the Las Vegas division), William Carlson, would arrive soon to study the program and make recommendations to university officials regarding its expansion. Wood told Dickinson that the "Nevada Southern" regional division (as he called it) would remain housed at Las Vegas High until a permanent campus could be established.

In 1954 Wood and Dickinson worked hard to make Nevada Southern more than the two-year junior college program it was. Indeed, the school moved beyond required freshman and some sophomore coursework and began hiring instructors to train more students for teaching careers. This had been a major goal of Maude Frazier during the 1940s when she began pushing for a Las Vegas program. The new curricular emphasis was immediately obvious. In summer 1954 a Colorado elementary school principal offered a class on teaching social studies in the grade school curriculum, while two Reno faculty members gave courses on teaching science at the elementary school level and the "non-instructional responsibilities" of a teacher.[4] By 1955, the school's faculty consisted of six professors and twenty-three part-timers. A year later, Dickinson hired seven more professors, including pioneers John Wright in history and Holbert Hendrix in education.

The faculty taught not only in the fall and spring but also in the summer. The latter was particularly important to local teachers. In fact, Nevada Southern's program of four summer sessions, each four weeks long, was, according to one source, "unique in American education"; the schedule, of course, reflected the need to jam in as much coursework as possible during the time when teachers and prospective education majors were able to take classes. In 1954 school officials expected the third summer session of education classes to draw more than 50 participants, a student body "made up mainly of teachers from all parts of southern Nevada," not just Las Vegas. Many of them spent the summer in town, because, as the registrar's office reported, "some 95 percent were enrolled in the first two terms."[5]

Staffing was also a concern. As the extension program grew, the university

CLARK COUNTY COMMISSIONER MANNY CORTEZ PRESENTS AN AWARD TO FORMER CLARK COUNTY SCHOOL DISTRICT SUPERINTENDENT R. GUILD GRAY FOR HIS EFFORTS TO PROMOTE EDUCATION IN THE LAS VEGAS AREA, 1981. SPECIAL COLLECTIONS, UNLV LIBRARIES #0277-0871

could not induce any more faculty to leave the Reno campus. Consequently, Dickinson increasingly recruited from the local community, seeking instructors with degrees in needed subjects. Already by 1954, a number of teachers from the Las Vegas Union School District were offering education courses at Las Vegas High at night. This group included school district head R. Guild Gray, who would play a key role in the 1955 campus fund drive.

Expanded offerings eventually forced Dickinson to schedule courses at locations other than Las Vegas High. As enrollment passed 300, he sought additional space, which he found with Gray's help. In December 1955, for instance, Dickinson announced that Nevada Southern's spring semester introductory course in physical chemistry would be taught in a chemistry classroom, using laboratory facilities at Basic High School in Henderson. But most of the courses were still held in the cramped dressing rooms of Las Vegas High's auditorium. In a 1970s interview, pioneer history professor John Wright recalled how classes had to be canceled whenever the high school staged a play, and longtime Nevada Southern registrar Muriel Parks remembered how she had to share an office with Dickinson and others at the school.

By the mid-1950s, as enrollment grew, it became more difficult to acquire space, and the student body began to coalesce into a community, the need for a campus became obvious. The first official recognition of the need for at least one building to house the extension program came not from the regents but from university officials in Reno. In August 1954 Dickinson's boss, William Wood, asked the regents for $359,616 in his biennial budget request for Nevada Southern. Wood planned to spend $172,000 for salaries, equipment, and supplies for the 1955–56 school year. He also requested $187,500 to construct

SEATED ARE JAMES DICKINSON (LEFT) AND LONGTIME
REGISTRAR MURIEL PARKS (SECOND LEFT) WITH OFFICE STAFF,
AT WORK IN THEIR CUBBYHOLE OFFICE AT LAS VEGAS HIGH
SCHOOL, CA. 1955. UNIVERSITY ARCHIVES, UNIVERSITY OF
NEVADA, RENO

a building exclusively for the extension program, citing Las Vegas's "soaring population" as the chief reason for enrollment growth.[6]

Tourism was the main engine driving the town's expansion, and by 1954 both downtown and the Strip (the old Los Angeles Highway) welcomed new hotels. On the Strip, the 1940s-era El Rancho Vegas, Hotel Last Frontier, Flamingo, and Thunderbird had been joined by five more, and at least three others were under construction or on the drawing board. Las Vegas's gaming and tourist economy, supplemented by heavy cold war defense spending and a thriving chemical industry in Henderson, all promoted Nevada Southern's development.

However, while Las Vegas's growth was the force pushing the creation of a campus, Nevada's anti-tax tradition constituted a powerful counterforce that led regents to cut Wood's $187,500 request. These opposing forces would continue to control the pace of campus development for the next fifty years. In the 1950s and 1960s the prevailing assumption, voiced even by Las Vegas regent candidate John Cahlan in his 1950 campaign, was that having only one main campus would save money,

While conceding that they had received "many letters from various groups" in Las Vegas supporting a campus there, regents were under pressure from state lawmakers to reduce the university's budget. For this reason, the board wanted more time to decide whether the enrollment warranted construction of a building. This position became clear in September 1954 when the regents advised everyone that their upcoming meeting in Las Vegas "indicated only a desire to acquaint themselves with the college education needs in the area, and did not mean that any definite plans have been made for building a college extension school there."[7] In the interim, the board cut the proposed budget for the next biennium, including Wood's building request. Of course, the Las Vegas program was not the only item to suffer budget cuts; regents also slashed $552,000 from the overall $6,429,000 university budget. Nevertheless, Las Vegas, with its smaller program of 200 full-time students, absorbed nearly 40 percent of the reductions. It was not just the penny-pinching approach of state legislators but also the growing concern of university officials and northern regents about the size of the Las Vegas program that determined the extent of the cuts.

The board's action served only to rouse the community. President Stout and the board, while not averse to constructing a building to house southern Nevada's program someday, had no intention of immediately buying land for a college campus. That all changed, however, at the first-ever regents meeting in Las Vegas on October 7, 1954. Besieged by an overflow crowd of 300 determined residents and impressed by chamber of commerce officials, who noted that the metropolitan population of 50,000 in 1950 had surged to 86,000 that month and was projected to pass 100,000 by 1960, regents agreed to reconsider their position. Other arguments eventually persuaded them to support the acquisition of land for a campus. As elected officials committed to promoting Nevada education, they had to be impressed by school superintendent R. Guild Gray's statistics indicating that while 50 percent of Reno high school graduates went to college, only 30 percent of their Las Vegas counterparts did. Clearly, the lack of even a junior college in a city whose population threatened to pass 100,000 was a deciding factor. A pledge by Clark County state senator Mahlon Brown and Assemblywoman Maude Frazier to support legislation appropriating money for a campus further convinced the four northern members of the five-person board.

With the 1955 legislature already in session, the regents met in February to discuss various sites for a campus. The lone Las Vegas regent, Archie Grant, was the chief advocate for a local campus. Grant, a successful Ford car dealer and Democratic Party activist, had been a member of the chamber of commerce and an active promoter of Las Vegas for many years. In the 1940s he worked to establish the Las Vegas Valley Water District and free the city from its dependency on the railroad's wells. In 1943 he represented Las Vegas in the state assembly, but in later years Grant's interests turned to higher education. Elected to the board of regents in 1952, he would serve for the next twenty years.

Grant worked hard, especially in the 1950s and early 1960s, to build a substantial college in the resort city. Once the board decided to build a campus, Grant, with his local business connections, was helpful in identifying suitable locations for his colleagues to discuss. In December 1954, Arnold Greenfield, a retired real estate broker, offered a parcel of 707 acres seven miles south of Las Vegas. Grant took this offer to his colleagues, but the land lacked paved roads. Boulder City and Henderson also offered sites, but they were too far from the main body of population in Las Vegas. University officials eventually entered into secret negotiations with the Union Pacific Railroad for a plot ranging from 80 to 480 acres in the "Old Ranch" part of town, near today's Rancho High School just north of downtown. The site, only vaguely described in university correspondence, included the old Mormon Fort, which President Stout proposed turning into a museum on the campus. In the summer of 1954, however, the railroad abruptly ended the negotiations after an employee leaked them to the press. This forced Stout and the regents to search elsewhere.

The process continued into 1955. In the end, the regents chose a 60-acre site offered by Howard and Estelle Wilbourn of Modesto, California. Mrs. Wilbourn wanted to give the land as a donation to honor her mother, Estelle Cornish, who had come to Las Vegas in 1918 during the city's pioneer days. A delighted Silas

Ross, chair of the board of regents, characterized Wilbourn's offer as "a gift to education and to the youth of southern Nevada."[8] The board promised a suitable memorial to honor Mrs. Cornish and her family, who had operated a small shoe store for several years in the Levy Building downtown. After brief negotiations, both parties signed an agreement in February 1955.

Ominously, press reports indicated that the 60 acres were part of a larger 280-acre parcel of federal land on which the Wilbourns had filed homestead rights in 1928. When Nevada became a state in 1864, the federal government allowed it to claim 1.5 million acres that it could later sell for money to build roads and government buildings. The agreement, however, put no time limit on the acquisitions and allowed officials in the state land office to wait and see where growth patterns raised land values the most. By the mid-twentieth century, tracts south of Las Vegas had appreciated, and the state exercised its option to acquire several large parcels west of Maryland Parkway between Flamingo and Tropicana. The land east of the road remained federal for a while longer.

As Las Vegas realtor and state assemblywoman (1957–61) Helen Herr remembered it, former state surveyor Wayne "Red" McLeod and a clerk in the state assembly recognized how much the land would appreciate if the board of regents chose it for a campus, but they could not personally buy the land from the state and sell it to the regents. So they served as silent partners for the Wilbourns, who did not own the land when they offered it to the board. Later, when regents expressed their willingness to sign a contract, the Wilbourns purchased the land for $1.25 an acre—a discount deal from the state land office arranged by McLeod and his ally in the assembly. Later, angry state legislators passed new legislation requiring that in the future all state lands be first appraised and then sold at market value.

Of course, regents and university officials had to determine how good a deal the Wilbourns' offer really was. As part of the agreement, the Wilbourns donated the 60-acre parcel on condition that the university buy an adjacent 20-acre parcel for $35,000. Everyone knew that if the Las Vegas campus developed, as many thought it would, 60 acres would not be enough land. So President Stout and the regents signed the contract. But it soon became obvious that they had overpaid. The officials reasoned that because nearby land sold for as much as $2,000 an acre at the time, getting 80 acres for $35,000, or $440 an acre, was a discount. Of course, all of this tract had been state land and should have been available to the university for free. Then, too, Mrs. Wilbourn could have given all 80 acres to the university for free, instead of trying to make a substantial profit off her "donation." Nevertheless, under existing laws the Wilbourns had acted legally, and university regents never contested the transaction in court.

With the legislature already meeting in February 1955, Las Vegans now thought they had a campus, since according to the contract with the Wilbourns, the university had until June 1956 to exercise its option to buy the additional 20 acres. There was plenty of time for lawmakers to appropriate the $35,000—but they never did. Mahlon Brown worked overtime to persuade members of the Senate Finance Committee to appropriate $35,000 for the land and $200,000 for the campus's first building. To be sure, the Wilbourns' 60-acre "donation" of land for a campus helped Brown in his lobbying, but his northern colleagues insisted that with revenues tight, money should be spent only for buildings on the main campus in Reno. Brown ultimately devised a strategy to break the deadlock: Tie the $200,000 for the building to a requirement that Las Vegans, not the state, pay the Wilbourns $35,000 for their additional 20 acres. Brown's bill contained a proviso mandating that this be done before the university's option to buy the land ran out in 1956. Convinced that local residents would not raise the money, northern lawmakers passed Brown's bill and Governor Charles Russell signed it.

Las Vegans accepted the legislature's challenge. In the spring of 1955, local business and political leaders established the Campus Fund Committee to help raise $135,000 for the Nevada Southern campus. The goal was to collect at least $100,000 beyond the state requirement, in order to buy supplies, books, and other equipment needed for the structure. The committee announced it was seeking 10,000 donors and would place the name of anyone who contributed $50 or more in a special donor book. Results were disappointing. By May 11 the group had raised only $4,000. The Elks Lodge, Business and Professional Women, Soroptimists, Central Labor Council, Schoolmasters Club, American Association of University Women, and Las Vegas Service League, as

a campus . . .
for Southern Nevada

IT CAN BE OURS NOW!

IF   *YOU ARE IN BUSINESS OR A PROFESSION — AN EMPLOYER OR AN EMPLOYEE*

IF   *YOU ARE A PARENT*

IF   *YOU ARE A CIVIL WORKER OR A TEACHER*

THEN   — you know the advantages of a University to your community — to Clark County and Southern Nevada.

HERE'S THE STORY OF HOW WE CAN DO IT—

well as individuals like former mayor Ernie Cragin (of Cragin and Pike Insurance), Mr. and Mrs. Henry Wick, and others all gave money, but it was not nearly enough.

The committee then pinned its hopes on a broad community fund-raising effort slated for the week of May 23, 1955. On May 24, KLRJ-TV and KLAS-TV aired a telecast featuring campus campaign organizers and Strip lounge acts. Hollywood movie star Jeff Chandler also volunteered his services to encourage viewer support for the so-called Porch Light Campaign being conducted that afternoon and evening. Organized by former Las Vegas school superintendent Maude Frazier and current school district director R. Guild Gray, seniors from high schools in Las Vegas, Henderson, Boulder City, and the county suburbs visited virtually every home and apartment in the budding metropolitan area. Even though it was late May and sunset was after seven thirty, the effort lingered into the night. As students knocked on doors, porch lights came on—hence the campaign's name.

The fund drive continued into June, with Archie Grant, Spencer Butterfield, and other leaders soliciting members of the business community. James Dickinson even hosted an all-night radio broadcast, imploring residents to support the effort. By early June they had raised only $23,000, largely because Las Vegas's resort industry, despite having $50 million of new construction in the works, contributed relatively little to the pot. In 1955, hotel executives regarded the campus campaign as a community issue and never saw how the college could benefit them. That attitude would dissipate in the 1960s, when corporate gaming and a popular hotel program changed minds on the Strip and in Glitter Gulch. Eventually the campaign netted almost $50,000, enough to purchase the extra 20 acres and guarantee state funding for the school's

LAS VEGAS MAYOR C.D. BAKER SIGNS THE CEREMONIAL FIRST CHECK FOR JAMES DICKINSON IN THE 1955 CAMPUS FUND DRIVE. UNIVERSITY ARCHIVES, UNIVERSITY OF NEVADA, RENO

first building. But little money remained for books and equipment, since the committee fell well short of its $135,000 goal.

As regents prepared to break ground for the construction of Nevada Southern's first building, scattered opposition to the school's location arose. In January 1956, President Minard Stout dismissed the complaints of the Las Vegas Home Siters, a group of real estate investors who objected to the university building a college on donated land. The group urged regents to put the campus on land bordering West Charleston near the Nevada State Highway Department's gravel pit, five miles west of downtown. Although regents went ahead with the Maryland Parkway campus, the state later purchased the 80-acre tract near today's intersection of West Charleston and Torrey Pines, currently the site of one of the Community College of Southern Nevada's campuses.

While some real estate interests, like the Home Siters, staunchly opposed Nevada Southern's location, others, like Jack Schofield, did not. Schofield, who later served in the state assembly and senate as well as on the board of regents, was then chair of the Paradise Valley Improvement Association. He denounced the Home Siters for not making their objection public "more than a year ago when the university officials were seeking a feasible site, and received no support from the Home Siters or anyone else."

The Home Siters and other opponents argued that the 80-acre parcel on Maryland Parkway was too small to allow for expansion. They were correct, but in 1955 no one, not even the Home Siters, could have dreamed that the Las Vegas metropolitan area would grow to more than 1.8 million people and that enrollment at what became UNLV would approach 30,000. Such projections could not have been made until the mid-1960s. Schofield therefore rejected the argument in 1955, contending that the regents' campus selection committee "consisted of qualified men whose business is educational planning." This group considered the question of size, but dismissed it. As Schofield reminded locals, the committee "pointed out that San Francisco State College recently purchased 39 acres for its new campus and Pasadena City College is on 20 acres, while City College in New York has 4 acres." For this reason, Schofield urged Las Vegans to support the chosen site, warning that "the necessary money to begin construction of Nevada Southern is now available and a change in plans could postpone further progress or knock it out completely."[9]

Aside from the campus's size, its proximity to McCarran Airport's north-south runway was also an issue. In 1955, though, the passenger jet was only in development. The Boeing 727's first commercial flight did not even occur until 1958. Nor could anyone have predicted that McCarran (the jetport on Paradise Road opened in 1963) would service hundreds of daily flights by the 1960s. Additionally, in the 1950s and for many years thereafter, the airport's main landing and takeoff pattern was on the longer east-west runway. Finally, the occasional propeller flights of 1955 hardly posed a problem for instruction in classrooms along the west side of Maryland Parkway, although in the 1990s one small plane crashed on campus land near the apartments at Swenson and Harmon.

With state appropriations secured for the first building on the new Maryland Parkway campus, Las Vegans prepared for construction to begin. On April 30, 1956, several hundred residents and visitors gathered near Maryland Parkway and Harmon for the groundbreaking ceremony for Nevada Southern's first building. Gray was the master of ceremonies, and turning over the first spade of dirt for the 13,000-square-foot building that would

FIRST FLAG-RAISING CEREMONY AT THE MARYLAND PARKWAY
ENTRANCE, JANUARY 11, 1958. *EPILOGUE, 1958*

someday bear her name was Maude Frazier. Following the groundbreaking
and a few words by Gray, who assured the crowd that his committee would
provide the state with money for sinking a well at the site and for soil testing of
groundwater, the crowd adjourned to the Thunderbird Hotel on the Strip for a
celebratory banquet.

Construction progressed and on March 17, 1957, with Estelle Wilbourn in
attendance and regent Silas Ross delivering the keynote address, Nevada's
Grand Lodge of Masons laid the cornerstone. By May the building was ready for
occupancy, although it would be a while before the Sahara Hotel donated money

to plant a lawn in front. The campus opened for limited operations in June, and the first day of fall classes was September 10, 1957.

As school officals prepared to greet the first students for the fall semester, workers added the final touch—large black lettering on the building's front wall that proudly bore the name: "University of Nevada, Southern Branch," a shortened version of the school's longer title. Later that year, Nevada Southern (still formally called the Southern Regional Division until 1965) became a college of the University of Nevada, thanks to Frazier's determined efforts in the legislature. During that fall, the local chapter of the Veterans of Foreign Wars donated money to erect a flagpole at the school's entrance, on Harmon Avenue and Maryland Parkway. On January 11, 1958, with classes canceled for part of the day, several hundred students, faculty, dignitaries, and ordinary Las Vegans heard Las Vegas mayor C. D. Baker deliver the keynote address at the ceremony marking the first-ever flag-raising at Nevada Southern.

Even before the campus opened in 1957, a university spokesman announced that William Carlson, dean of student affairs at Reno, would replace Dickinson as head of the Las Vegas program. Dickinson had requested relief from his administrative duties as early as 1954; he still had to finish the research for his dissertation at Stanford and needed the time. In addition, his immediate superior, Dr. William Wood, felt that the young English professor was not aggressive enough as resident director and said as much in conversation and written evaluations.

Of course, it was unlikely that Dickinson, without a doctorate, would have gotten the job anyway. Running a campus required someone with more administrative experience, which Carlson had. Additionally, President Stout viewed Carlson as a talented and loyal subordinate who would promote growth at Nevada Southern without threatening funds for the Reno campus. Carlson, a former elementary school teacher, college professor, and dean, knew how to carry out orders and was a perfect choice for Reno officials in 1957. In many respects, he would be a good selection for Las Vegas, too. Carlson's determined effort in the early 1960s to begin the long process of making Nevada Southern an equal partner with Reno would raise few eyebrows on the mother campus.

Dickinson had done his job, scheduling a growing number of classes, hiring qualified faculty (many of whom remained more loyal to him than to Carlson), boosting enrollment, and working harmoniously with school district and community members. For six years Dickinson nurtured the infant program. Most important, he enlisted the support of a growing number of prominent business and political leaders to help the school grow. He was the vital link between university officials in Reno, the Las Vegas community, and its fledgling "college" at Las Vegas High. It was Dickinson who lobbied leaders of the local media, especially the *Las Vegas Sun*'s Hank Greenspun and the *Review-Journal*'s Al Cahlan, to keep Nevada Southern in print and on the public's mind. Over the course of those six years, Dickinson's efforts helped build a sense of pride in Nevada Southern and create a momentum that inspired residents to demand that regents give the school a more permanent home—a campus all its own.

CHAPTER TWO

Developing a Campus

WILLIAM CARLSON

The job of developing the arid, 80-acre campus bordering the two-lane dirt road called Maryland Parkway (the "park" was three miles away, near Charleston Boulevard) fell to William D. Carlson, whose experience would serve him well. Carlson, a prison guard in his youth, had been an authoritarian dean of students on the Reno campus, known for his enforcement of rules and for expulsions. He was even hanged in effigy from the arch in downtown Reno, along with President Stout and the dean of women, for canceling an annual dance at Lake Tahoe. Put simply, the students and even some faculty were glad to see Carlson go.

Carlson began what eventually became a forty-eight-year career in education as an eighteen-year-old teacher in a one-room schoolhouse in northeastern Minnesota. He received his bachelor's degree at St. Cloud University and later a doctorate from the University of Minnesota. Hired in 1953 by the University of Nevada, he taught educational psychology and other courses before President Stout, an authoritarian in his own right, made him a dean.

From his office in the new, and as yet unnamed, building on Maryland Parkway, Carlson set about the task of planning more facilities for the rapidly expanding number of students and faculty. He had to act fast because the entire college—the two-thousand-book library, all of the offices, all of the classes, and even the science labs—was jammed into the one building. In a 1975 reminiscence, registrar Muriel Parks remembered: "Thanks to our lovely air vent system, we all knew exactly when the chemists were doing experiments. Sometimes the whole place smelled like rotten eggs." The biologists were not much better; because "there was little room for storage, cages of lizards, frogs, and snakes lined the hallways."[1] To the relief of many, Carlson moved quickly to get the scientists out of the building and into trailers.

During his eight years as dean of Nevada Southern, Carlson struggled to get the basic buildings that every campus needs. His first goal was to erect a large classroom facility with faculty offices to ease the already crowded conditions. But there would be some delay in opening what eventually became Nevada Southern's second building, Archie C. Grant Hall.

DEAN WILLIAM CARLSON, 1957–65. SPECIAL COLLECTIONS, UNLV LIBRARIES 0062-0428

One of the major obstacles to the construction of Nevada Southern's early buildings was the state requirement that only bids from Nevada architects could be considered. The problem was that Las Vegas architects, like Zick and Sharp, the firm that won the contract, had never designed large structures before and were less experienced than some out-of-state competitors, which could have done the work faster. In November 1957, state planning board secretary M. George Bissell accused Zick and Sharp of needlessly delaying construction on the new classroom building, because the firm had missed deadlines for preparing blueprints—clear evidence that the architects were struggling to handle what was for them a big project.

Despite the setbacks, the classroom building opened in time for the fall 1959 semester. Earlier that spring, regents had finally named the buildings, partly to make it easier for students and faculty to refer to them and partly to honor two

TOP: MAUDE FRAZIER HALL IN 1958. THE SCHOOL'S MOTOR POOL BRIEFLY OCCUPIED THE SOUTH SIDE OF THE BUILDING ON THE LEFT. SPECIAL COLLECTIONS, UNLV LIBRARIES 0062-0135

BOTTOM: STUDENTS AND STAFF IN THE LOBBY OF MAUDE FRAZIER HALL, 1958. ALL CLASSES WERE HELD IN THIS BUILDING UNTIL 1959, WHEN ARCHIE C. GRANT HALL OPENED. *EPILOGUE*, 1958

AERIAL VIEW OF NEVADA SOUTHERN CAMPUS, CA. 1960. NOTE
THE SANDY MEDIAN ON MARYLAND PARKWAY AND THE DIRT
PATHWAYS CONNECTING THE BUILDINGS. SPECIAL
COLLECTIONS, UNLV LIBRARIES 0062-0958

of the key figures who had fought to create Nevada Southern and its campus.
In March 1959, two years after the first building opened, regents designated the
school's administrative center as Maude Frazier Hall. Confined to a wheelchair
by a recent hip fracture but still a member of the state assembly, Frazier attended the ceremony. A month later, in another cornerstone-laying ceremony
conducted by Nevada's Grand Lodge of Masons, regents acknowledged the
efforts of one of their own, Archie Grant, by naming the new 33,500-square-foot
classroom building for him.

The added space came just in time. Fed by Las Vegas's spiraling population,
growing enrollment forced Carlson to expand course offerings and hire more
teachers, despite having only two buildings on campus. Through his program-

matic efforts, in December 1958 the Northwest Association of Secondary and Higher Schools awarded both the University of Nevada and Nevada Southern unrestricted accreditation. This milestone provided the latter with a degree of respectability and served as a useful recruiting tool. To be sure, the accreditation team made allowances for Nevada Southern's youth, but everyone knew the school needed a library, a gymnasium, and more classroom buildings. Carlson spent the rest of his term trying to get them, and by and large he was successful.

During the school's early years, physical education classes had been conducted at Las Vegas High's gymnasium and field, but Carlson moved quickly to provide an on-campus venue for these activities. Planning for the gymnasium began in 1959, just as Grant Hall neared completion. In February 1960 Governor Grant Sawyer presided over a brief groundbreaking ceremony for the new Physical Education and Health Center—popularly called the Gym, which today houses the Marjorie Barrick Museum of Natural History. The $500,000 project, built by the Robert Gordon Construction Company of Las Vegas, included two classrooms, storage facilities, locker rooms, and a "full college-sized basketball court."[2] The court, immortalized in a dance scene featuring Elvis Presley and Ann-Margret in the 1964 film *Viva Las Vegas,* served as home to the Runnin' Rebels until the 1962–63 season.

Two hardpan pathways, one running due west from the south side of Maude Frazier Hall and the other cutting laterally (through what would today be the site of Wright Hall) from today's University Road intersection with Maryland Parkway, provided early access to the Gym. As late as 1961, Harmon Avenue dead-ended at Maude Frazier Hall and did not run westward through the campus. By 1964, however, the state had constructed University Road from Maryland Parkway along the campus's southern property line and had also finished Harmon Avenue, which began just behind the science and technology building (today's Lilly Fong Geoscience). To link both thoroughfares and provide an east-west route through the campus to Paradise "Valley" Road, the state also built a connecting artery, Gym Road. In 1994 when the classroom building complex (CBC) (today the Harter Classroom Complex, or HCC) opened, school officials tore out this portion of Gym Road to create a broad sidewalk for students walking to classes there, but for thirty years, Gym Road occupied this space and

ELVIS PRESLEY AND ANN-MARGRET IN THE FAMOUS DANCE
SCENE UNDER THE BASKETBALL SCOREBOARD AT NEVADA
SOUTHERN'S GYM IN THE FILM *VIVA LAS VEGAS*, 1964. SPECIAL
COLLECTIONS, UNLV LIBRARIES 0062-0598

AERIAL PICTURE OF NEVADA SOUTHERN, CA. 1961. THE FIRST
FLOOR OF WHAT BECAME JAMES DICKINSON LIBRARY IS UNDER
CONSTRUCTION. SPECIAL COLLECTIONS, UNLV LIBRARIES 0062-
0407

AERIAL VIEW OF NEVADA SOUTHERN IN 1962. HARMON
AVENUE BARELY MAKES IT TO PARADISE ROAD. SWENSON
STREET DID NOT APPEAR UNTIL THE LATE 1970S. THE LOW-
RISE TROPICANA HOTEL IS AT THE TOP OF THE PICTURE.
SPECIAL COLLECTIONS, UNLV LIBRARIES 0062-0421

ran just west of the old athletics field (replaced in 2002 by the Central Desert
Complex), where Nevada Southern conducted its physical education classes and
various sporting events.

In 1960 planning also began for the $612,000 science and technology build-
ing (today Lilly Fong Geoscience), built by Sierra Construction and partly owned
by longtime UNLV donor Kitty Rodman. A year later, as the science facility
opened, Carlson was already at work helping to plan the library, another structure that the school desperately needed. The nearly two thousand volumes that
Dickinson had collected for Nevada Southern since 1951 had been temporarily
moved to the larger Grant Hall from their original home in Maude Frazier Hall
to escape the problems of that building,which included occasional rattlesnakes
in the hallways, under the desks, and on the bookshelves. The growing collec-

tion remained in Grant Hall until the new library opened. Groundbreaking took
place in October 1961. Nevada Southern built its original library in stages. The
first, which opened in 1963, consisted of a one-story building (the round south
wing of today's William S. Boyd School of Law) that could hold 75,000 volumes,
microfilm, and other materials.

By 1960, with the metropolitan population approaching 130,000 and the obvious need for more buildings, it had become clear that Nevada Southern's campus had to be expanded. In March 1961 state legislators appropriated $145,000
to purchase 80 acres of adjacent land, which effectively doubled the campus's
size. The vote, however, was not without controversy. One Elko assemblyman
protested that former state surveyor general Wayne McLeod, the Wilbourns'

silent partner in the 1955 deal that created the campus, had purchased the nearby land several years earlier from the federal government for only $1.25 per acre. A legislative investigation of McLeod's land transactions in the early 1950s had so angered lawmakers that they took steps to abolish his office by 1954. But as Assemblyman George Harmon correctly pointed out, under the laws of the time, McLeod had obtained the land legally. Henderson assemblyman Jim Gibson placated lawmakers, assuring them that portions of the land could be sold off if values rose and the school failed to grow. That never happened, and the legislature's acquisition proved a wise investment.

Still, the amount of money appropriated for the Las Vegas school was relatively small compared to the overall university budget that mostly funded the Reno campus. This bred increasing resentment, especially as Clark County became the largest revenue producer in the state by 1955 and Las Vegas became the largest city. In a May 1962 editorial, the *Review-Journal* reminded readers that "this newspaper has contended for a long time that Nevada Southern has failed to receive its rightful share of funds."[3] The column cited budget figures for the 1962–63 fiscal year to buttress its case. Out of a university budget of $7,180,000, Nevada Southern's share was only $445,000—even though the Las Vegas campus accounted for almost 20 percent of the university's enrollment (1,100 of 5,800 total students). Worse still, the regents and the president actively restrained Carlson from raising money locally, fearing that such efforts would divert potential contributions for the main campus in Reno. Pressure for supplemental, private money for Nevada Southern's development came mainly from the local community.

After telling residents that regents and legislators needed to be convinced that southern Nevada's growth demanded "an outstanding facility" of higher education for the future, the *Review-Journal* advised: "We are going to have to begin building the university today." Recognizing the need for supplemental private giving, the editorial urged the Las Vegas community to donate to the newly formed Nevada Southern Foundation. This nonprofit fund-raising corporation, created in 1962, was run by a seven-member board of mostly local businessmen. The newspaper implored residents to join the organization. "Southern Nevadans themselves must get behind the university with dollars and cents," the editorial declared, because, given the lack of state funding by northern interests, "the Foundation holds out the best hope in many years to actually accomplish something in building the University here."[4]

In October 1962 the Nevada Southern Foundation announced plans for its first fund drive, a $100,000 campaign to complete the new library. In a brief ceremony, Las Vegas mayor Oran Gragson gave the first donation to fund chair Shelby Ostensen. The latter told residents they could participate in a coupon pledge drive by cutting out a book coupon from local newspapers and mailing in their offering to buy a book for Nevada Southern's new library. Ostensen warned residents not to donate directly to the school, lest Reno officials siphon off most of the funds. The foundation's purpose, he explained, was to funnel all monies collected to Nevada Southern; "otherwise, all contributions would have to go to the Reno campus, and we'd probably get only three cents on the dollar down here."[5]

Small gifts poured in. Many were little more than enough to purchase a book or two, but others were quite generous. In 1963, for instance, an anonymous donor gave a parcel of land, on the Salt Lake Highway north of Las Vegas, worth $90,000. He stipulated that the proceeds be used to establish an economics library at the school as well as an endowed chair for a "distinguished professor" of economics. In 1964 the foundation targeted the proposed performing arts center for a fund-raising drive led by millionaire developer Wing Fong. In April the Service League of Las Vegas contributed $4,000 to the foundation, which was then chaired by attorney and businessman Bill "Wildcat" Morris.

Encouraged by this outpouring of community support, Carlson continued to press for more buildings. In 1964 planning began for the proposed social science building (today John S. Wright Hall) between Maude Frazier Hall and the Gym. In April of that year the regents also announced plans to build a dormitory. They recognized that Nevada Southern was no longer just a commuter campus but was attracting a growing number of students from out of town and out of state. The regents also targeted library expansion. University officials asked the state planning board to allocate $4.8 million for the Las Vegas program over the next biennium, out of a total university budget of $12.2 million. Part of Nevada Southern's share was to be used to build two more floors onto the round library, erect a fine arts building, and construct a $1 million addition to the physical sciences building.

As the Las Vegas Strip continued to grow with new resorts, Nevada Southern's campus obviously would undergo even more development in the future, and Carlson recognized the need for a master plan. At his prodding, university officials commissioned a 1963 report on the future development of the campus by Skidmore, Owings, and Merrill Architects and Planners. The consultants wasted little time recommending the purchase of 40 acres along Flamingo Road (the northwest portion of the campus, where the Paradise Elementary School, the Bennett Professional Development Center, and the Stan Fulton Building are today), plus 82 acres on the south and east, the current location of the Harter Classroom Complex, Reynolds Student Services Building, and part of the Thomas & Mack parking lot. The consultants emphasized the importance of buying these tracts before land prices went higher. "A revolving fund of $200,000 every two years," they estimated, "could purchase approximately 16 acres of land at the going rate and would take approximately 11 years."[6] Carlson proposed establishing a fund to do it, but ultimately his successor, Donald Moyer, formed what became the Nevada Southern Land Foundation.

Diagrams in the report show part of the existing north-south mall running from "Frazier Humanities" and the new social sciences building (later Wright Hall) toward the one-story round library, with trailers north of that. In 1963 there was no east-west mall. The consultants called for the construction of both malls, featuring the familiar parallel sidewalks of today, landscaped with trees and shrubs, to beautify the area. Plans called for the new, and as yet unbuilt, "Life Science Building" to be the "terminal building" on the west mall. The plan allocated a site for a large humanities building (today Flora Dungan Humanities) and at least one dormitory to the south. It also designated sites for a possible fine arts building and an "addition" to Maude Frazier Hall. The report

even outlined a plan for more construction in the event that Nevada Southern's
student population might someday exceed 1,700!

In addition to his ambitious building agenda, Carlson mounted impressive
administrative and programmatic initiatives. In a 1981 memoir to the faculty
senate commemorating UNLV's upcoming twenty-fifth anniversary, Carlson
detailed his strategy in 1960 for turning the young extension program on
Maryland Parkway into a degree-granting institution, the crucial prerequisite for
attaining autonomy from the Reno campus. He began by noting that even after
the "Southern Regional Division of the University of Nevada" became a college
among the various colleges in Reno, university administrators "desired to have
a measure of control, even to the extent of faculty selection and nomination."
However, the Las Vegas campus "successfully resisted" the effort, although
all proposals and recommendations for promotion, tenure, and new courses
required the approval of the university's Academic Council of Deans in Reno.[7]

At the same time, Carlson remembered that for political and legislative reasons, members of the University of Nevada administration always spoke of Nevada Southern as having "junior college status" and described Nevada Southern to Reno's faculty as just a feeder school for the big campus. Most of Nevada Southern's coursework, Carlson conceded, was lower division, although once the campus was established in 1957, "a limited number of upper division and graduate courses" were offered. Even a few basic education courses were available at Las Vegas High in the mid-1950s. According to Carlson, he employed the "claw-hammer technique" to get new courses past the deans in Reno.[8] Sometimes he assured them that the courses were absolutely required by the local school district; at other times he just scheduled the classes and relied on the deans' trust in him for tacit approval.

Since Reno campus officials barely considered Nevada Southern a college in the 1950s and early 1960s, there were no "colleges" on the Las Vegas campus in which to house programs. Carlson recalled that when he replaced Dickinson in 1957, faculty were organized into "committees" of business administration, education and physical education, humanities and fine arts, science and mathematics, and social sciences. Carlson appointed a "coordinator," later referred to as a "chairman," for each group. There were no departments until 1965, because "departmentalization was neither feasible nor desirable at that point." Eventually, the committees became areas and divisions "and later became Schools, with a 'Director' and finally moved into College status, with deans as heads." Business, for example, was an "area" in the late 1950s, a "division" in the mid-1960s, a "school" by 1967, and a "college" in 1968.[9] Planning, budget requests, and course approvals at Nevada Southern began with faculty in the affected subject area, who later forwarded them to Carlson and his superiors in Reno for approval.

University officials expected Nevada Southern's early faculty to emphasize teaching and service, because the college was still being formed. Every faculty member sat on committees that organized and reorganized the campus and its curriculum. In these early days, chairs had little or no secretarial help, so they spent hours typing up minutes, reports, and correspondence relating to their committee's or department's activities. Carlson expected faculty to meet college guests at the airport, drive them to their hotel, and shepherd them around campus as well. Faculty were also obligated to give public lectures, attend service club meetings, and solicit scholarship donations. In the 1950s and 1960s, the granting of tenure rested heavily on classroom performance and one's willingness to engage in many time-consuming service activities. But teaching was burdensome, too. Since university officials regarded Nevada Southern as little more than a junior college and because enrollment always exceeded the money available to hire more teachers, the faculty taught a 5–5 (five courses each in the fall and spring semesters) course load in 1957 when the campus opened. In 1958 Carlson got the load reduced to 4–4, where it stayed until the early 1970s.

Summer school teaching was another obligation that hindered faculty research. After James Dickinson began the extension program in 1951, there was always some coursework in the summer. Once the school moved to Maryland Parkway in 1957, summer study was structured in four four-week sessions of intensive coursework, especially in education. Carlson remembered, "Since most of the summer students were teachers, the summer sessions had to be geared to the public school calendar resulting in the ultimate two five-week summer sessions."[10] Although the longer five-week, double summer sessions became

the standard in the 1960s, the school retained the three-week winter Miniterm to let students earn one or two credits; the Maxson administration finally ended it in 1988. The popularity of a short, three-week session among students eventually gave birth to today's Summer Session A in 1992, although a few instructors had been teaching an unofficial version of it since the 1970s.

During Carlson's tenure as head of Nevada Southern, Reno officials approved three important proposals "of immense value in the furtherance of the institution." The first was the creation of "Off-Campus and Evening Division programs." In 1957 Carlson appointed Dr. Herbert Derfelt, a former Kansas school superintendent and an education professor at Reno, to run this operation. The off-campus classes primarily served Nellis airmen on base, although Nevada Southern instructors also

HERBERT DERFELT, EARLY HEAD OF DISTANCE EDUCATION.
SPECIAL COLLECTIONS, UNLV LIBRARIES 0062-1162

traveled to outlying communities, driving as far as Pioche and Panaca to offer coursework. Fortunately, there were many qualified teachers in science, mathematics, and even foreign languages who were Las Vegas residents. Indeed, Nevada Southern offered the first Russian-language course in the state, because a former instructor happened to live in the area and responded to the school's continuous community appeal for qualified college teachers. Carlson remembered that in most cases these part-timers received "only a token honorarium," but he credited them with being "truly interested in furthering the academic growth of the institution."[11]

The second important initiative promoting Nevada Southern's development was creation of the so-called Evening Division. Usually, Carlson observed, the university defined evening classes as those starting after five P.M., but he listed *most* of Nevada Southern's courses under the Evening Division, which was "deliberately a misnomer." "Using that particular title," he explained, "made it easier to secure approval for the operation, and great care was taken not to mention the time for that instruction."[12]

In this way the school began offering upper-division courses and even a few graduate classes by the early 1960s. Carlson noted that because Nevada Southern listed most of its upper-division and non-required coursework in the Evening Division, "it was at first somewhat confusing for the Regents, the President (Reno), the Comptroller (Reno), and deans (Reno), to discover that some Evening Division classes were being taught at 8 a.m." But because Carlson was a trusted administrator from the Reno campus—one of their own—Reno officals (including new university president Charles Armstrong, who replaced Minard Stout in 1958) never suspected anything. All the while, precedents accumulated and the "accretion" of coursework eventually created a "critical mass" of curricular development that allowed Carlson and his faculty to push for the third great initiative of his administration, degree-granting status for the Las Vegas campus.[13]

Carlson's ingenuity also advanced program development, a key prerequisite to winning support for degree-granting status. For example, the x-ray technician program (Nevada Southern offered many technical courses until the community college took over most of them in the early 1970s) began when local radiologists advised Carlson of the need for more trained technicians. They proposed the standard two-year program of coursework leading to a certificate. Because no such program existed on the Reno campus and university regulations in those days required "approval by the faculty concerned," which Nevada Southern lacked, the proposal appeared to be dead. In fact, this would have been the major roadblock for many new programs that the school would have liked to create. But Carlson told Derfelt, his director of the Off-Campus and Evening divisions, that he constituted the sole "faculty concerned." At the dean's behest, Derfelt endorsed and voted for the submission of the program to Reno. Carlson then recounted how "with a straight face" he presented the radiology program to the university president "with the approval of the faculty concerned," and Armstrong endorsed the rad tech program for the Las Vegas school, where it still thrives today.[14]

Carlson also devised the pay mechanism for part-time instructors, for many years called the P-99 (now the PTI) system. Since the Evening Division had to be completely self-supporting, Carlson proposed that Reno officials designate all fees paid by part-time students for the Evening Division, whose wide range of courses increasingly "bolstered and filled gaps in the academic programs" that Nevada Southern was not supposed to have. Carlson assured Reno authorities that the fees of all regular, full-time students would continue to go into the university's General Fund. "Any mention of the fact that the majority of students at NSU were part-time was studiously avoided."[15]

Thanks to this administrative chicanery, Nevada Southern generated lots of extra money to hire more part-time instructors to offer an even broader range of coursework in more subject areas. These additional funds permitted "a marked increase in the hiring of part-time instructors, enabling certain areas such as history, biology, art, education, English, and others to flesh out their offerings to more closely approach baccalaureate requirements." In addition, enough money was left over to buy desperately needed instructional supplies as well as audiovisual and other equipment that was normally "not available through ap-propriate fund budgets" for the Las Vegas campus.[16]

Carlson's major triumph was convincing skeptical regents and reluctant administrators that they should make Nevada Southern a degree-granting institution. When the campus opened in 1957 the board had designated the Southern Regional Division as a college, one of six in the university, but the

Las Vegas program enjoyed little autonomy. As historian Robert Davenport has noted, the two campuses shared the same curriculum, and by 1959 "it was possible to fulfill all requirements for a degree at Las Vegas, at least in education."[17] But university officials, perhaps concerned that Las Vegas students might slip through with a degree by meeting lower standards than their counterparts in the north, required the former to be in residence for at least one semester, or its equivalent in summer sessions, at Reno before receiving a university degree.

Two Las Vegas seniors, George Widner and Jeanne Chretien, challenged the rule, but lost. Chretien, a thirty-five-year-old housewife with a young daughter, was an honor student at Nevada Southern who wanted to become a teacher. Even though she had earned twenty-six credits beyond what she needed to graduate, appealed to the state legislature, and presented a petition signed by six hundred southern Nevada residents supporting her cause, the regents rejected her request and ultimately forced her to spend a semester at Reno. Chretien should have been Nevada Southern's first graduate.

Having now lived three years in Las Vegas and recognizing the growing problem with Reno's position, Carlson by 1960 was determined to secure degree-granting status for his school. He understood that because the Las Vegas college was only a few years old, "most deans at the Reno campus would not be in favor" of degree-granting status. In addition, every administrator in Reno knew that giving Nevada Southern this power would eventually pose "appropriation and budgetary threats." Carlson therefore executed an end run by appealing directly to the regents. He knew that all of them were either native Nevadans or longtime residents of the state who were devoutly proud of its heritage. So in July 1960 he embarked upon an audacious plan to persuade the board to let Nevada Southern issue its first degrees in 1964 to commemorate Nevada's hundredth anniversary as a state. The idea of designating a "Centennial Class" in southern Nevada immediately appealed to the regents, and Carlson took pains to reassure them that "it would take four years of preparation."[18]

At their July 29–30, 1960, meeting, the regents endorsed Carlson's plan by authorizing him to establish a baccalaureate program. The board's action delighted the faculty, who immediately set about revising old courses and inventing new ones to finally liberate Nevada Southern's curriculum from Reno's control. Carlson, however, opposed the faculty's approach, but not its goal. As a former dean at Reno and an old hand at dealing with Reno's administrators and faculty, he championed a less controversial strategy. Since all modified or new courses and each altered baccalaureate program required approval by the affected faculties and deans on the big campus, Carlson suggested merely submitting the university catalog of courses verbatim. Otherwise, he warned, Nevada Southern's faculty "could anticipate a long, drawn-out, and not necessarily conclusive process." Even though many, if not all, of the professors on the Las Vegas campus detested this approach, they eventually agreed. They accepted Carlson's view that, as he put it, "the Reno faculties would not veto programs they had already adopted." As he explained, once Nevada Southern's faculty "had received approval of programs and had become degree-granting in status, they could exercise their faculty prerogative and introduce course and program changes."[19]

First, Carlson and his faculty worked to expand the number of degree areas, in preparation for the school's first-ever graduation. In 1963 Nevada Southern launched what Carlson called the first phase of its four-year degree program by announcing that students could now major in elementary and secondary education in the Education Division (there were still no colleges at the school), while majors in the Social Science Division could obtain degrees in history, political science, and psychology. Science students could graduate with a degree in biology, botany, mathematics, pre-medical, pre-dental, and zoology, with English becoming a major in 1964—the same year that Nevada Southern graduated its inaugural class.

In 1965 Nevada Southern, the old Southern Regional Division created in 1954, became Nevada Southern University (NSU), with its own curriculum. It remained a "coordinate campus" of the University of Nevada, but as of 1965, the institution began to reorganize, renaming the former "divisions" of fine arts, social sciences, and education "schools" by 1967 and "colleges" by 1968. In 1965 the old "concentrations" in biology, history, and English became formal departments serving their "majors." The symbol of this new partial autonomy from Reno was the first edition of NSU's general catalog in 1966 (up to then Reno's catalog had been used for both campuses). NSU's Division of Graduate Studies, directed by English professor Charles "Chuck" Adams, even published a small graduate bulletin in 1966.

UNIVERSITY PRESIDENT CHARLES ARMSTRONG CONGRATULATES
ACCOUNTING MAJOR DOMINIC DAILEDA, FIRST WINNER OF THE
CENTENNIAL MEDALLION AWARD AT NEVADA SOUTHERN'S FIRST
COMMENCEMENT. JUNE 3, 1964. SPECIAL COLLECTIONS, UNLV
LIBRARIES 0062-0283

Of course, granting its first degrees in 1964 hastened the march toward partial and eventually, in 1968–69, full autonomy. Nevada Southern's first graduation ceremony, on June 3, 1964, was a significant event, thanks in no small
part to the commencement address delivered by Governor Grant Sawyer. He
had supported the school as a regent, and as governor he had worked to provide
more money for both the Reno and the Las Vegas campuses. The twenty-nine
members of the centennial class, which included future state senator and dental
school advocate Ray Rawson, heard more than an inspirational speech imploring them "to take your place in a new America." Sawyer also used the occasion

to trace the school's development. The former Elko County district attorney re-minded his audience that the original University of Nevada at Elko was "a lone building surrounded by a desert waste," much like Nevada Southern in 1957. Then, several minutes later, Sawyer became the first person to officially refer to the Maryland Parkway school as the "University of Nevada at Las Vegas"; he would use the term a second time before concluding.[20] Five years later, the regents would give Nevada Southern that name, along with the UNLV acronym. It was a memorable and emotional day for everyone. Longtime English profes-sor Charles Adams sat near James Dickinson at the ceremony, and Adams remembered that as the students stood up to receive their degrees, "There were tears in Jim's eyes. It was a day he had fought for and dreamed about for nearly a decade."[21]

It was Dickinson's day as much as Carlson's, but a year later Carlson would pay a price for his crafty leadership. The regents had adopted a new organi-zational structure: Nevada Southern would become a small university within the state university system, with the Reno and Las Vegas campuses led by chancellors serving under University of Nevada president Charles Armstrong. In September 1964 Carlson withdrew his name from the list of candidates for the position of Nevada Southern's first chancellor because he believed that he lacked Armstrong's support. Armstrong quickly denied the claim, but it was obvious that Carlson was out. It was just easier for regents to select a more qualified out-of-state candidate without antagonizing Las Vegas and pro-Carlson regents Ray Germain and Archie Grant, who would have charged northern regents with imposing their will on the south. Later Carlson tried to reenter the race, but, even with the active support of the *Las Vegas Review-Journal,* it was to no avail.

Sources on the board correctly attributed Carlson's downfall to lack of NSU faculty support. Indeed, a faculty screening committee that interviewed can-didates for the chancellor's position gave Carlson its lowest rating. The body, composed of Charles Sheldon (political science), Herb Wells (engineering), Floyd Scritchfield (education), Reuben Neumann (accounting), and Jerry Craw-ford (speech and drama), overwhelmingly supported Donald Moyer. Despite Carlson's active effort to make his school independent of Reno, most Nevada Southern faculty believed he was too subservient to Armstrong. They wanted a strong advocate who would publicly challenge the president for more buildings and programs in the south.

In addition, many faculty, like John Wright in history and James Deacon in biology, saw Carlson as an "educationist" who wanted to make Nevada Southern into a teachers college. After all, Carlson came from an education background. He ran the campus more like a high school than a college—with bells ringing to signal the beginning and end of each class, for instance. And many of his proposals were aimed at training teachers rather than emphasizing research in the sciences and humanities. Carlson was even heard to say that Nevada Southern's inadequate library would never support advanced research. Deacon actually left Nevada Southern briefly in 1963 for a position at the Desert Research Institute, because he disliked what he considered the myopic, "educationist" direction of Nevada Southern under Carlson.[22]

For those who wanted Nevada Southern to evolve into the research university it is today, Donald Moyer's selection as chancellor was a major victory. Indeed, Deacon returned to the school in 1965 and stayed for the next thirty-five years. He and the others were not disappointed. Even though Moyer would serve as chancellor for less than four years, he would accomplish much during his tenure.

Carlson's problems persisted during the lame duck period before Moyer officially took over in June 1965. Inadequate funding continued to wreak havoc upon operations at NSU, prompting student complaints about a number of issues, including "muddled" class schedules. Carlson attributed the problem to lack of enough faculty and classrooms to handle soaring enrollment. He predicted that more state funding would solve the problem, but it never did.

One local newspaper bemoaned the number of closed classes. What the press did not realize was that the spectacle of students by the hundreds standing in line or sitting on a gym floor trying to register for class sections closing right in front of them was a familiar sight on campuses across the country in the 1960s, as the baby boom overwhelmed colleges from Maine to California. In Las Vegas the class shortage was not the faculty's fault; many were volunteering to teach five-course loads to ease the crisis—a practice hardly conducive to the greater research emphasis that Wright, Deacon, and other professors wanted the young college to pursue.

While some critics pointed to California, where UCLA and UC-Berkeley limited enrollment, Carlson opposed that option. "The University of California's program can include this method," he explained, "because those not admitted there may still attend their state colleges. In Nevada where would they go?"[23] But the Silver State's growth and the legislature's unwillingness to fund higher education at California levels to maintain low teacher-student ratios continued for decades. Future efforts by later presidents Robert Maxson and Carol Harter to raise admission standards by raising the minimum GPA would spark controversy over access even with a community college and later a state college system in place.

But Nevada Southern's enrollment crunch in the 1960s had other dimensions. First, it was not just the booming resort economy and in-migration that swelled Las Vegas's population and Nevada Southern's enrollment. The postwar "baby boom" also played a role, as residents themselves contributed their share to the growing population. At the same time, the state's failure to expand the faculty to meet student demand discouraged not only research but new programs as well. As one local editorial complained, "Because the faculty is taxed to capacity by student enrollment, the possibilities of expanding the fields covered is remote. This despite interest in the scientific community developed in southern Nevada by space rocketry and other research programs and the desire for a graduate school for persons teaching in the county school district."[24]

Clearly, Las Vegas would pay a price for delayed curricular development. The late 1950s and 1960s were precisely the decades when the University of Arizona, Arizona State, and the University of New Mexico were spending millions to upgrade their science and technology programs to attract cold war defense contractors to Tucson, Phoenix, and Albuquerque. All the while, department chairs in Las Vegas struggled to staff survey courses. Nevada's sluggish response to the challenge ultimately cost the metropolitan area. Despite the best efforts of Leonard Goodall, Robert Maxson, and others in the 1980s and 1990s to create an engineering school and attract high-tech companies to the Las Vegas Valley, these efforts came late in the game. By the 1960s, universities in California, Arizona, and New Mexico had already established research facilities and programs for training scientists and engineers, and the migration of computer firms to those southwestern and coastal cities was well under way.

LONGTIME HISTORY PROFESSOR JOHN WRIGHT (1956–76)
STANDS ON THE GYM'S ROOF IN 1964 AND WATCHES
CONSTRUCTION OF THE SOCIAL SCIENCES BUILDING (NAMED
IN 1976 JOHN S. WRIGHT HALL). UNLV OFFICE OF PUBLIC
AFFAIRS

In fact, during the 1960s, when contractors at the Nevada Test Site pleaded for advanced degrees in engineering at Nevada Southern, the Reno campus established a brief extension program at Camp Mercury, flying qualified instructors down to teach the classes. NSU played no part in the program.

Nevada Southern had neither the time nor the money to compete with rival schools for students, because it was too busy coping with soaring enrollment. While Dean Carlson agreed with those who suggested that closed-circuit telecasts would allow one instructor to teach many students, he cautioned that it would take a small army of teaching assistants to service the students. Staffing would be difficult, since Nevada Southern had no formal graduate programs in 1964. "If somehow capable aides could be obtained," Carlson explained, "the problem of keeping pace with pupil population would be lessened."[25] But that was not yet feasible. Moreover, television was not an effective way to teach foreign languages, science, and mathematics, disciplines in which student questions for the professor could not be easily answered. Technology would not surmount this problem until the 1990s when television, the Internet, and e-mail converged to make distance education more practical.

Carlson's solution to crowding in 1964 was the construction of large lecture halls. Later that spring, the dean would accept a check from Smith Barney for $1.45 million in state bonds to build the new social science building, which contained the school's first two large lecture halls. The facility (named for historian John Wright upon his retirement in 1976) opened for classes in fall 1965 and went a long way toward easing the classroom crunch. Wright Hall came just in time to eliminate the need for Carlson to limit 1965's freshman enrollment to 500 students, a move that the Las Vegas community opposed.

But the shortage of funds only continued, made worse by Las Vegas's unrelenting growth, which fed still more students to Nevada Southern. Carlson was no doubt relieved to let Donald Moyer handle the problem. In 1965 the beleaguered dean retreated to the newly created Division of Education, where he trained teachers for the rest of his career. Carlson, who had arrived to head the new campus in 1957, and Professor Holbert Hendrix, who had come to Nevada Southern a year earlier, both retired in 1980. To honor the men for their contributions to NSU/UNLV, President Leonard Goodall named the education building for Carlson and its adjacent lecture hall–auditorium for Hendrix—a fitting tribute to two dedicated pioneers.

Carlson guided the young campus through its formative years. Had some university officials had their way, Nevada Southern would have remained an academic backwater—little more than a feeder school for Reno and, at best, a junior college. Like his predecessor, Carlson never openly challenged his superiors. But he devised an agenda for Nevada Southern's development and engaged in skillful diplomacy with university officials and his own faculty to implement it. Clearly, he was more than a caretaker; he quietly laid a firm foundation for Donald Moyer to build upon.

CHAPTER THREE

The Struggle for Autonomy

DONALD MOYER

By the mid-1960s, the regents believed that Nevada Southern needed a more dynamic leader than Carlson, but still one who would not challenge them. They would get more than they bargained for in Donald Moyer. After voting 6–3 not to offer the Las Vegas chancellorship to Carlson, the board selected Donald C. Moyer as the third head of Nevada Southern. With a doctorate in higher education administration from the University of Chicago, where he served as director of alumni development, Moyer had pursued a career in administration. For more than a decade, he held various educational positions, including executive secretary of the New Mexico Board of Educational Finance before becoming president of Eastern New Mexico University in 1960. Upon hearing of Moyer's appointment as NSU's new leader, Carlson urged Las Vegans to close ranks behind his successor. "I feel that we all owe the new Chancellor our loyalty and cooperation," Carlson declared. "He certainly has mine."[1]

Following his selection, Moyer told reporters that he was impressed by the "potential" of fast-growing Nevada Southern. Guiding a campus of 2,800 students for five years at Eastern New Mexico had prepared him for the challenges of a school with an enrollment of 1,500 that, he believed, would quickly surpass

Eastern New Mexico. Moyer resembled later presidents like Robert Maxson and Carol Harter in that he brought an ambitious vision for the Maryland Parkway school, and he was quick to articulate it. "Those persons who have been planning campuses haven't been thinking big enough," he insisted in a 1965 interview. "We have to lay out a big broad view of the campus which will be adequate for future needs."[2]

The 1963 master plan report by Skidmore, Owings, and Merrill Architects and Planners had suggested setting up a revolving fund to buy more land, but university officials regarded the idea as a bit premature. At that time, real estate south of today's University Road was worth about $14,000 or $15,000 an acre.

The need to begin buying land became obvious in 1966 when developer Lloyd Tupper filed an application to rezone the tract along Maryland Parkway

UNLV'S FIRST PRESIDENT, DONALD MOYER, 1965–68.
SPECIAL COLLECTIONS, UNLV LIBRARIES 0062-0964

just south of NSU's property line (at today's University Road intersection) from residential to commercial so he could build a small shopping center and a McDonald's. Fred Anderson, chair of the board of regents, met with Clark County commissioners, who agreed to hold the request in abeyance until Anderson showed county planners NSU's master plan. But Anderson had to concede that there was none and none was under way, explaining, "It would be extremely difficult at this time [because] we do not know what the legislature will give us."[3] While Anderson and Moyer both pleaded for more time to devise a way to buy the real estate, its owner, Gerald Leavitt, was no longer willing to wait. Although school officials blocked the fast-food restaurant for several decades, they could not block the commercial development. The acreage along Maryland Parkway from University Road to Tropicana was lost in 1966 because there was no state money to buy it.

Concerned that this scenario might be repeated all along the school's perimeter, Moyer worked with banker Parry Thomas and other Las Vegas businessmen to form the Nevada Southern Land Foundation. They were literally in a

FIRST MEETING OF THE NEVADA SOUTHERN LAND FOUNDA-
TION, WITH E. PARRY THOMAS AT THE HEAD OF THE TABLE.
(FROM LEFT): J. KELL HOUSSELS JR., ARCHIE GRANT, UNIDEN-
TIFIED, NEIL HUMPHREY, HERMAN WESTFALL, HERB GRIER,
PROCTOR HUG JR. TO PARRY THOMAS'S RIGHT ARE DONALD
MOYER, HAROLD JACOBSEN, TOM BELL, WILLIAM HANCOCK (OF
THE STATE PUBLIC WORKS BOARD), UNIVERSITY ENGINEER
EDWARD PINE, JAMES CASHMAN JR., AND ART SMITH (OF FIRST
NATIONAL BANK). UNLV OFFICE OF PUBLIC AFFAIRS

race against time to acquire some key parcels bordering the campus before land values soared even higher. The trustees held their first meeting on January 27, 1967, just one day after the foundation's incorporation and three months *before* state lawmakers passed legislation authorizing university officials to operate such an organization. By statute, the foundation was a nonprofit corporation authorized to "hold land for later sale to the State for the University."[4] President Moyer chaired the board of trustees, which consisted of businessmen Herb Grier, James Cashman Jr., J. Kell Houssels Jr., regent Juanita White, and bankers Parry Thomas and Jerome Mack. Thomas served as foundation president; regent Procter Hug functioned as treasurer, and Nevada Southern's business manager, Herman Westfall, was the secretary.

At their first meeting, the trustees conceded defeat on Leavitt's costly Maryland Parkway tract and instead focused their efforts on purchasing less-expensive parcels. The foundation bought numerous tracts that today constitute much of the campus north and west of the old Dickinson Library (today's William S. Boyd School of Law). Some of the acquisitions, however, did not become part of the campus. According to the statute, regents were not obligated to buy all of the foundation's properties. So, for instance, when the board decided not to purchase the site of today's Terrible's Hotel and Casino at the corner of Paradise and Flamingo Roads, the foundation sold that tract to private interests for $814,000, which it then gave to the university. Sometimes there were missed opportunities. Witness the abortive effort to purchase the local Boy Scout headquarters, today the parking lot on University Road and Brussels Street. The Boulder Dam Area Council had used the property as a training facility since 1965. In April 1974 the foundation offered the council $350,000 for its 2.2 acres and building, but the Boy Scouts wanted $400,000, which the foundation rejected. In 2001 UNLV paid $1.5 million plus other costs for the same property.

Part of the problem in expanding the campus lay in the university's tardiness in creating the land foundation. As maps in Skidmore, Owings, and Merrill's 1963 campus plan clearly demonstrate, nearby property was available.[5] In October 1972, for example, the foundation tried to buy parcels of land owned by the University Park Apartments on Cottage Grove, northeast of the campus. It got little more than an acre. Unfortunately, lands bordering the south side of Flamingo Road and the southwest corner of Maryland Parkway already contained apartments and some businesses, and those properties had already become too valuable to acquire. The opening of Caesars Palace in 1966, the Boulevard Mall in 1967, and the MGM Grand Hotel (today Bally's) in 1973 had stimulated building and traffic up and down those arteries for several miles, appreciating land values beyond the university's budget capabilities. This was the same problem encountered by regents in 1966 when the Tropicana Hotel, the new 1963 jetport, and other developments along Tropicana Avenue raised front-foot values on Gerald Leavitt's property to the point where the university could not afford to buy it.

Nevertheless, Moyer's land foundation made significant progress. The trustees met from 1966 until 1977, when the state finally completed its purchase of

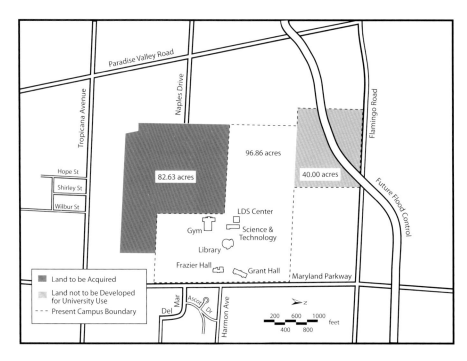

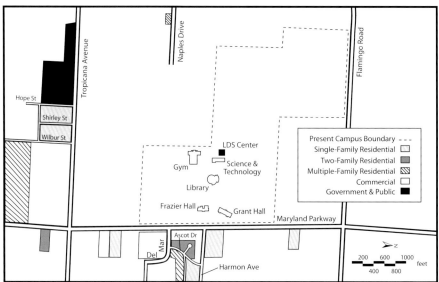

TOP: LAND ACQUISITIONS, 1963

BOTTOM: LAND USE—CAMPUS VICINITY, 1963, UNIVERSITY
OF NEVADA, LAS VEGAS CAMPUS

all of the foundation's landholdings, giving UNLV most of its present-day campus. During these years, the foundation bought 164.51 acres, using $2,284,000 in bonds authorized by the legislature. The trustees acted just in time; as early as 1975, Herman Westfall reported the lands' appraised value at $12 million. Trustees Parry Thomas and Jerry Mack were particularly helpful in using their financial expertise and their Bank of Las Vegas (later Valley Bank) to handle the sometimes complicated transactions affecting the acquisition of these tracts. According to future president Leonard Goodall, their dedicated service to the land foundation was the major reason why he and the regents named the Thomas & Mack Center for them in 1983.

Aside from securing more land for the campus, President Moyer also worked to satisfy community needs. In 1965 he supported creation of the Division of Continuing Education "to meet the demand for classes off campus." "A university," he declared, "ought to support its community in providing programs which would help the community to grow." To this end, he promised to "meet local people and discuss Las Vegas's needs and problems and what the university might do to solve them."[6] This was the approach he had witnessed at the University of New Mexico, where upgraded science and engineering programs promoted the growth of the nearby Sandia Laboratories and the cold war economy that keyed Albuquerque's postwar development. Having seen this phenomenon in New Mexico, Moyer looked to replicate the process in Las Vegas.

Moyer emphasized science as one way that an improved Nevada Southern curriculum could help Las Vegas. And while he did not specifically mention them, the connections were obvious. Having taught mathematics in Tennessee, and having received a doctorate from the University of Chicago, whose physics faculty helped build the first atomic bomb, and having observed in Albuquerque the symbiotic relationship between the university's science departments and that city's atomic economy, Moyer eagerly prepared to develop the university in the city nearest the site where America tested its nuclear weapons.

Part of Moyer's building program would include the expanded library, dedicated to the school's first leader. Less than two weeks after Carlson lost the chancellor's post to Moyer, Nevada Southern's first head, James Dickinson, suffered a massive heart attack and was rushed to Sunrise Hospital. The professor of English and chair of the school's Humanities Division died after a second

A STUDENT WATCHES THE SECOND AND THIRD FLOORS OF THE JAMES DICKINSON LIBRARY UNDER CONSTRUCTION, 1966. *EPILOGUE,* 1966

coronary a week later. For Las Vegas residents, including Nevada Southern's alumni and current students, Dickinson was the beloved figure who had shepherded the extension program through its salad days and transformed it into a school large enough to justify a campus. He registered and taught most of the early students and hired all of the early faculty. Upon completion of his Ph.D. at Stanford, Dickinson had returned to Las Vegas to head the English program and the Humanities Division. Veteran English professor Felicia Campbell remembered Dickinson's meeting her at McCarran Airport in 1962 and helping her get settled in Las Vegas, where she began a career at the school that would span more than forty years. Nor was she the only one who benefited from Dickinson's assistance.

In a touching eulogy, regent Juanita White described Dickinson as "the man who built Nevada Southern," while the *Review-Journal* added, "The memory of Dr. Dickinson should remain a source of pride for the students and faculty."[7] In 1965 the students dedicated their annual yearbook to him. So it was no surprise when regents, students, faculty, and residents gathered that same year to dedicate the school's library to the man who had started it all on a small bookshelf at Las Vegas High in 1951. The old library, now part of the Law School, would proudly bear Dickinson's name until 2001, when the new Lied Library opened. And while the new library would honor Ernest Lied, whose foundation contributed the millions needed for its construction, President Carol Harter named the large plaza fronting the entrance for Dickinson in 2002 as a continuing tribute to his memory.

The year 1965 was notable not only for Moyer's arrival at Nevada Southern and Dickinson's death but also for a dramatic restructuring of the University of

NEVADA SOUTHERN'S SECOND COMMENCEMENT IN THE GYM, NOW PART OF THE MARJORIE BARRICK MUSEUM OF NATURAL HISTORY, 1965. SPECIAL COLLECTIONS, UNLV LIBRARIES 0062-0211

Nevada's organization that created a chancellor position at both Las Vegas and Reno. Other administrative reforms created new entities for faculty governance and more efficient management. As President Armstrong explained, on the Nevada Southern campus "we want a reorganization of the faculty itself. We want a faculty organization—elected by faculty—to advise the chancellor on education policy."[8] This change in policy resulted in the creation of a faculty senate, which would play a major role in curricular development. Armstrong also indicated the need to appoint a dean of faculty, a position that later evolved into vice president of academic affairs in the 1970s and provost in the 1980s. After university officials briefly saddled Moyer with the irascible Harold Hammond, an associate dean and historian on leave from New York University, Moyer fired him with Armstrong's blessing and selected thirty-one-year-old Jerry Crawford.

It proved to be a wise choice. Crawford was a popular and innovative theater arts instructor, who, among a host of other accomplishments, taught the first-ever honors course at the school, with John Bailiff (philosophy) and Charles Sheldon (political science). As dean of faculty, Crawford played a helpful role in developing Nevada Southern's curriculum. This included frequent skirmishes with as many as nine deans from the Reno campus over curricular issues. At the same time, Crawford also had to keep some of his own faculty in line. As President Moyer noted, through "negotiation and arbitration"[9] Crawford persuaded some senior faculty, who in the past had pushed their own curricular and other initiatives directly with state officials, to respect the chain of command and allow Moyer, with the advice of the faculty senate, to set policy and represent school positions with regents and lawmakers. Crawford also persuaded the faculty to approve student evaluation of courses, which only reinforced the importance of good teaching as a factor in tenure, promotion, and merit decisions.

Moyer and Crawford had more than their share of problems. The class and faculty shortages that plagued Carlson during his last months as dean continued into Moyer's years. When he arrived to take over Nevada Southern in June 1965, the new chancellor emphasized the need to raise more public and private funds for expansion and predicted a huge enrollment increase by century's end. "It may sound impossible," he declared in May 1965, "but in planning we should anticipate 25,000 students here by the end of the century." Moyer's statement reflected the breadth of his vision. He reassured those concerned about anti-tax legislators not providing enough funds for expansion by asserting that campus development would be more rapid "with strong local support."[10]

In this vein, Moyer used Carlson's Nevada Southern Foundation to raise thousands of dollars to help fund the new library expansion and construct the performing arts center's first building, the Judy Bayley Theatre, which opened in 1972. Moyer actively led fund-raising efforts in the business community with the help of Wing Fong, who chaired the Grand Founders' Committee. Moyer also required that to be eligible for a seat on the foundation's prestigious board of trustees, each member had to contribute a minimum of $10,000, which local businessmen willingly did. On another front, Moyer viewed the creation of programs promoting local economic expansion as crucial to help-ing the foundation raise funds. To this end, he suggested establishing a hotel and motel management school for Las Vegas's "unique" economy. At the time, little did anyone realize how significant this would be for the university's future fund-raising efforts.

A few resort executives had raised the idea of creating a hotel program at the Las Vegas campus in the late 1950s, but nothing ever came of it other than a ho-tel accounting class and a few other courses offered in the Division of Business during the mid-1960s. In January 1966, the Nevada Resort Association (NRA) rewarded Chancellor Moyer's efforts to create a hotel school at Nevada Southern by pledging $280,000 to fund a "department or school of hotel management," with courses in hotel-motel administration, and some coursework in gambling. While there was no overt effort to establish a dealers school, university officials were quick to reassure the public that the department's "courses relating to gambling will provide generally, an orientation" in gaming mathematics and accounting procedures.[11] There would be no formal degree in gaming manage-ment at the campus until 2003.

The gaming industry was cautious, too. Although Gabriel Vogliotti, execu-tive director of the Nevada Resort Association, also minimized the gambling dimension of the program, he reminded residents that no major Las Vegas hotel without a casino had yet succeeded. Indeed, the Aladdin had replaced the failed Tally-Ho, a non-gaming resort, that year. Vogliotti then pointed out that at most Las Vegas resorts, hotel, food, convention, and other guest service operations were becoming larger than the casino business itself. And while it would not be until the 1990s that Las Vegas resorts actually made more money in non-gaming revenue than from their casinos, the 1966 trend made a hotel department with gaming courses more appealing.

Advocates helped cement public and faculty support for the department by never mentioning that their ultimate goal was to make hotel administration anything more than a program within the Division of Business. Efforts to ensure quality reassured the faculty. University and NRA officials wisely hired Dr. Howard Meek, executive director of Cornell University's Council on Hotel and Restaurant Education and former dean of its College of Hotel Administration, as a consultant to help plan Nevada Southern's program. The fact that Cornell had offered a well-respected hotel administration program since the 1920s, financed initially with money from the Statler Hotel chain, made the NRA's proposals more palatable to Nevada Southern's faculty. In addition, since the NRA offered to fund all operating expenses until the fourth year, when the state would take over, the new program and its projected student enrollment of 150 would not drain Nevada Southern's budget. Vogliotti also declared the NRA's support for constructing a building to house the program, using resort gifts and donations "from wider segments of the hotel industry," including the big chains.[12]

In an editorial supporting the NRA's proposal, the *Review-Journal* argued that "in the true sense of the word, the Nevada hotelman is becoming just that—not just a casino manager with some rooms on the second floor." Recognizing that a hotel program would be good for the community and good for the hotel business, the editor noted: "It marks the first major gift to NSU by private industry. We hope it attracts other gifts so direly needed by the young school." The benefits were obvious. Nevada Southern would provide Las Vegas with "a labor pool of specially trained men and women . . . ready for integration into local hotels at all levels of management." The editorial added that "perhaps even large motels will exhibit an interest" in the graduates, too.[13] No one at the time expected the program's alumni to diffuse nationally throughout America's hospitality industry, but that would change in a few years.

The program needed a strong leader, and it got one in Jerome Vallen, who had applied for the position at Meek's urging. After interviewing Vallen in Chicago, Jerry Crawford recommended him to Moyer. In 1967 Vallen launched the program in NSU's business college with just 16 students. Over the next quarter century, he was instrumental in expanding the curriculum, raising private funds, persuading local hotel executives to teach classes, and securing internships at Strip resorts for advanced students. It was Vallen's leadership that helped make the hotel administration program, which became a department in 1968 and an independent college in 1969, nationally prominent.

Donald Moyer pushed not only for more programs like Vallen's, but also for new construction. In fact, space was still so scarce at the overcrowded campus that faculty in the fine arts and humanities regularly held their meetings at the bar of the Tropicana Country Club (where the MGM Grand Garden is today). Of course, the availability of cocktails and the club's ambience also influenced their choice of location. Former English professor Charles Adams recalled that his department regularly held its meetings there, with James Dickinson always buying the first round of drinks. Their colleague Felicia Campbell remembered that while faculty members moved through their agenda, celebrities like comedian Buddy Hackett would often stroll by or performers like Sammy Davis Jr. would sip drinks with friends at the next table. Crawford recently noted that Davis once jumped up on the bar and danced while the department tried to vote on an issue. Well aware of the space problem, Chancellor Moyer worked tirelessly to end the delays that slowed construction of new buildings on campus. This was particularly true of the school's first residence hall, today's north wing of Tonopah Hall, which opened in September 1966 along with the original dining commons (today part of the UNLV bookstore).

Moyer also lobbied President Armstrong and regents for a student union. In June 1965 Armstrong pleased Moyer and student leaders when he finally endorsed the creation of a committee to develop plans for a student union at Nevada Southern. Students voted to charge themselves a $27 fee to help finance the project. Later that year university officials won partial federal funding for the building, which opened in 1968.

There was progress on other fronts as well. In September 1965 Nevada's U.S. senators, Howard Cannon and Alan Bible, secured $529,500 in federal funds, roughly one-third of the money needed to finance construction of two additional floors to the Dickinson Library. Money came from the Higher Education Facilities Act of 1965, part of Lyndon Johnson's Great Society. Clearly, the friendship between the two senators and Johnson, including their support for the president's war in Vietnam, helped pry the money out of Congress.

Besides the added space, Dickinson Library also needed to expand its collections. Although the Reno campus had donated duplicate sets of books and journals over the years, they were not enough to support graduate and advanced undergraduate research. In the mid-1960s, library head Harold Erickson pleaded with southern Nevadans to contribute books, microfilm, and periodicals, especially older issues of *Nevada Highways,* the *Nevada Education Bulletin, Nevada Historical Society Quarterly,* and *Nevada Business Review.* He also asked local doctors, lawyers, and builders to donate old copies of professional journals from their personal collections. The two new floors that Moyer added to the library provided vitally needed space for these and thousands of other items until 1981, when UNLV constructed a rectangular building with a pedestrian bridge connecting both structures.

Nevada Southern's rapid development and its commitment to excellence with new buildings and programs brought other benefits. In November 1965, for instance, efforts of the Moyer and Crawford team to improve academic quality received another boost when officials of Sigma Xi, the Scientific Research Society, established the first national honor society on the Las Vegas campus. Founded in 1886, Sigma Xi was the honor society of research scientists and engineers, representing the disciplines that President Moyer deemed crucial to NSU's advancement as a research institution.

Of course, hindering Nevada Southern's development and pursuit of excellence was its dependence upon the Reno campus for approval, funding, and direction. Dean Carlson had begun the process that awarded Nevada Southern more independence by securing degree-granting status. But even after 1965, the main campus still held NSU's purse strings. All state revenues for Nevada Southern passed through the office of university president Charles Armstrong. Not only did all purchase orders from the south have to be approved in Reno, but NSU's business manager, Herman Westfall, continued to report to his counterpart in Reno until 1968. Westfall ordered items but had no control over the outcome. Indeed, Reno's business office frequently purchased items that were below NSU's specifications just to save money. Historian Robert Davenport recalled that during the construction of Tonopah Hall in 1966, Reno authorities chose all of the furnishings. Incredibly, the committee formed to plan the new chemistry building in 1968 included no members from Nevada Southern until regent Juanita White forced the inclusion of chemistry professor Robert Smith.

The need for complete autonomy was obvious to an administration, faculty, and student body who felt victimized by what they considered Reno's academic colonialism. Chancellor Moyer continued to lobby regents, sometimes enlisting the aid of Nevada Southern faculty and even student leaders to support the cause. Victory came in July 1966, nine years after the Maryland Parkway campus opened, when Moyer proudly announced: "We have it in writing now; each campus is a full-fledged university in its own right."[14] Nevada Southern's faculty finally became a governing body with the creation of a senate.

The Las Vegas campus had enjoyed a measure of autonomy with its own chancellor since Moyer's arrival in 1965, but votes on curricular reform and other academic measures still required approval by faculty committees in Reno. Now the Las Vegas school had its own faculty senate and academic council, both of which reported directly to Moyer. Of course, the chancellor, like his counterpart in Reno, still had to report to the University of Nevada president. But under the new plan, Moyer had control over local educational and administrative policy as well as legislative appropriations for the campus. In addition, NSU faculty could finally organize their own curriculum. By 1967 the school already had twenty-two academic departments, but Nevada Southern still had to meet the overall admission and graduation requirements of the Reno campus. Full autonomy from Reno, when the Nevada Southern chancellor became a real university president independent of the Reno president, would not occur until 1968.

The process moved forward when President Armstrong resigned under pressure in December 1967 and left to head a consortium of private colleges in Ohio. Once Armstrong vacated his position, regents discussed whether to abolish the university president's job and let the two chancellors run their own campuses or to preserve the status quo. In the end, pressured heavily by southern Nevada officials, students, faculty, and business leaders, the board chose a third option. Under the 1968 reorganization, one chancellor would head the university (and eventually the community college) system, with a president running each university campus.

Moyer was jubilant about his school's new freedom and wasted no time in exercising his new authority. In 1968 he and Crawford led a reorganization effort that transformed NSU's six schools (Business Administration, Education, Science and Mathematics, Fine Arts, Social Science, and Humanities) into colleges. Also in 1968, two years before the 1970 reaccreditation visit by the Northwest Association, Moyer authorized the preparation of a development plan by the respected Palo Alto consulting firm Davis, MacConnell, Ralston to guide campus development for the next decade. The consultants offered numerous recommendations, including converting Jerry Crawford's dean of faculty

GOVERNOR PAUL LAXALT AND REGENT FRED ANDERSON SIT
BEHIND DONALD MOYER AT NEVADA SOUTHERN'S FOURTH
COMMENCEMENT, 1967. SPECIAL COLLECTIONS, UNLV
LIBRARIES 0062-0971

position to vice president of academic affairs. The school immediately enacted this reform, which brought future president Donald Baepler to campus in 1968 after Crawford returned to the faculty. Crawford had helped pave the way for Baepler's hiring by recommending him to Moyer and the regents after the two had met during a conference in Seattle.

The consultants also insisted that each campus president "must have sufficient autonomy to carry out the program of the institution under his own leadership so that the institution may move forward."[15] The wording undoubtedly pleased Moyer, who was probably still concerned that the regents might someday rescind some of the authority they had given him. But the consultants missed the real internal problem: too much power for the senate and the colleges at the president's expense—something that the 1970 reaccreditation team would emphasize.

Regarding programs, the consultants suggested that Nevada Southern consider establishing a law school, an idea that Moyer had emphasized in his initial meetings with them. This 1968 report represents perhaps one of the earliest documented statements recommending a law school on the Las Vegas campus. The consultants reasoned that "in the years to come Clark County will continue to outstrip other areas in a) its need for legally trained men and women and b) its continually expanding urban 'critical mass' which will increasingly provide the necessary milieu of attorney's offices, courts, cases to be tried, and so forth."[16]

The consultants also urged Nevada Southern to begin emphasizing research from its faculty rather than just teaching and service. "An emphasis on research is . . . justified," the report asserted, "because of the need to offer and to maintain programs of excellence; programs which must continuously thrust forward in order to stay at the 'cutting edge' of inquiry."[17] In an ambitious agenda, the consultants advised the creation of a Ph.D. degree in English by 1970–71 (the M.A. had just begun in 1967–68) and doctorates in German, Spanish, French, education, and sociology by 1971–72. But in 1971, education became the only doctorate offered at the Maryland Parkway campus; no others were instituted until the 1980s. The report also urged Ph.D. programs in political science, physics, and mathematics by 1972–73, and history the following year. The consultants even advocated creating a dental school, offering a D.D.S. degree by the 1976–77 school year. The timing of their agenda was a bit ambitious. As late as 2007, political science still did not have a doctoral program; history waited until 1991, and the School of Dental Medicine did not open until 2002.

The consultants also recommended more vocationally oriented degrees. This included a police science degree, which evolved into the Department of Criminal Justice during the 1970s. In addition, the evaluators suggested a technical degree in stage production. "While Las Vegas is certainly endowed with casinos and top name stars," the report declared, "it certainly cannot lay claim to great emphasis in the serious or legitimate theater." But, "in an effort . . . to provide personnel for technical programs in the performing arts and . . . to establish and enhance serious theater in the Clark County Area," the consultants strongly recommended that a "full range program in the practical aspects of the performing and cultural arts be instituted."[18] This idea fell by the wayside for decades until 2004 when the Harter administration finally implemented a more comprehensive version of it. The consultants' assumption that Las Vegas could not support legitimate theater eventually proved false; by 2000 the Department of Theater offered nationally recognized master's of fine arts degrees in playwriting, performance, and design.

Perhaps the most dramatic portion of the 1968 report was not the programmatic vision of the future or, in the case of some programs, the cracked crystal ball effect of events that never came to pass, but the consultants' major conclusions. After considerable study, they argued that "the geographical and socio-economic area of Southern Nevada not only can but should support . . . a full-scale and first-rate program in higher education ranging from courses usually associated with the community junior college through upper division courses and on through programs at the masters' and doctors' degree level." In short, the consultants were "convinced of the need for a full-fledged and full-scaled university in Las Vegas which Nevada Southern University may and should become."[19]

Moyer was eager to enact many of the new programs, including the law school. Increasingly, however, the northern-dominated board of regents became concerned about his aggressive approach. As early as April 1968, rumors began to circulate that Moyer would resign. On May 1 he made it official in a vaguely worded statement, asserting that he could "no longer afford to remain in higher educational administration." Moyer gave every indication that his $25,000 annual salary was not enough to secure his "family's future."[20] Some regents speculated that the president had more lucrative offers from private industry that he could not pass up.

But money was not the main factor behind Moyer's decision. Put simply, he was tired of battling with northern regents over budget requests for his school. And many of the regents were tired of him. The creation of a hotel program was a major step toward Moyer's goal of building a university that would serve the city, but it was more the result of a generous grant from the NRA than state action. Even later, when Nevada had to assume the operational expenses for running the program, it was done by legislators who relied on casino campaign contributions for their reelection.

For Moyer, the hotel program was a necessary first step, but he came from a science background. His dream was to do for his campus what Sandia Laboratories and millions in federal defense spending had done for the University of

New Mexico. He wanted to expand graduate education and in-service training for area science projects and spend the money necessary to build an impressive science complex. But it never happened. Northern regents had little interest in making Nevada Southern into a high-quality science school or research center. By 1968 their attention had already turned to availing themselves of Howard Hughes's original $6 million offer to build a medical school on the main campus in Reno (approved by the state legislature in 1977).

Undeterred, Moyer and Crawford pushed hard to expand graduate programs, arguing that a quality faculty could not be recruited without them. In April 1966, Moyer announced that the Clark County School District and the local business community needed advanced degree programs for their employees. To this end, that fall the Moyer-Crawford team launched the first master's degree programs, in the Divisions of Education, Science, and Business Administration. Nevada Southern awarded its first graduate degree in 1967. Progress was rapid; by 1969 UNLV offered master's degrees in seventeen disciplines, almost half the Reno figure.

But the only large investment in science was the construction of five buildings on Harmon Avenue, which the state leased to the U.S. Public Health Service to house the Southwestern Radiological Laboratory. In addition to testing for natural and man-made sources of radiation in the environment, the laboratory's purpose was to raise public awareness of the dangers posed by radiation. Research conducted at Nevada Southern and other facilities would later result in the Public Health Service's questioning the position of Atomic Energy Commission scientists that nuclear testing was safe. Begun during the Carlson administration, the complex opened its first building just west of the science and technology building (later called Science Hall) in 1961; the state built additional facilities in 1966. The only advantage for Moyer was that in the early years, some "Rad Lab" personnel voluntarily taught regular courses in biology, chemistry, physics, and engineering, which helped supplement the university's understaffed departments. The laboratory became part of the Environmental Protection Agency in 1970. When the EPA's twenty-five-year lease expired during the mid-1980s, the space crunch on campus led President Robert Maxson to consider asking the EPA to seek an off-campus facility, but complaints from regular science faculty and the administration's realization that the laboratory strengthened UNLV's appeal to prospective science students kept the EPA on campus.

Moyer attributed most of his problems with the regents and university officials to his battle for autonomy. In a 2002 interview, he recalled that in 1965 the university president, administrators, and even the faculty in Reno still exerted substantial control over Nevada Southern's academic programs, hiring, budgeting, and planning. Until 1968, they were in a position to control and even block the school's expansion, and often did. Moyer complained that Reno enjoyed an 8-to-1 student-faculty ratio while Nevada Southern's was 25-to-1, an advantage that allowed the big campus to recruit the best students by promising them more individual attention and a better education. The situation changed slowly, beginning with Las Vegas assemblywoman Flora Dungan's successful suit in federal court to force the legislature's reapportionment. The resulting decision, *Dungan* v. *Sawyer* (1965), awarded Clark County a majority of seats in both houses of the legislature, a crucial first step toward giving Nevada Southern its share of appropriations. In appreciation for her effort, UNLV named the new seven-story humanities building for Dungan in 1974 and art professor Rita Abbey sculpted a likeness of her, which the university still displays in the lobby.

Moyer's conflicts with regents and lawmakers over autonomy issues eventually took their toll. "I only stayed three years," he remembered, "because when you really work hard to get emancipated, you make a lot of enemies." And he did. He was also frustrated by the perennial lack of money. In 1966, the English department had to turn away more than 400 students from freshman courses because of insufficient funds to hire staff. Moyer's plans for America's first twenty-four-hour college, designed to service the course needs of Las Vegas workers on swing and graveyard shifts, also foundered for lack of funds, as did many of his other initiatives. When asked in 1968 how NSU would secure enough funds for the new buildings and faculty it needed, Moyer told reporters: "My personal approach must be working within the system, but I believe STRUD [Students to Remove Upstate Domination] can help us in educating northern legislators as to NSU's needs."[21] STRUD was a group of militant students whom the northern regents detested, and Moyer's words hardly reflected the kind of rhetoric the board expected from NSU's president.

Additionally, once the state legislature had been reapportioned to give Clark

County virtual control, Moyer flagrantly violated the system's policy that allowed only the university president to lobby lawmakers for appropriations. He also antagonized northern officials by plying Howard Hughes, who was sequestered in the penthouse of the Desert Inn from 1966 to 1970, with various academic schemes designed to secure a fragment of the billionaire's fortune for the Las Vegas campus. In the end, Hughes chose to fund a medical school in Reno. Moyer also supported a proposal, instituted in New Mexico, to establish separate boards of regents for the Reno and Las Vegas campuses, a controversial idea that university officials opposed. For these and other reasons, most regents were glad to see Moyer go. In fact, after his departure, regents such as Fred Anderson, a supporter of departed university president Armstrong, initially balked at student requests that UNLV's new student union be named for Moyer. Eventually, student body president and later attorney Bill Terry, along with Wing Fong, convinced the board.

Besides campus expansion and the autonomy fight, Moyer took fund-raising to new heights in an effort to supplement state funds and buy land for expansion. "We had to do everything at the grass-roots level," he recalled. "It was very difficult to raise money back then." Part of the problem was that, before Nevada legalized corporate gaming in 1969, "the hotels . . . were not big contributors." Much of the $1.5 million the school raised to build the Judy Bayley Theatre came from $10,000 and $1,000 donations from all over the community. But, Moyer added, the momentum generated by the small gifts was crucial, because "a large number of small donations persuaded others to make larger donations," including $65,000 from Judy Bayley herself.[22]

After resigning in May 1968, Moyer eventually left for Alaska, where he worked on university expansion in that state before returning to Southern Nevada in the mid-1970s as a marriage and family counselor. Despite his relatively short tenure at Nevada Southern, Moyer's accomplishments were significant. By securing full autonomy from Reno, he completed the process begun by Carlson when he won degree-granting status for the school. It was Moyer who brought the right people together in the gaming community to begin what became the hotel college. It was Moyer who took Carlson's small Nevada Southern Foundation, harnessed the fund-raising energy of Bill "Wildcat" Morris, and used both to get the money to expand the library and move closer to building the Judy

Bayley Theatre. Moyer also began the foundation that acquired enough land to sustain the school's development for the rest of the century.

Moyer, along with his dean of faculty, Jerry Crawford, emphasized academic credibility by initiating honors classes and student evaluation of teaching. In a state with limited funds, the Moyer-Crawford team worked with faculty to target select subject areas for accelerated curricular development, including desert biology and ecology, the performing arts, and hotel management. In addition, to "meet the demand for classes off campus" they pushed for creation of the Division of Continuing Education in 1965, resurrecting William Carlson's off-campus program begun in 1957 by Herbert Derfelt, who was now an education professor. They also boosted the importance of intercollegiate athletics by hiring Bill Ireland to establish a football program at the school. As Crawford has noted, all of these efforts were designed to increase Nevada Southern's national visibility.

But, most important, it was Moyer, Nevada Southern's first "president," who, in his speeches and press comments, was the first to emphasize the importance of science in building the Maryland Parkway campus into the serious research institution that it is today.

CHAPTER FOUR

The End of "Tumbleweed Tech"

ROMAN ZORN AND DONALD BAEPLER

For Moyer's successor, the next logical step was to begin the long process of transforming UNLV into a research university by placing greater emphasis on scholarship. Regents again hired the right person, or in this case, persons, for the job. Just days before Donald Baepler was scheduled to become President Moyer's academic vice president, Moyer resigned. Taken by surprise, the regents hurriedly appointed Baepler interim president. Baepler, a respected ornithologist and scholar, took the reins for almost a year—a "baptism of fire," as he described it—before Roman "Jay" Zorn arrived in March 1969 to assume control. Together, these two would begin to make UNLV into more of a research institution.

While regents were probably more interested in Zorn's ability to control a faculty given too much leash by Moyer and a student body increasingly restive over civil rights, Vietnam, and northern domination of their school, Zorn was more concerned about UNLV's future direction. Ever the dedicated scholar, Zorn was well qualified to push UNLV toward a greater research emphasis. With a bachelor's degree in history from Wisconsin State College, Zorn began his career as a high school teacher during the Depression. After a stint in the army

UNLV'S SECOND PRESIDENT, ROMAN "JAY" ZORN, 1969–73.
SPECIAL COLLECTIONS, UNLV LIBRARIES 0062-0963

PRESIDENT DONALD BAEPLER, 1973–78. SPECIAL
COLLECTIONS UNLV LIBRARIES #0062-0965

during World War II, he earned a Ph.D. in history from the University of Wisconsin. He taught in a variety of colleges, including the University of Arkansas–Fayetteville, Ohio University, the University of Missouri, and the University of Wisconsin, where he got his first administrative post. After serving as dean of the College of Arts and Letters at the University of Wisconsin, Zorn became president of Keene Teachers College in New Hampshire in 1965 before regents selected him as UNLV's second president in October 1968.

Students welcomed Zorn with little enthusiasm. The new president served during the most tumultuous time on campus in all the twentieth century. The late 1960s and early 1970s were deeply affected by national and international events. It was an age convulsed by violence, as the passions unleashed by the civil rights movement and the Vietnam War radicalized large numbers of students. During this period when the usual campus quiescence yielded to protests and, in some places, rioting, many an ulcer-ridden college president opted for retirement.

Zorn had already experienced a measure of conflict at Keene State, and it carried over to UNLV. Even before he arrived, a group of student rights advocates working for the *Rebel Yell* published stories about how Zorn had dismissed a popular Keene State instructor who had actively supported Senator Eugene McCarthy's 1968 campaign against Lyndon Johnson in New Hampshire's presidential primary. According to the story, Zorn had "snubbed" students at Keene State who wanted to discuss the firing with him. Student activists did what they could in the *Rebel Yell* to stir the cauldron and poison the atmosphere against the incoming president, whom they regarded as another stodgy traditionalist. Zorn knew he had a public relations problem, so, even before taking office, he met with the press, including student reporters, to discuss recent controversies at Keene State. Asked about class boycotts and faculty complaints, Zorn explained that "whatever movement exists at Keene State consists of 20 students and a tightly knit group of close friends in the faculty."[1] It was hardly a mass uprising reminiscent of Berkeley's Free Speech Movement or the huge protests that other campuses experienced.

Zorn reiterated his support for student participation in the campus governing process and made it clear that as president of UNLV, "I'm opening the door to any responsible student who wants to talk with me."[2] And he did, even supporting the creation of a university senate in 1971 that allowed student senators to take their seats next to faculty representatives. The students would remain, voting on university matters, for most of the decade, until faculty and professional staff decided to reestablish a faculty senate in spring 1978. At that time, student representatives returned to the CSUN Senate (CSNS, the Consolidated Students of Nevada Southern, had become CSUN, the Consolidated Students of the University of Nevada in 1969, once Nevada Southern changed its name to UNLV).

Before Zorn's inauguration as president, militant staff members on the *Rebel Yell* continued to do all they could to raise questions about his selection by what they considered the ever villainous regents. *Yell* reporters even went to New Hampshire to interview Keene State students and faculty. In a ten-page special edition of the newspaper, based on interviews of a "cross section" of students and faculty, the investigators came to the predictable conclusion that while Zorn had numerous admirers in the faculty and student body, many other students and professors were concerned about his management style. One anonymous administrator noted that Zorn was "a constant nit-picker" who "can't keep his fingers out of any pie."[3] Of course, as the president of a small college, Zorn knew that if there were problems with any of the "pies," it would be he, not the students, faculty, or administrators, who would ultimately be held accountable.

In time, the attempts at vilification subsided, thanks for the most part to Zorn's conciliatory remarks and capable leadership. When asked, for example, if he would approve hiring counselors for minority students who needed help in adjusting to college life, the president responded positively. Indeed, Zorn was sensitive to minority student needs and was the first president to reach out to Las Vegas's growing Hispanic community. In 1973 he authorized publication of a lengthy recruitment booklet printed in English and Spanish that highlighted the achievements of UNLV's Hispanic students and urged Spanish-speaking high school seniors and other qualified residents to apply.

New buildings also appeared, and just in time, as the campus struggled to serve a metropolitan population that passed 275,000 in 1970. With construction scheduled to begin in late 1969 for what became the seven-story Flora Dungan Humanities Building (FDH), Zorn predicted that the structure "will not only solve problems of space shortages, but will also allow us room to expand our curricular programs in the coming years."[4] The new space was sorely needed, since in fall 1969, after two years of austere budgets, UNLV had 25 percent more faculty than in 1968. The seventh floor of the Dungan Humanities Building became the home of UNLV's head. William Carlson's office had been in Maude Frazier Hall. Donald Moyer moved it to the second floor of Dickinson Library when that new addition opened in 1967, while Jerry Crawford's dean of faculty office was in the two-year-old social science building. Both offices remained at those locations until Zorn and Baepler moved them to the humanities building in 1972.

In 1969–70, construction and hiring almost kept pace with the school's spiraling enrollment. "During this academic year," Vice President Baepler announced, "we will complete new chemistry and faculty office buildings." In spring 1970, the school sold bonds for what would become the Judy Bayley Theatre; later that year, the chemistry building opened. Baepler also noted that new faculty and the hiring of 59 graduate assistants "will permit us to expand our upper division and graduate offerings, and still enable us to give greater attention to beginning students."[5] This was the key. Zorn got new buildings, but he also hired more faculty and at higher salaries than ever before. Making the process easier was the 1970 election of Democrat, and former Basic High School history and government teacher, Mike O'Callaghan to succeed conservative Paul Laxalt as governor. Program development and restructuring also were important. It was Zorn and Baepler who established the graduate college in a 1971 reorganization plan. Even though English, history, biology, and other departments already offered some graduate courses and even master's degree programs, the creation of the graduate college gave these initiatives added momentum.

Increases in faculty salaries, the hiring of more faculty, the construction of more buildings, and the creation of the graduate college all contributed to UNLV's maturity and growing quality. Sometimes, however, this commitment to excellence sparked controversy. For example, the termination of popular instructors triggered conflict. This was especially true in departments like political science, which, unlike history, gave students no representation or vote in tenure decisions. Eventually, the firing of several popular teachers for failing to earn their terminal degrees inspired majors to form the Political Science Student Association.

But standards were changing at UNLV. Zorn and Baepler argued that the campus had been established. Gone were the old pioneer days when faculty taught heavy course loads and spent hours on committee work. UNLV was now a university and had to get about the business of developing a good research faculty, whose scholarship would allow the school to rise to the next level and begin earning respect among its peer schools nationally.

As Vice President Baepler noted in a recent reminiscence, contracts were not renewed for any faculty who failed to earn the terminal degree in their field (for most the Ph.D. or the Ed.D.). This policy even extended to administrators. In 1969, when hotel administration became an independent college, Zorn and Baepler refused to appoint the program's head, Jerome Vallen, a dean until he earned his doctorate. Since no university offered a Ph.D. program in hotel administration in 1967 when Vallen arrived at NSU, his promotion had to wait until the early 1970s when he finished his doctorate at Cornell.

Under Zorn and Baepler, the standards quickly rose beyond mere possession of a terminal degree. By 1970 faculty in some departments were also denied tenure for failing to publish. In the early 1970s Zorn and Baepler applied this policy selectively at first, focusing on departments with graduate programs. Their position was that faculty who taught advanced coursework should themselves be publishing scholars in their field. So in departments like English and biology, publications were required. In others, like philosophy, which lacked a graduate program, the old rules applied for several more years. But by the late 1970s third-year reviews of faculty requiring documented progress of research activity leading to publication or its equivalent became the rule in virtually all departments.

In a 1973 statement published in the *Rebel Yell,* Baepler summarized the administration's position: "We have emerged from a bleak period in our history when salaries were not competitive and our overall lack of excellence reflected that deficiency."[6] Recognizing that some students remained disappointed that a few of their favorite teachers had been dismissed, Baepler assured them that the decisions were made in the interests of academic quality and that the degree UNLV's graduates worked so hard for would become more valuable as the school's prestige rose. After noting that 70 percent of the university's 250 faculty members now held doctorates, Baepler proudly declared: "There has been an exodus of marginally qualified instructors during recent years and their replacements have been men and women with outstanding credentials."[7] Of course, not all of the faculty who left were deadwood. In some years during the late 1950s and 1960s, nearly 20 percent of the school's full-time faculty quit— many of them talented academics who simply grew tired of the heat, isolation, lack of resources, and low pay. Others left after the efforts by some faculty in 1967–69 to form a union and engage in collective bargaining with the regents failed to win broad support from their colleagues.

Nevertheless, Zorn and Baepler did all they could to promote scholarship, with the goal of making the struggling university better. In 1970–71, they effectively reduced the teaching load to three courses for each regular semester to promote more research and match the 3–3 standard at most comparable universities of the time. They accomplished this quietly by forcing departments to teach larger classes, which the big lecture halls in new buildings, such as the social science building and Flora Dungan Humanities, made possible. In this way, professors still taught increasing numbers of students, but did it more efficiently.

Zorn and Baepler not only encouraged more publication but pursued their commitment to excellence on other fronts as well. They wasted little time in implementing many of the reforms suggested by the Northwest Association's accreditation team in 1970. This report called for streamlining UNLV s organizational structure to promote orderly development. In the document, reviewers complained that "the University seems overly structured and departmentalized." As they saw it, UNLV's development had "been accompanied by decentralization that has tended to defeat collaborative assessment of problems and positive administrative leadership." They faulted UNLV's lack of adequate support staff for the president and his academic vice president and suggested that "the intangible cost associated with excessive fragmentation of university policy-making may be a much more important item to explore." Put simply, the departments, colleges, and faculty senate had as much or more control over curricular development and other matters than Zorn or Baepler did. "It appears that the colleges and their departments may control the senate and, if they wish, unite against change or promote their own programs and expansion. There is no graduate faculty to interfere and the University Code gives the faculty and colleges much authority."[8]

The implications were serious for UNLV's progress, because in 1970 the majority of UNLV's faculty were still dominated by those who emphasized teaching and service over research. They were in a position to stymie the selection of new applicants with a scholarly emphasis and block advanced graduate programs that would give further momentum to hiring top-quality scholars. For the most part, however, this did not happen. Still, the accreditation team expressed concern about the president's lack of power to combat this danger: "Apparently, the university president can withhold budget or his approval as new programs go to the regents. However, he is in a relatively poor position to actually block undesirable curricular and structural change."[9]

In the end, UNLV was reaccredited. The Northwest Association's evaluators agreed that the school "has much promise." The committee members complimented the administration, faculty, students, and programs, but warned that UNLV needed to "adjust its structure [and] bring its hopes and plans more in line with current size and budgetary capabilities."[10] Zorn responded to the report by ordering an overhaul of UNLV's organizational framework. He appointed the Ad Hoc Committee on the Developing University, chaired by history professor Paul Burns, to study the matter. In early 1971 the committee submitted an eighteen-page report, which became the basis for university-wide discussions. The administration scheduled numerous faculty-staff meetings and encouraged students to attend.

Zorn's and Baepler's effort was remarkably similar to the initiative by Carol

Harter and her provost, Douglas Ferraro, in the mid-1990s to reduce the number of colleges and stand-alone programs at UNLV. The goal in 1970 was to reduce the university's ten academic units, which included eight colleges (Business and Economics, Education, Fine Arts, General and Technical Studies, Hotel Administration, Humanities, Science and Mathematics, and Social Sciences) and two divisions (Graduate Studies and Continuing Education and Summer Session). After all, the university had fewer than 6,000 students, and Zorn wanted to leave room for the new colleges that would surely come with expansion. The committee proposed to merge all existing colleges into four: a college of cultural and environmental studies, a college of professional studies, a graduate college, and a university college. Even as UNLV won official reaccreditation in January 1971, debate raged on about the changes.

Clearly, the committee was too ambitious about compressing the number of colleges. There was little sentiment on campus for merging fine arts, letters, the sciences, and other traditional disciplines into one college. Faculty were familiar with the massive College of Arts and Letters on the Reno campus, and many wanted to avoid creating a similarly cumbersome structure. And while the idea of a professional college might have worked for hotel and perhaps business (the latter still offered typing and stenography classes until 1967), many of the programs that Maude Frazier, Carlson, Moyer, and others had once seen as the province of the Maryland Parkway campus went to Clark County Community College (today the Community College of Southern Nevada) after that institution opened in 1971. However, the Graduate College and the University College for incoming freshmen won approval later in the year.

After much debate about the committee's suggestions, Zorn and the faculty senate reorganized UNLV into eight colleges that served the campus, albeit with some name changes, for the rest of the century: the Graduate College, University College (abolished in 1982 and reestablished in different form in 2004), the College of Science and Mathematics ("Engineering" was added to the title in 1974), the College of Allied Health Professions, the College of Business, and the College of Hotel Administration. There was also some compression. Burns's committee had suggested merging the humanities, social science, and fine arts colleges into the university's largest unit, the College of Arts and Letters, which

Zorn approved in 1971. In the 1990s, the fine arts and some social science departments left, and what is today the College of Liberal Arts became smaller.

Besides the reorganization, Zorn also supported the creation of new academic programs. In 1970, for example, regent Helen Thompson put up $30,000 of her own money to expand a black studies program, staffed by part-time instructors, and it began in 1969. In 1971 Zorn secured funding for the first full-time faculty member for ethnic studies. This subject, taught for more than twenty years by Notre Dame graduate Roosevelt Fitzgerald, reflected the importance of black history and the civil rights movement years before the anthropology and history departments hired specialists with doctorates in the field. By 1972–73, the program also offered Chicano, Asian American, and Native American courses, taught mostly by members of the anthropology department.

Doctoral programs at UNLV also started with Zorn and Baepler, who began lobbying regents for them in 1970, even before the university established its Graduate College. In January 1971, Dr. William "Thomas" White, dean of the College of Business and Economics, told reporters that Las Vegas already had a number of graduates who were qualified to enter a doctoral program. "Right now," he explained, "they must leave the state to attend other universities. But their homes are here in Nevada."[11] Las Vegas's population provided a compelling reason for regents to approve an M.B.A. program, which they soon did. In fact, the city's development into a large metropolitan area provided a compelling rationale used by dozens of departments and colleges into the twenty-first century to justify new degrees and other initiatives.

The administration's championing of doctoral programs did not escape the notice of College of Education officials, who used the feverish expansion of the local school district to enlarge their graduate offerings. After all, one of Maude Frazier's major reasons for creating Nevada Southern was to train local teachers, and by the 1970s the Clark County School District could barely hire enough to keep pace with enrollment. As early as 1971, College of Education dean Anthony Saville pushed for the Ed.D., arguing that "a doctoral program offered locally can do much to upgrade the qualifications of everyone associated with our educational system—its teachers, principals, counselors and central staff."[12]

Groundbreaking in December for what became the William Carlson Education Building only contributed to the enthusiasm. With its 121 offices, 35 classrooms, 29 seminar rooms, 15 study areas, and large lecture hall, this facility
finally liberated education students and faculty from their cramped quarters in
Wright Hall and Grant Hall. As J.A. Tiberti Construction began work on the
building, President Zorn observed that "the appearance of the entire campus is
changing rapidly in preparation for the growing number of students who will
be seeking a higher education in the coming years."[13]

James Dickinson's dream of establishing a performing arts center on campus finally came true when the 575-seat Judy Bayley Theatre opened in April 1972. Thanks to the work of the Nevada Southern Foundation and especially Wing Fong, Las Vegans raised more than $750,000, the amount that state legislators required before they made their allocation. Nevertheless, the building opened two years behind schedule, after construction was delayed by a sharply reduced federal grant and a tight college bond market occasioned by a national recession. The *Rebel Yell* celebrated the occasion with a column touting the theater's Green Room, scenery shop, and other features. But there was more. Zorn not only presided over this event but also began serious discussions about replacing the old 1960 Gym with a larger facility. In 1972 regents approved plans for a six-building complex that ultimately opened in 1975 and was named for late Las Vegas regent Paul McDermott.

FOUR UNLV BUILDINGS ARE NAMED FOR PEOPLE OR FAMILY REPRESENTATIVES IN THIS PHOTOGRAPH. (FROM LEFT): ART HAM JR., JUDY BAYLEY, ROMAN ZORN, MRS. ART HAM SR. (ALTA HAM), AND WING FONG AT THE GROUNDBREAKING CEREMONY FOR THE JUDY BAYLEY THEATRE, 1970. SPECIAL COLLECTIONS, UNLV LIBRARIES 0062-0189

JUDY BAYLEY THEATRE UNDER CONSTRUCTION, 1971. SPECIAL
COLLECTIONS, UNLV LIBRARIES 0062-0925

While Zorn neither built nor named the $3.4 million Las Vegas Stadium for
UNLV's football team, he did support the construction program and planning
effort to give the Rebels a spacious facility in which to play. Built by the Las
Vegas Convention and Visitors Authority in 1972, the stadium originally seated
8,000 fans. This capacity served the football program well for many years
until the school's and city's growth required several expansion projects. While
not considered a sports-oriented president, Zorn appreciably helped student
athletes, building facilities for the school's sports programs, hiring talented
coaches, and endorsing creation of the Intercollegiate Athletics Council during
the 1970–71 school year to handle appeals, waivers, and other matters affecting
student athletes.

Still, academics was Zorn's first priority, and his building program reflected
this emphasis. Zorn was also president during construction of the seven-story
humanities building. Of course, neither he nor Baepler dared to interfere when
in 1973, regent Helen Thompson donated $9,000 to build a three-foot hill
west of the building because she felt UNLV's campus was too flat and that every
respectable college needed a hill somewhere. The hill, partially obliterated in

the 1990s during construction of the alumni ampitheater on the lawn fronting FDH, still remains embedded in the last few rows of seating.

While Zorn did not interefere with Thompson's project—although he probably wanted to—he was proactive in ensuring that the expanded campus being acquired by Donald Moyer's land foundation was not threatened by urban development. In June 1971 Clark County commissioners announced plans to extend Swenson Street from Flamingo southward. That intersection is today located between the Desert Research Institute and the Stan Fulton Building. In an effort to cut costs, county officials wanted to route the thoroughfare due south across the campus, but Zorn, working with county commissioner Tom Wiesner and others, fought to ensure that the road veered sharply westward almost to Paradise Road (at Harmon), as it does today, to avoid having the campus cut in half. Throughout his presidency, Zorn was very active in negotiations with local property owners, regents, and the university's land foundation in acquiring numerous parcels to give UNLV the 343-acre campus it had by the late 1970s.

All of these initiatives—better faculty, academic reorganization, new programs, new buildings, and more land—required more funding. The 1970 accreditation report made the obvious point that lack of funds for staff and operations hindered the development of a large and growing physical plant. While the reviewers judged UNLV's plant as adequate, they questioned the absence of architects, landscapers, and professionals in the planning process. Because of budgetary constraints, a school committee for years had done much of the planning.

Like his predecessors and successors, Zorn faced an uphill battle to secure enough state appropriations for his campus. In 1971, when Chancellor Neil Humphrey complained about proposed cuts in the university budget, powerful Senate Appropriations Committee chair Floyd Lamb bluntly told him: "There is no money." Later, President Zorn explained to Lamb's committee that the governor's $4.5 million cut in UNLV's proposed budget was disastrous because the school's enrollment was growing at almost 25 percent annually, and the campus needed more faculty, books, and equipment. Zorn also fought for higher faculty salaries as part of his own commitment to improving academic quality and increasing the number of faculty scholars on campus. Arguing that UNLV ranked fourth among comparable schools in the West for faculty salaries and that he didn't want the school to "slip backwards," the president insisted on a 6.5 percent raise for the biennium, most of which he got.[14]

In 1973 Zorn again appeared before committee members in Carson City, pushing for UNLV's budget. This time he emphasized new programs more than salaries, although he still defended the need for cost-of-living increases. He had to, because the early to mid-1970s experienced some of the highest inflation in American history. Colleges and universities across the country struggled to retain good faculty when the cost of living far outdistanced salaries. At the time, endowment funds also suffered, as the stock market lost more than 50 percent of its value. For places like UNLV, whose endowments were still small and whose local economy seemed recession-proof, the 1970s brought relative prosperity. The opening of the first MGM Grand Hotel (today Bally's), the Holiday Casino (today Harrah's), the Imperial Palace, the Marina (today the site of the new MGM Grand), and other resorts generated increased gaming revenue for the university to tap. In addition, Democratic governor Mike O'Callaghan, while hardly a big-spending liberal, was more flexible than his conservative predecessor, Paul Laxalt.

During Zorn's four years, UNLV progressed not only in terms of its physical plant, staff salaries, quality hires, faculty retention, and academic programs but on other fronts as well. Zorn initiated an effort to enhance the campus landscape with a sculpture worthy of UNLV's growing maturity. In March 1972, he announced plans to seek a $45,000 grant from the National Endowment for the Arts to commission a sculpture that would serve as a signature landmark for the growing campus. The effort was not immediately successful. Numerous snags delayed the process. Debate also raged over where to locate the sculpture—on the mall, by the humanities building, at the library, or near the original entrance at Maude Frazier Hall. Finally, in 1978, the donors and UNLV officials designated the site for what would become the *Flashlight* where it deserved to be: at the heart of the performing arts center between Judy Bayley Theatre and Artemus W. Ham Concert Hall, where students and the public could enjoy it.

Despite his accomplishments, Zorn's tenure as president was relatively short, barely exceeding Moyer's. Zorn suddenly resigned on May 19, 1973. But why? Initial reports in the Las Vegas newspapers implied the reason was a May

1 drug bust in which twenty-five officers from the state narcotics division and the sheriff's office raided Tonopah Hall at one o'clock in the morning and arrested twenty-one people, including the student body vice president-elect, the Rebels' starting quarterback, a member of the baseball team, three basketball players, and even a UNLV policeman, for the sale and use of marijuana. The damaging story was front-page news even in the *Los Angeles Herald-Examiner,* where narcotics officers reported how the suspects had offered to sell their undercover agent amphetamines, heroin, and cocaine. The newspaper also detailed how, upon breaking in, the police found drugs everywhere, as well as grown men and students in bed with underage girls, including one fourteen-year-old. It got worse the next day when the CSUN Senate voted to use $2,500 in student money as a "loan" to bail four of the suspects out of jail, a move that angered the regents.[15]

Clearly, the administration was embarrassed, but regents were quick to dismiss the raid as a cause for Zorn's resignation. Several factors contributed to the president's decision. While he did not publicly say so at the time, it is clear from his private comments that his reluctance to hire Jerry Tarkanian as UNLV's new basketball coach was a crucial reason for his departure. As Donald Baepler remembers, once Tarkanian agreed to come to UNLV in March 1973, Zorn opposed the action. The president had not participated in the screening process, and years later he told an interviewer that by the time he interviewed Tarkanian, the decision was a "fait accompli."[16] The Rebel Boosters played a dominant role in selecting the coach. Baepler and Las Vegas advertising executive Sig Rogich, as well as local businessman and booster Dave Pearl, traveled to Southern California to woo Tarkanian. They believed he would make the UNLV basketball program nationally prominent and, in Baepler's words, "put UNLV on the map."[17] As Baepler noted in a recent conversation, when he and Zorn went to national and even regional meetings in the early 1970s, many officials from other colleges often did not even know what the UNLV acronym stood for. Tarkanian changed all that.

For his part, Zorn became disenchanted with the entire process of hiring the coach. He signed off on Tarkanian's contract under intense pressure from regents and resigned after graduation at the end of that school year. Although regents chair Harold Jacobsen later told reporters that Zorn was not forced to resign but could "see the writing on the wall," Jacobsen probably never understood the full meaning of his words.[18] What Zorn saw was that UNLV's intended road to national prominence differed significantly from the course he envisioned. To some extent, Baepler, who would succeed Zorn as president, represented the course favored by regents and many locals.

Zorn and Baepler were both quality scholars who believed in academic excellence and in making UNLV the fine research university it has become. Zorn believed that academic quality was the road to greatness. He advocated the Harvard model of attracting excellent faculty, promoting quality scholarship, and then using that quality to appeal to donors, private foundations, and federal grant-giving agencies to raise the millions needed for the programs, schools, and colleges that Nevada's legislature would never completely fund. Zorn had seen this model work many times over in higher education, at the University of Wisconsin, Ohio University, and other respected schools where he had served.

Baepler's model for building UNLV into a nationally prominent university followed a different course. As he explained it in a recent conversation, he felt the UCLA, USC, and Notre Dame models would be more practical for transforming UNLV. After all, Las Vegas was not Boston, Madison, or Athens, Ohio. Baepler believed that by bringing Jerry Tarkanian to Las Vegas and building a nationally prominent sports program in basketball and perhaps also in football (several weeks earlier, UNLV had hired the dynamic Ron Meyer to replace the school's first football coach, Bill Ireland), more local businessmen could be lured into funding UNLV's academic needs. As in the case of Notre Dame and UCLA, "first they'd give to athletics, and then they could be led to discover academics."[19] And many big UNLV donors did just that. Elaine Wynn would observe that Tarkanian's Runnin' Rebels first attracted her and her husband, Steve, to UNLV. Later, in the 1980s, they began actively supporting the new UNLV Foundation and the school's development.

Las Vegas's gaming community and other boosters felt the same way. It was not just about having a good local team to root for. As public relations wizard and former owner of R&R Advertising Sig Rogich told historian Richard O. Davies, "For us to appear in every newspaper in America every day with the University of Nevada, Las Vegas, it might just prompt someone in a windstorm or a rainstorm in Buffalo to visit the town."[20] Tarkanian was better, he felt, than the old Live Wire Fund, the Desert Sea News Bureau, and other expensive advertising campaigns, because the Runnin' Rebels would splash Las Vegas onto every sports page in the nation for free. "For a town that's selling its name, and spending millions of dollars to do it, having the University of Las Vegas," as he then called it, "on the front of jerseys and in box scores was the right kind of name for us to be successful."[21]

For Zorn, the price of fame was not worth the risk, and he stuck to his position. He feared that if Tarkanian was successful, UNLV would soon acquire the unwanted reputation of being a basketball college. The jock campus label was something Zorn wanted no part of. In the late 1970s, as a member of the UNLV history department, he merely chuckled when asked about the school's latest problems with the NCAA.

But there was perhaps another force at work that drove a wedge between Zorn and the regents. At the time of his hiring in 1969, the board had not yet been reapportioned. He had been hired by a board composed primarily of northern regents. As Zorn told longtime history professor and colleague Robert Davenport in a 1995 interview, when the regents interviewed him in 1968, it was clear they felt power was too diffuse at UNLV. The 1970s accreditation report said as much. Despite the efforts of Moyer and Crawford, the faculty senate, deans, and even individual faculty members contacted state legislators at will and exerted influence beyond their respective positions. Regents wanted a strong president who would centralize power on campus and channel new proposals and budget requests through himself to them. This is what Zorn set out to do. Those regents probably would have been unenthusiastic about bringing Jerry Tarkanian to UNLV. They certainly would have cracked down on any maverick sports program in Las Vegas—no matter how successful the coach was.

But the 1971 reapportionment of the board of regents shifted control to southern Nevada. Paul McDermott and other regents were part of the political and business networks of the Las Vegas area. They personally knew many of the major boosters, like Rogich and Tom Wiesner, and, like them, wanted to "put UNLV on the map." They saw no problem with a prominent basketball program giving UNLV national visibility. They were proud that Las Vegas was now the largest city in the state—even bigger than Reno—and were willing to make UNLV larger and more prominent than UNR. While certainly not opposed to

UNLV's becoming larger than UNR, Zorn was concerned about how it was done. For these and other reasons, he was no longer the person that southern regents wanted as head of UNLV; Don Baepler was more their choice.

For his part, Zorn was diplomatic about the whole affair and expressed no bitterness about it. Up until his death in 2002, Zorn was still publicly vague about his reasons for stepping down. At the time of his retirement from the history department in 1982, he told a student reporter that "the wear and tear factor becomes accumulative and you become somewhat disenchanted. The whole situation is extremely abrasive."[22] A few months after his resignation, Zorn was a bit more candid, declaring, "A university [administration] that isn't willing to rock the boat doesn't develop academic strength."[23]

In his more private 1995 interview with Davenport, however, Zorn was unusually frank, asserting that "the constant friction with the chancellor [Neil Humphrey] was a grinding thing. . . . Plain and simply, that little nest in Reno was not interested in UNLV." The former president also indicated that while he felt Tarkanian would be a distinct improvement over his predecessor, Rolland Todd, he "never expected a cult to emerge." Zorn expressed no regrets about leaving Tarkanian to his successors: "I suspect that sooner or later, had I stayed on, I would have been trampled under by the Tarkanian army."[24]

While Zorn has often been portrayed in print and conversation as a colorless, office-bound president whose contributions were minor, the evidence suggests otherwise. Zorn attended numerous meetings in the community to raise money for student scholarships and for projects like the Judy Bayley Theatre. He lobbied for higher faculty pay to attract the best young scholars. Working with Baepler, Zorn effectively reduced the teaching load to three courses each regular semester to allow enough time for serious research. He even adjusted the criteria for merit pay to reward scholarship more—a vital incentive for research faculty in a state where cost-of-living increases historically have never kept pace with inflation. In 1971, Zorn approved UNLV's first doctoral program, in education, and encouraged more departments to begin master's degree programs. After his resignation from the presidency, Zorn joined UNLV's history department, where he taught for nine years and continued to champion both teaching and research in tenure and promotion decisions. His dedication to excellence so impressed his colleagues that after his retirement in 1982, the department created the Roman J. Zorn Award, given annually to the best graduate student in history.

When Zorn resigned, regents immediately appointed his academic vice president, Don Baepler, as interim president of UNLV. Baepler, who had just pleased students and Rebels fans by helping to recruit Jerry Tarkanian, decided that this time he would be a candidate for the presidency. His credentials were solid. A graduate of Carleton College with a Ph.D. in biology from the University of Oklahoma, Baepler had taught at Central Washington University before chairing its biology department. His administrative skills soon attracted the interest of that school's president, who appointed him an assistant and eventually vice president for business. After Moyer hired him as academic vice president in 1968, Baepler served as interim president for almost a year following Moyer's resignation. During that year and the next four, which he spent under Zorn, Baepler immersed himself in the university's operations and, given lots of autonomy and decision-making power by Zorn, played a role in shaping UNLV's transition from a local college to a small but increasingly respected university.

Baepler was fortunate to serve during Mike O'Callaghan's second term as governor. O'Callaghan was one of the first governors to recognize the importance of keeping state salaries in line with inflation. This was crucial, because the cost of living rose significantly during the Nixon and post–Vietnam War years. Thanks to generous cost-of-living increases for faculty and staff, Baepler was able to recruit talented faculty by offering competitive starting salaries. Indeed, he described 1975 "as a very good stable year. . . . A significant increase in money from the state legislature has kept us a little ahead of the rate of inflation, which is good, because most universities haven't kept up with it."[25]

Baepler had always championed the need for more faculty research, and so he was especially disturbed by the lack of money for faculty travel, a problem that not only discouraged talented young scholars from applying for positions at UNLV but also caused many of the school's publishing faculty to leave. Throughout the 1970s, the state's contribution for travel to major academic conferences was embarrassing: $50 or less per faculty member for the year. Legislators never quite understood that faculty participation in conferences was essential to advancing their careers and contributing to the university's prestige. "I think it's hurting the university," Baepler told reporters in 1976. Pointing to

UNLV's relatively isolated position in the desert Southwest, he explained: "Our need is different than universities in areas such as Los Angeles or the Bay Area because we don't have many conferences in Nevada."[26] But legislators were unmoved, and the problem continued into the 1980s, when the Maxson administration finally tied faculty travel funds to departmental revenues derived from summer school.

Baepler was as committed to program development as his predecessors were. In a 1974 speech at the Silver Nugget, he told a receptive audience that with 7,000 students enrolled, UNLV had reached a "plateau of maturity" and predicted that the campus would soon have a law school. He also suggested that UNLV would have a substantial women's sports program, fielding teams in volleyball, tennis, gymnastics, swimming, and track and field.

New construction also symbolized UNLV's progress and growth. Indeed, UNLV passed UNR in total enrollment during the 1977–78 school year, but the younger campus had far fewer buildings to accommodate its students and programs. The Department of Athletics welcomed the opening of the $5.3 million Paul McDermott Physical Education Complex in fall 1975. With its 50-meter indoor swimming pool, two gymnasiums, eight handball courts, locker rooms, classrooms, and offices, it liberated students, players, and coaches from the confines of the old 1960 Gym. Additionally, Baepler looked forward to the completion of two other major buildings in spring 1976, the $5.5 million life sciences building (later named for regent Juanita White) and the $4.5 million Artemus W. Ham Concert Hall, a 2,000-seat addition to UNLV's Center for the Performing Arts.

In March 1976 Baepler requested $9 million for a new rectangular addition to the Dickinson Library and $1 million to remodel Tonopah Hall into offices and classrooms. Baepler actually opposed dormitories on campus and, even in

FACING PAGE:

TOP: PAUL MCDERMOTT PHYSICAL EDUCATION COMPLEX UNDER CONSTRUCTION, 1974. THE NATATORIUM IS ON THE LEFT, AND THE CLASSROOM BUILDING IS ON THE RIGHT. SPECIAL COLLECTIONS, UNLV LIBRARIES 0062-1118

BOTTOM: JUANITA GREER WHITE HALL, THE HOME OF LIFE SCIENCES, UNDER CONSTRUCTION, 1975. SPECIAL COLLECTIONS, UNLV LIBRARIES 0062-1017

later decades, felt that the lands stretching along Gym Road from Tonopah Hall to Tropicana could have been put to better use. But regent Lilly Fong successfully blocked his efforts to close the dormitories. On other fronts, Baepler also requested money for additions to the chemistry and life sciences buildings, as well as funds to pave more parking lots and upgrade lighting.

As a biologist, Baepler recognized the need for a modern facility, besides the 1970 chemistry building, that would promote faculty and student research in that discipline. At the same time, he also pushed another project that he would someday head. In 1975, when the Athletics Department moved into the new McDermott Complex, the president approved plans to renovate the old Gym to house an expanded Marjorie Barrick Museum of Natural History. The museum, which had begun operations across the street from Nevada Southern during the 1960s, now had a place on campus where students and residents could examine the archaeological wonders of the Mohave, including its ecology, wildlife, and native peoples. The staff moved in to supervise renovations in 1975, although the facility did not open to the public for another two years. In 1988 the museum unveiled its "Xeric Demonstration Garden" of drought-resistant

LONGTIME NSU-UNLV LIBRARIAN CELESTA LOWE, AT WORK IN
SPECIAL COLLECTIONS, 1973. SPECIAL COLLECTIONS, UNLV
LIBRARIES 0062-0950

plants on land it shared with Wright Hall. A year later, President Maxson named the museum for Marjorie Barrick in appreciation for her gifts and service to the university.

As UNLV improved its physical plant and academic quality, some called for raising admission standards. Baepler, however, expressed concerns that establishing a GPA requirement might limit enrollment. In 1975 all Nevada high school graduates were eligible to attend UNLV in one way or another. "It has been shown," Baepler argued, "that when you raise only the grade point average requirement, high school teachers adjust to the change and give higher grades, so you end up with the same students anyway." The president preferred beefing up UNLV's remedial programs. It was a practical policy at the time that helped maintain the school's enrollment growth and further diversified its student body, both of which were politically appealing. As Baepler noted, "Historically it has worked out that when you raise one or two criteria, you discriminate against minority students."[27]

In addition to programmatic development, Baepler endorsed a number of reforms. Two of the most popular with students were the adoption of pass/fail grades in 1971 when he was vice president and the 1975 abolition of the physical education requirement from UNLV's core curriculum. The latter became necessary as UNLV's size and population increased. For years, students at the Las Vegas campus had had to complete four courses of physical education as part of their core requirement. While some enjoyed the challenge, many, especially summer students taking sports classes in Las Vegas's sizzling heat, objected strongly. The requirement became more difficult to service as UNLV's student population far outdistanced the number of qualified instructors. Moreover, beginning in 1975, the new Paul McDermott Physical Education Complex, at the far western end of the campus, was simply too far from the major buildings paralleling Maryland Parkway. The old Gym (today's Marjorie Barrick Museum of Natural History) sat at the center of the campus and students could make it to their next class in ten minutes, but that was no longer the case in 1975. For these and other reasons, the university senate voted in 1978 to make physical education an elective rather than part of the school's core curriculum, much to the relief of the student body.

While Baepler was flexible regarding this liberalization of requirements, he continued to insist upon scholarly publication as a necessary prerequisite for tenure. With the end of America's military presence in Vietnam in 1973 and the easing of civil rights tensions, student protest on UNLV's campus had largely ended. But minor protests continued over the termination of popular instructors. In addition, regents continued to provoke controversy with the faculty over concerns about student complaints regarding unpreparedness, poor teaching, and other abuses of tenure by a small number of instructors. As a result, the board seriously considered abolishing tenure in the University of Nevada System during the late 1970s.

It took all of Baepler's considerable skill to fend off this action. He was trying to attract good scholars to UNLV at this time, and he knew the abolition of tenure would threaten this effort. After conceding that tenure was "a national problem," the president warned that "if tenure is abolished, a suitable alternative to it must be found to ensure our ability to attract top-notch teaching personnel."[28] The regents backed off eventually, and the issue did not surface again until the university code battle of 1982–83.

Finally, Baepler played a decisive role in one more major event: naming the school. This occurred while he served as interim president following Donald Moyer's resignation. After the 1968 reorganization that granted Nevada Southern full autonomy, the school was free to choose its own name. Many locals, like Archie Grant and Jim Bilbray, preferred to keep it Nevada Southern University, but Baepler felt that name carried the connotation of an agricultural school. Others complained that to many out-of-state people, "Nevada Southern" sounded like a private school or even a railroad. Baepler recalled that he had spent endless hours trying to explain to academic officials around the country that Nevada Southern was part of the University of Nevada System. He felt the campus needed a more distinct identity—one that identified the school with its famous hometown. This would be accomplished by adding "Las Vegas" to the university's name. So he lobbied regents to adopt the California model that had distinguished the two big campuses in the Golden State's major northern and southern cities as UCLA and UC-Berkeley. By a vote of 6–2, the regents decided at their January 11, 1969, meeting to implement Baepler's idea. Much to the dismay of the northern campus, Nevada Southern University officially became the University of Nevada, Las Vegas (UNLV), and the mother campus became the University of Nevada, Reno (UNR).

Clearly, President Baepler contributed significantly to the improvement of UNLV. The regents were impressed with his leadership and administrative abilities and chose him to be acting chancellor of the University of Nevada System in 1978 following Neil Humphrey's departure for the University of Alaska. For almost a year, Baepler served both as chancellor and as president of UNLV. After

he was selected as the permanent chancellor, he resigned his UNLV position.

Even after he left UNLV to become chancellor of the University of Nevada System, Baepler still supported a law school for the campus. In 1980 he convinced regents that they should allocate $37,000 for a consulting firm to study the feasibility of creating such an institution. But he was pessimistic. With inflation high in 1980, with gaming revenues relatively stagnant after the opening of Atlantic City's casinos two years earlier, and with the likely passage of Question 6 shifting the state's chief revenue source from property taxes to the more unstable sales tax, Baepler told reporters: "We will have a law school—the question is not if, but when."[29]

After serving as chancellor for three years, Baepler returned to Las Vegas in 1981 to become director of the Marjorie Barrick Museum of Natural History and the Harry Reid Center for Environmental Studies. Over the next two decades, he secured millions of dollars in research grants and recruited dozens of talented scientists to the highly successful center.

When Baepler left UNLV for the chancellor's job, regents selected Dr. Brock Dixon, dean of administration since 1971, as interim president. The fifty-nine-year-old Dixon, with a doctorate from USC, had enjoyed a diverse career, teaching political science at the high school and college levels and serving as an IRS agent as well as a naval officer. He was therefore experienced in fiscal affairs, teaching, administration, and leadership. Dixon's first contact with UNLV came in 1970 when he was part of the Northwest Association's accreditation team assessing the school's condition. Impressed by UNLV's progress and potential for growth, he applied for the dean of students position and got it. Three years later, he became vice president of administration. In these capacities, he served presidents Zorn and Baepler. By 1979 Dixon was more than qualified to head UNLV when the opportunity arose.

As interim president, Dixon faced a tough, uphill fight to secure enough funding for his school. During the 1979 legislative session, he fought just to maintain existing positions at UNLV. Governor Robert List's higher education budget cut forty-two jobs at UNR and twenty-one at UNLV through attrition over the next biennium. Conceding that UNLV's FTE enrollment had dropped by 4 percent (from 5,827 in fall 1978 to 5,583 in 1979), Dixon correctly pointed out that UNLV had always been understaffed and underfunded and needed additional money to operate. He also criticized the state's 20-to-1 student-to-faculty funding formula, calling it "arbitrary." But his argument was to no avail. "It is clear we live in a world of numbers games," he complained. "I believe in a school like this that numbers and quality tend to vary with each other." Dixon knew that UNLV needed more students, so he considered instituting a master's degree program at Nellis Air Force Base, whose airmen and base commanders "were begging for one." By "putting programs where people want them," he could boost enrollment in time for the next legislature when the numbers game for UNLV would begin all over again. But UNLV did not begin a degree programs at Nellis until 1986.[30]

INTERIM PRESIDENT BROCK DIXON PRESENTS AN AWARD TO JUDGE ADDELIAR "DELL" GUY, 1978. SPECIAL COLLECTIONS, UNLV LIBRARIES 0062-0373

Dixon never applied for the permanent president's job. Clearly, he saw himself as a temporary figurehead. "If I were the real president, I would not have sat around a year and a half like I did without proposing and vigorously pushing new programs that would make this institution much more of a comprehensive university than it is."[31] Dixon, who remained at UNLV as vice president for administration until 1985, wondered aloud at one 1983 cabinet meeting about the state's commitment to UNLV and whether Nevada would have two universities or "one flagship campus supplemented by a regional college bearing a university title."[32] For their part, the regents saw Dixon more as an administrative manager than as a program-building chief executive. In searching for the latter, the regents found their person in Leonard "Pat" Goodall, vice chancellor of the University of Michigan–Dearborn.

CHAPTER FIVE

Laying a Foundation for the Future

LEONARD GOODALL

In the late 1970s UNLV had begun to drift noticeably. Weak leadership, inadequate state funding, and a lack of policy direction all greeted the new president upon his arrival in March 1979. Experienced and highly personable, Leonard "Pat" Goodall immediately brought a new sense of energy and vision, which the campus desperately needed.

Like his predecessors, Goodall possessed solid academic credentials as well as an important new component: big-city experience. Although a native midwesterner with a bachelor's degree from Central Missouri State, a master's degree from the University of Missouri, and a Ph.D. in political science from the University of Illinois, Goodall was no stranger to the Southwest. He had lived in the Phoenix area for six years during the mid-1960s, serving as a political science professor and an administrator at Arizona State University's Bureau of Government Research. He returned to the Midwest in 1968 to become a professor and vice chancellor at the University of Illinois, Chicago Circle campus, where he stayed for three years before his appointment as vice chancellor at the University of Michigan–Dearborn. After six years in Phoenix, three years in Chicago, and eight years in the Detroit area, Goodall understood the problems

involved with running a rapidly developing urban campus.

The UNLV job was a challenge he embraced. Despite the many similarities between UNLV and Dearborn, Goodall believed that the two schools differed in several respects. As he explained to Las Vegas reporters in 1979, "This is the major university in the area and is a very visible school in the community," while "Dearborn was one of many campuses in the Detroit area." And he noted one more important distinction: "There's a lot of growth in this area, and not a lot of growth in Michigan."[1] As a specialist in urban affairs, Goodall understood what it would take to run a university in a metropolis whose 1970 population of 273,000 had surpassed 450,000 just nine years later.

The new president clearly recognized the crucial new factor in the equation that would vault UNLV upward over the next three decades. Las Vegas was no longer the relatively small community it had been in the days of Carlson, Moyer, and Zorn, and UNLV was no longer the little college at the south end of town. By 1986 Las Vegas would become the fastest-growing metropolitan area in the United States, and, in an odd contrast with its counterparts elsewhere, UNLV remained the only real university for miles around. This situation would enable the school to raise hundreds of millions of private dollars over the next thirty years.

Upon taking office in July 1979, Goodall announced that he would conduct a review of UNLV's administrative structure and academic programs to prepare for the decennial accreditation process in 1980. He also ordered an analysis of enrollment. "I think we ought to know a lot more about our student body, their backgrounds, how many came straight from high school, [and] the increasing numbers that are coming from other kinds of non-traditional settings." In particular, he emphasized the "need to see if there are clientele groups out there that we ought to be serving, but we're not."[2] Additionally, Goodall had to recruit a new academic vice president, a Graduate College dean, and an athletics director.

The president was realistic about the challenges facing UNLV: "I think . . . the 1980s [are] going to be a difficult decade for higher education." But he also sounded a note of optimism that presaged his commitment to encouraging more university research. "If one believes that things like energy and inflation are going to be dominating problems in the future, people are going to look for ways to handle that." Goodall also believed UNLV would fare better than many colleges in the face of budget cuts and declining enrollments: "If Las Vegas continues to grow . . . then I think this campus will continue to grow."[3]

In August 1979 Goodall outlined his concerns for the first year of his presidency. Specifically, he predicted that UNLV would face tight budgets over the 1979–81 biennium, given Governor List's tax shift and his modest university

AT THE TWENTY-FIFTH ANNIVERSARY OF NSU-UNLV IN 1982. (FROM LEFT): ROMAN ZORN, WILLIAM CARLSON, HENDERSON MAYOR LORIN WILLIAMS, FORMER UNIVERSITY OF NEVADA DEAN WILLIAM WOOD, LEONARD GOODALL, AND DONALD MOYER. SPECIAL COLLECTIONS, UNLV LIBRARIES 0062-0186

budget. Indeed, thanks partly to List's fiscal conservatism, Nevada in 1981 ranked fifty-first among the states and the District of Columbia in per capita spending for higher education—a dubious distinction that hardly bothered the Republican governor.

Goodall also noted that because of the NCAA's suspension of the Runnin' Rebels from postseason play for the next two years for recruiting violations, "We will be watched very carefully by [the] NCAA and other institutions." "Whether or not that is fair," he said, "it is imperative that we be especially careful in all of our activities relating to athletics."[4] So it was vitally important to hire a skilled athletics director. Goodall also outlined other goals, including marketing university programs more effectively, improving transfer arrangements with the local community college, and completing existing construction projects while planning for new ones.

Goodall, like Baepler, also supported creating a law school at the campus. "Every state should have a law school," he declared, "to provide a place to document legal history." While the president recognized that "many of our students won't want to practice law," he predicted they would instead "be employed in other professions and will come here to study the law they need to know for their jobs."[5]

Goodall realized that new academic initiatives like a law school would be expensive, so he looked to cut waste. In an effort to save money and streamline bureaucracy, he eliminated the position of dean of admissions in the wake of Muriel Parks's retirement after twenty-two years in spring 1979. He also reduced the number of administrators reporting to him from twelve to eight and gave more responsibility to his academic vice president, who would soon be Dale Nitzschke. Additionally, Goodall decided to separate the coordinator of research development from the graduate dean's office, a move that gave an important new position vital autonomy.

Goodall also recognized the importance of improving UNLV's fund-raising efforts. With state spending slowed nationwide by taxpayer revolts and the growing popularity of the "Reagan Revolution," Goodall energized UNLV's fund-raising, announcing in August 1980 the first-ever alumni fund drive to encourage the school's graduates to make regular financial contributions. He recognized that NSU/UNLV had graduated only seventeen classes, so, unlike more established schools, the pool of potential donors was relatively small, young, and not yet wealthy. "I recognize this drive won't be a financial bonanza," he declared. "Our alumni are young and in their early years." Nevertheless, he suggested, "if our former students can give us only $5 or $10 or $15 now, they can get into the habit of giving and will be likely to provide us more money in the future."[6] Goodall's prediction would prove correct. In future years alumni would contribute millions of dollars in gifts to the school, and future presidents would transform Goodall's initial fund drive into today's Rebel Ring Phonathon.

But Goodall did not just seek funds from graduates; he reached out to the Las Vegas metropolitan community in 1981 to create the modern UNLV Foundation of today. In 1962 university officials and local businessmen, along with William Carlson, had created the Nevada Southern Foundation. But, as former president Baepler observed in a recent conversation, it was a small vehicle used primarily to raise money to build the Judy Bayley Theatre and the new library addition of 1967. The organization was too limited in scope and purpose for what Goodall wanted to do. Also, Carlson's foundation had lost much of its early momentum. It was time to form an exciting new entity and start from scratch.

Over the next twenty-five years, the UNLV Foundation would generate more than half a billion dollars for the school. Several major donations soon fattened the school's coffers. In February 1984, a group of landowners, including future state supreme court justice Miriam Shearing and her husband, prominent ophthalmologist Steven Shearing, donated a 1,470-acre tract near Pioche to UNLV. The land, valued at $882,000, was one of the largest gifts to the school up to that time.

But it was Marjorie Barrick's $1.2 million donation to the Maryland Parkway campus in 1980 that gave the president's fund-raising efforts a critical boost. Her gift was significant for several reasons. First, it provided enough money to fund a lecture series whose generous honoraria attracted major national and world figures to the school, thereby contributing to UNLV's quest for national prominence. Second, it provided the funding to reward academic excellence by faculty and students. Beginning in the 1980s, UNLV annually gave the Barrick Scholar Award to those faculty with fewer than ten years of service whose research publications or creative activities were "extraordinary" in terms of quantity and quality. The school bestowed the Barrick Distinguished Scholar

Award on those faculty with more than ten years of service whose body of work met these criteria over a longer span of time. Barrick's 1980 donation and her subsequent gifts also funded the Barrick Graduate Fellowships, granted to outstanding doctoral students "who have demonstrated excellent scholarship during their graduate study at UNLV."[7] Not only did Marjorie Barrick's donation reinforce the commitment to excellence made by every president since Donald Moyer, but, more important, in giving such an unprecedented sum, she made it fashionable for wealthier Las Vegans to give the campus much larger amounts than ever before, setting the bar at $1 million. While it is true that in the early 1970s President Zorn helped negotiate the $5 million DeVos gift for student scholarships, that money came in over time as the family sold various real estate properties. Barrick's gift came in a lump sum and was designated for multiple purposes.

PHILANTHROPIST MARJORIE BARRICK WITH PRESIDENT LEONARD GOODALL, CA. 1980. SPECIAL COLLECTIONS UNLV LIBRARIES 0062-0974

In addition to fund-raising, Goodall and his academic vice president, Dale Nitzschke, were both active in promoting research and expanding UNLV's curriculum. Goodall insisted that he would push for a 15 percent cost-of-living increase to retain talented faculty hired before the 1978–79 recession. He also announced his determination to secure more funding for faculty research and travel to conferences. In his 1980 State of the University address, Goodall reiterated his commitment to support professional development. But under the tight-money policies of Governor List and the legislature, this goal proved difficult to accomplish.

Regarding academic programs, Goodall told faculty that "architecture and law should be our highest priority areas for new professional colleges when the time comes to move into new program areas."[8] Regents, however, again postponed a law school, considering it premature and expensive. The same was true of architecture. Earlier, Goodall had talked a group of local architects into laying the foundation for such a school on the campus. But once again, regents, anxious about voter concerns over higher taxes, were not supportive. Ultimately, it would be left to Robert Maxson and Carol Harter, who led UNLV during more prosperous times, to draft the proposals, raise the money, and build the schools. Goodall, however, made greater progress on his third initiative: to create a stand-alone engineering school. In February 1984 regents approved preliminary plans to establish an engineering and computer science school, dismissing the concerns of fiscal conservatives that it would merely duplicate UNR's program. Goodall recruited Dr. David Emerson, a dean at the University of Michigan–Dearborn, to guide the school's development. The next step, to erect a building to house this prestigious addition to the university, proved to be a difficult task. In May 1984 Las Vegas regent Joan Kenney voted with northern Nevada regents to keep UNLV's proposed $15.2 million engineering building in twelfth place rather than moving it up to first on the system's construction priority list. A discouraged Bob Gore, who helped lead the Nevada Development Authority's push for the school, was at a loss for words. "I don't know what it means. We didn't get what we wanted out of this obviously."[9] Kenney, who as a sitting Las Vegas regent donated $1 million to her alma mater, Stanford University, rather than to woefully under-endowed UNLV, felt the building was premature and supported the position of her fellow Stanford graduate Chancellor Robert Bersi.

Goodall strongly disagreed. "I thought it should have been moved to No. 1," said Goodall, who now had to negotiate with other system presidents to get the building moved higher on the priorities list.[10] The president was clearly disappointed. After all, the project had the endorsement of a broad spectrum of the community, including North Las Vegas mayor James Seastrand and other prominent politicians and business leaders who saw a UNLV engineering program as the key to attracting high-tech business to southern Nevada. In defense of the board's actions, regent chair Frankie Sue Del Papa reminded everyone that the system's presidents set the priority list and they alone should be the ones to change it. But there were no changes. The list eventually went to the state public works board and the governor, with UNLV's engineering building a low priority. As a result, the facility did not open until 1988. Once it did, the school finally had the room to expand its course offerings and attract more students, which it succeeded in doing. A year later, the regents made engineering a college.

JAMES DICKINSON LIBRARY ADDITION UNDER CONSTRUCTION, 1980. THE BUILDING, WHICH OPENED IN 1981, IS NOW PART OF THE WILLIAM S. BOYD SCHOOL OF LAW. SPECIAL COLLECTIONS, UNLV LIBRARIES 0062-0946

Even without a building on the way, in the summer of 1984 UNLV's civil and mechanical engineering programs won certification from the National Accreditation Board for Engineering and Technology. Dr. William Wells, director of the Howard R. Hughes School of Engineering, observed that the endorsement, held by only 275 other schools in the nation, came several years sooner than expected. Kelly Chuma, a senior in the civil engineering program, explained the significance of the accreditation from the students' viewpoint when he said: "It means I will probably be able to get a better job when I get out of school." Additionally, "it means more money and respect."[11]

Besides programmatic initiatives, there was also new construction during

Goodall's years as president. In 1973, the year of Tarkanian's hiring, Rebel Boosters had formed a committee, supported by more than eight hundred members, to raise funds for the construction of a large basketball arena on campus. By the late 1970s, the project had gained momentum, with bankers Parry Thomas and Jerry Mack contributing $500,000 for architectural renderings of the facility. President Goodall spent months helping to plan the $30 million Thomas & Mack Center, which soon became the largest building on campus. The success of Jerry Tarkanian's Runnin' Rebels and their need for a large on-campus venue so more students and residents could see them play, encouraged large donations. Helping Goodall to fund this sprawling sports and events center were myriad influential boosters led by Bill "Wildcat" Morris, then part owner of the Holiday (today Harrah's) Casino on the Strip and a former director of the old Nevada Southern Foundation. When the 18,500-seat Thomas & Mack

THOMAS T. BEAM AT THE CORNERSTONE-LAYING CEREMONY
FOR FRANK AND ESTELLA BEAM HALL, 1983. SPECIAL
COLLECTIONS, UNLV LIBRARIES 0062-1701

JERRY MACK, PARRY THOMAS, GOVERNOR RICHARD BRYAN,
AND PRESIDENT GOODALL AT THE THOMAS & MACK CENTER'S
OPENING CEREMONY, 1983. UNLV OFFICE OF PUBLIC AFFAIRS

CHAPTER SIX

The Rise of UNLV

ROBERT MAXSON

After a year of bitter conflict over the university code, a situation made worse by inadequate state funding, it was obvious that UNLV desperately needed more buildings, books, faculty, and a measure of prestige. It was also obvious that the beleaguered campus needed dynamic leadership. To the surprise of some, the regents turned not to any number of qualified western, midwestern, and eastern candidates, but to the senior vice president of the University of Houston System, whose dynamism impressed them.

A graduate of Arkansas A&M College, Robert Maxson had received a master's degree from Florida Atlantic University in Boca Raton and a doctorate in education from Mississippi State. With an ingratiating southern style and a talent for administration, Maxson quickly moved up the ladder, serving as a dean at Auburn and at Appalachian State. He then headed to the University of Houston at Victoria, Texas, where he was chancellor before becoming senior vice president at the university's main campus.

UNLV's previous heads had been westerners or midwesterners with university experience in all parts of the nation, but Maxson was different. He was a southerner who had remained in the region throughout his career. The regents

were especially impressed with his Houston experience. The Texas city was not only home to NASA's flight operations but also a center of high-tech industry. The University of Houston played a vital role in training engineers and scientists for these activities, and many regents felt this was just the kind of experience that UNLV's next president should have.

In Texas, Maxson saw firsthand how universities raised funds on a massive scale to support new and existing programs. From the time he arrived at UNLV, on August 1, 1984, he understood that fund-raising was crucial to the process of transforming UNLV into a large and respected university, and he built up Goodall's foundation into a potent fund-raising machine. But there were immediate conflicts with the first director, Burke "Buck" Deadrich. The two clashed for a variety of reasons, the most public of which was the quarters from which the foundation staff operated. Deadrich, who had assumed his post in July 1982, had worked in an office at the Paradise Development Company provided by trustee Irwin Molasky. Meanwhile, the foundation's staff operated in a storefront space. Even though Maxson set aside rooms in the humanities building on campus, Deadrich considered the accommodations unsuitable for negotiating with high-profile donors. And there were other differences. Maxson preferred to have UNLV handle the accounting of funds, while the foundation's board of trustees retained control over the money. Maxson also believed that allowing UNLV employees to manage some operations would cut the foundation's overhead. "I guess I thought we ought to have a leaner staff than we presently have," Maxson told reporters in 1984, and "utilize resources we have at the university."[1]

Deadrich's successors, Bob Gore (1984–86) and Lyle Rivera (1986–95), proved to be effective directors (although Rivera never officially held the title). With considerable help from Maxson's network-building and well-publicized promotional efforts, Las Vegans began contributing record amounts of money. Large gifts also became more commonplace. In December 1985, for instance, former regent Lilly Fong and her family gave $150,000 to the UNLV Foundation for a variety of needs, including $50,000 to upgrade the old geoscience building. In recognition of this and the Fongs' longtime support of the campus, Maxson later named the structure for Lilly. Another $80,000 of the family's gift equipped the business college with a computing center of forty machines in Beam Hall, and the remaining money went to the hotel college and the alumni association.

AERIAL PHOTOGRAPH OF UNLV LOOKING SOUTH, CA. 1985.
SPECIAL COLLECTIONS, UNLV LIBRARIES 0062-1007

Not only did science and business benefit from Maxson's efforts, but so did the arts. Insisting there was no reason why UNLV could not become nationally known for its fine and performing arts, Maxson designated the 1986–87 school year as the "Year of the Arts." This meant that UNLV would raise public awareness of the arts through special exhibitions, concerts, and other events and would emphasize the arts in its fund-raising. Indeed, the president noted that in 1984, UNLV's fund-raising priority had been engineering, and in 1985 business and economics; now the arts would be highlighted. To celebrate the occasion, Maxson announced that UNLV would spend $200,000 to double the size of the Alta Ham Fine Arts Gallery and predicted, "It will be the finest fine-art galley in the state of Nevada."[2]

Maxson used private donations not only to expand programs but also to recruit gifted students. In his 1986 State of the University address, the president trumpeted UNLV's growing ability to attract the "best and the brightest" students. After noting that in 1985 the campus had registered 14 high school valedictorians, all of whom were returning for their second year, the president announced that 22 new valedictorians were coming to UNLV in the current semester. All of them took advantage of the Elardi Scholarship program, which awarded each valedictorian $2,000 annually for up to four years.

By 1986, as UNLV's academic image in the state continued to improve, gifted students from Nevada's high schools applied. But as nursing professor Myrlene LaMancusa, chair of UNLV's financial aid committee, explained, "We have money for valedictorians. But if a high school student has a grade point average of 3.95 and they aren't the valedictorian, they may not receive a scholarship." Of the two hundred requests for scholarships received in 1986, seventy-five were from "high quality" students, but UNLV barely had the money to fund half. At the time, the entire UNLV scholarship program amounted to $649,466, compared to UNR's $1.4 million. Clearly, UNLV would lose some of the state's top students to schools that had the money. As David Emerson, dean of the College of Science, Mathematics, and Engineering, explained, "A large percentage of the applicants want to take engineering or computer science." So the Elardi Scholarship directly benefited his college's recruitment efforts. Although he lamented, "We won't be able to provide funds to all the qualified applicants,"

THOMAS T. BEAM ENGINEERING BUILDING UNDER
CONSTRUCTION, 1987. SPECIAL COLLECTIONS,
UNLV LIBRARIES 0062-1022

Emerson consoled himself with the thought that "at least we have eleven more scholarships than last year."[3]

Clearly, with its Elardi Scholarships for the state's valedictorians, UNLV had drawn the interest of students who graduated near the top of their high school class. But as one faculty senate member remarked, "I think we made so much of the Elardi Scholarship, some students have been misled into thinking more money is available than there really is." Fortunately, Maxson's commitment to quality created a contagious enthusiasm in the Las Vegas community. In May 1986 Palace Station owner Frank Fertitta pledged $500,000 in cash and real estate over five years to strengthen UNLV's "scholarship endowment." "I'm aware of the value of leaders like Bob Maxson," Fertitta declared, "and I want to support his efforts in carrying out his goals for UNLV by giving him the necessary tools for the job."[4] Four months later, local developers John Midby and Daniel Byron gave the school $1 million, $300,000 of which Maxson earmarked for the scholarship fund.

While appreciative of their generosity, the president was quick to caution Las Vegans and "friends of the university" that much still needed to be done. In a 1986 speech, Maxson emphasized the need for UNLV to offer more degree programs in the coming years to give students a wider range of choices at both the undergraduate and the graduate levels. He estimated that UNLV had about half the number of degree programs found at other universities of comparable size. Doctorates in English and sociology, and master's degrees in the visual arts and fine arts were on the way, but he told faculty and regents that UNLV needed more.

To help push the development effort, Lyle Rivera, who became vice president for development and university relations in 1984, announced a new capital campaign in 1987 that included direct mail and personal appeals to alumni, parents of students, and parents and friends of the university to raise more money to support scholarships, faculty travel, development, and the arts. The purpose of the campaign, given the title "Private Dollars, Public Scholars," Rivera said, was to "be letting people know that they can make a difference. Their donations can provide the scholarships that enable Nevada's best students to take advantage of UNLV's educational opportunities."[5] Eager to boost the momentum that had propelled the foundation to new heights during the Maxson era, Rivera used the opportunity to point out that of the nearly $23 million in gifts and pledges raised since 1981, more than $20 million had come since Maxson's arrival.

Clearly, Maxson was the talented fund-raiser that UNLV desperately needed. Thanks to his leadership and the fruitful efforts of the foundation, UNLV attracted $12.3 million in 1989, more than double the $5 million figure of the previous year. As foundation board chair Elaine Wynn noted, "I have a sense that UNLV is becoming much more stable and mature."[6] The largest gift in 1989 came from the Holiday Corporation and William Harrah's widow, Verna, who donated $5 million to the hotel college, which Maxson renamed for her late husband.

The president understood the symbiotic relationship between fund-raising and creating a quality university, and he pursued both. At UNLV, he worked to build new programs and strengthen old ones. In 1985, for instance, interim business college dean Thomas White told reporters that Maxson had pledged $500,000 to hire more faculty and to use a $250,000 grant from First Interstate Bank to further strengthen the program. White declared, "We are finally starting to get the support we need from both the university and the community," with evident enthusiasm.[7] An economics professor at the school since 1967, White appreciated the growth of supplemental funding from the private sector under Maxson.

The president also recognized the importance of building enrollment by catering more to off-campus constituencies. In 1986 UNLV began offering degree programs at Nellis Air Force Base. While the school had scheduled courses at the installation for years, this was the first time that service personnel could pursue degrees there. The university joined the Servicemen's Opportunity College, a national program that allowed soldiers, sailors, and airmen to earn their degrees even if they transferred to several bases during their education. There was no loss of quality in the off-campus instruction at Nellis. Indeed, UNLV officials noted that the same faculty teaching at Nellis taught on campus, and more than half had doctorates. Maxson took an important first step, but it would be almost twenty years before the Harter administration finally established an Air Force ROTC program at UNLV.

Maxson also reached out to minority groups and daytime workers to make it easier for them to earn college credit. In April 1985 the president addressed members of the Nevada Black Chamber of Commerce and explained his plans to streamline UNLV's bureaucracy and make more classes available to local workers. He also promised to schedule more evening classes for those with daytime jobs: "We cannot make adults jump through the same bureaucratic hoops as 18-year-olds," he said. As for those workers who had to rush over to UNLV and deal with its bureaucracy on their lunch hour, he promised to reform the process, declaring, "We simply cannot send them from office to office."[8]

Maxson's encouragement often resulted in the creation of new programs. This was the case with sociology, which got its Ph.D. program in 1988; at the same time, regents approved master's degrees in theater arts and fine arts. The process for creating a doctorate in history (1991) as well as many other graduate

AIRPLANE SUSPENDED FROM THE LOBBY CEILING IN THE NEW
THOMAS T. BEAM ENGINEERING BUILDING, CA. 1989. SPECIAL
COLLECTIONS, UNLV LIBRARIES 0062-1764

and undergraduate programs began with encouragement from Maxson and his provost, John Unrue.

Sometimes Maxson's efforts benefited existing programs. In 1987 the president began lobbying federal officials for a "supercomputer" for the campus. The effects were immediate when combined with other events. In January 1988 the Howard R. Hughes School of Engineering moved into its new $14.7 million building. Enrollment soared. As Dean William Wells pointed out, in just two years the number of majors increased from 600 to more than 1,000, and that number was expected to swell as UNLV negotiated with federal officials to acquire a $10 million supercomputer.

In October 1989 Maxson announced that UNLV had been awarded the machine as part of a Department of Energy appropriations bill. He proclaimed, "Scientifically speaking, this computer will put UNLV on the world map. I honestly believe that this is one of the most significant events in the history of the university." To get it, UNLV resorted to good old-fashioned pork barrel politics. In May 1990 UNLV dedicated the new machine. At the ceremony, Maxson proudly declared, "UNLV won the NCAA [basketball] championship, and we also won the pork bowl."[9] Explaining that there were just thirty-four "supercomputers" in the world (only seventeen of which were in the United States), the president credited Senator Harry Reid with getting the machine as part of a federal funding bill for the DOE to study the suitability of building a high-level nuclear dump at Yucca Mountain. However, Nevada's other U.S. senator, Richard Bryan, boycotted the ceremony to protest what he considered the DOE's efforts to win southern Nevada's support for the dump by giving UNLV the supercomputer.

Reid and Maxson both dismissed Bryan's concerns. The president was quick to point out that because Reid got the computer through a DOE spending bill, UNLV's application did not have to go through the normal review process, which was controlled by the National Science Foundation, where senior academics surely would have rejected UNLV's proposal. As Senator Reid correctly pointed out, "The peer review is slated toward the Harvards, the MITs, the Yales."[10] The president saw the supercomputer as UNLV's first step toward building the advanced science program that Donald Moyer had envisioned. But Maxson's expectations were premature. In its first few years on campus, the supercomputer would, in the words of Provost Unrue, "eat us alive" with maintenance and other operational costs. Presidents Kenny Guinn and Carol Harter eventually turned the situation around by renting out the machine and putting its operation in the capable hands of Joseph Lombardo, who became director of UNLV's National Supercomputing Center for Energy and the Environment.

Maxson was on a roll in 1989, and he used the momentum to push two new initiatives that he had earlier announced in his State of the University address in September. While in Washington, D.C., at a December luncheon with Nevada's congressional delegation to thank its staffers for their help in securing the supercomputer, he announced that private donors had just given $1.5 million to help establish an architecture school at UNLV. He was quick to promote "the next two major programs" at the university, the architecture and law schools. Although conceding that he had yet to obtain state funding for either program, he nonetheless predicted, "You will see a school of architecture . . . within the next two years" and a law school "in the very near future." His confidence was unshakable: "I just know that we'll work hard enough at it and we'll get the support."[11] The law school would take longer than he thought. The William S. Boyd School of Law would not open until 1997, and it would cost millions more than Maxson projected.

While the law school was still a dream, the Maxson administration continued to create many new programs. In April 1990 regents approved a Ph.D. program in physics and a master's degree in architecture. The president spent thousands to equip laboratories and studios for both degrees, which he considered crucial to transforming UNLV into a research university. And the initiatives kept coming. In August 1990 regents approved creation of the Hank Greenspun School of Communication (today's Greenspun School of Journalism and Media Communications) following a $2.6 million donation from that family in memory of Hank Greenspun, the flamboyant publisher and founder of the *Las Vegas Sun*. Later, Carol Harter merged the school into a new college that is today's Greenspun College of Urban Affairs. Prime Cable, a Greenspun subsidiary, also gave $150,000 to operate a channel at UNLV, where communications faculty could train students in television broadcasting skills. The money also helped the former communications department to expand and strengthen its course offerings in print and broadcast journalism, public relations, and advertising.

All of these new programs and degrees contributed to UNLV's reputation as an "up-and-coming" university. Under Maxson, UNLV both expanded and improved its graduate degree programs. Thanks to enrollment and faculty growth as well as to the increased number of graduate programs, UNLV surpassed UNR, the state's traditional degree-granting institution, in the annual number of master's degrees offered. In the 1990–91 school year, UNLV awarded 332 master's degrees, and UNR awarded 284. From 1988 to 1991, UNLV had a 42 percent increase in graduate degrees, from 233 in 1988–89 to 332 in 1990–91. UNR still led in doctoral degrees, with 67 awarded in the 1989–90 and 1990–91 school years, compared to just 10 at UNLV. However, that imbalance would eventually change, too. Before Maxson arrived in 1984, UNLV had only one doctoral program, education, and had awarded only two doctorates by 1976. The university granted its first Ph.D. (English) in 1991. Three years later, there were ten doctoral programs, and then twenty, and then more. By 2004 UNLV had granted 397 doctorates, not including law degrees.

Quality also improved in the 1980s and early 1990s. In physics, for example, Dr. John Farley, who left the University of Oregon in 1987 to join UNLV, told reporters, "I've been able to do things here that there is no way I could have done in Oregon where they have chronic financial problems." His enthusiasm was evident. "The growth here is phenomenal. We are filling our new positions with young, dynamic, active faculty."[12] Farley, a specialist in laser spectroscopy, used laser beams to study the properties of atoms and molecules. In particular, he praised UNLV for the advanced laser equipment purchased for the physics laboratory, mostly from federal grants for his research and that of three other colleagues.

As one local newspaper reported, Farley's research and scholarly reputation drew a number of talented graduate students to the department, including Quian Tu, a graduate of an optical engineering program in China. Tu learned about Farley from newspaper reports describing the 1987 International Conference on Lasers held in China. Farley attended that meeting, thanks partly to travel funds raised by Maxson, and his department secured the equipment he used from a research grant operation funded and improved by the president.

Tu spent the next two years as a graduate student working with the laser equipment acquired for the physics department by Farley and others. For his master's degree project, Tu built an instrument that produced lasers used to study ions, a useful innovation in the field. Tu's impression of UNLV kept him in the program. "The academic standards at this university are high," he told one reporter. "Some universities just kind of give master's degrees away after you spend two years in a program. Here you have to produce and be of high quality."[13] Tu's story, while somewhat exceptional, nevertheless mirrored the experience of many graduate students in the 1980s and 1990s, when UNLV began the long transition process from small college to research university. Moyer, Zorn, Baepler, and Goodall definitely set the process in motion, Maxson gave it a major boost, and Harter would take it dramatically forward.

As UNLV grew in enrollment, faculty, and prestige, UNR officials became increasingly concerned. UNLV's enrollment surge, which put its numbers for 1990 well past UNR's (18,192 versus 11,487), the law and architecture school initiatives, the basketball titles, the new doctoral programs, and a dozen other factors all contributed to growing unease on the Reno campus. In September

1990, UNR president Joseph Crowley blamed politics for what he considered "inequities" in the university system budget that he believed favored UNLV. Be assured, total state spending per student still favored the older campus. Nevertheless, Crowley argued that "it has been suggested on occasion that as an institution gets larger, it inevitably gets better. The facts of the matter are otherwise."[14]

Crowley, of course, never mentioned that UNR's enrollment growth rate was currently 3 percent compared to UNLV's 13 percent, but he played to fiscal conservatives by criticizing the huge increase in the university budget. The president inferred that much of this new spending involved UNLV's exaggerated projections of future growth and its ambitious pursuit of expensive Ph.D. programs already offered by UNR. Then, adopting a more conciliatory tone, Crowley observed: "We realize that we have been around for 116 years and that other institutions must be allowed to mature and develop." But, he insisted, "we also understand the reality of resource limitations"—an argument that resonated with constituencies outside of Clark County and fiscal conservatives within it.[15]

Maxson responded to Crowley's statement with one of his own. In October 1990, he suggested that both UNLV and UNR raise the minimum GPA for admission from 2.3 to 2.5. "We feel that it is imperative that both of Nevada's universities have the same requirements," he declared, "because their missions and functions are identical."[16] UNLV's fall enrollment of 18,216 was an 11.3 percent increase over 1989, and Maxson knew well that if the trend continued, the student body would exceed 20,000 by 1992. His proposal was designed to ease the legislature's concerns over excessive growth and costs. The reform would also affect UNR's enrollment even more than UNLV's, because the 2.5 GPA would wipe out most of Reno's 3 percent growth rate, creating the impression of stagnancy. In December 1991 regents raised the standard for admission. Concerned about the threat posed by UNLV's spiraling enrollment and overall aggressiveness, Crowley opened a recruiting facility on West Charleston Boulevard to lure as many Las Vegas–area students to his campus as possible.

Maxson's reform proposal also addressed the high freshman attrition rate that critics emphasized. The time had come, he insisted, to make UNLV's entrance requirement the same as it was for acceptance as a major in many of UNLV's colleges. This would eliminate academically weaker students who often dropped out in frustration after receiving their grade reports. As the president explained, "Now we are enrolling so many top students that we are becoming concerned about the fate of those who are not as well prepared academically for university level work."[17] In effect, Maxson's proposal was designed to kill two birds with one stone.

While many professors applauded the president's suggestion to tighten enrollment standards, minority spokespeople quickly voiced opposition. As Wayne Nunnely, former UNLV football coach and now (in 1990) director of the school's minority affairs office, contended, "To deny the minority students the opportunity to go to one or the other university in the state would be a gross injustice." Nunnely spoke for many in the city's black and Hispanic communities. He cited statistics demonstrating that if the GPA requirement had been 2.5 or 2.6 in 1989, three-quarters of the minority students admitted to UNLV would have been rejected. "That," he emphasized, "is a significant concern."[18] Then in

IMPRESARIO CHARLES VANDA BROUGHT MANY PROMINENT SPEAKERS AND PERFORMERS TO UNLV. SPECIAL COLLECTIONS, UNLV LIBRARIES 0062-0966

a conciliatory vein, he suggested making it easier to transfer community college credits to UNLV and establishing programs to help all students make the transition from community college and high school to university-level work. In the end, UNLV did raise its admission standards, but it also improved its commitment to remedial programs to help students adjust to the new requirements.

Aside from creating new programs and raising admission standards, UNLV became a better institution by hiring the best people to staff key positions. No one exemplified this trend better than Charles Vanda, whom Baepler hired in 1975 to serve as director of UNLV's new performing arts center. Vanda, a consummate professional who had worked for years in New York in both radio and television, was originally responsible for programming at the newly opened Artemus W. Ham Concert Hall. One of his first actions was to establish the Master Series, which brought immediate prestige to the campus. Under Vanda's

watchful eye, Isaac Stern, Itzhak Perlman, Andre Previn, Aaron Copland, and major symphony orchestras performed on campus. When Marjorie Barrick established the Barrick Lecture Series as part of the Barrick Endowment in 1980, she chose Vanda, a close friend, to select the speakers. He soon used his connections at CBS to bring a former colleague, Walter Cronkite, to campus.

Vanda served UNLV well, enhancing the prestige of the school, the Barrick Lecture Series, and the Master Series by booking the great and the near great for appearances—a tradition that continued long after his departure. In June 1988 Vanda died, and Maxson took his time trying to replace an almost irreplaceable figure. In September 1989 the president finally appointed a talented Vanda associate, Richard Romito, to serve as director. In this position, Romito not only supervised the Charles Vanda Master Series, which was the center's presenting arm, but also managed the Black Box Theatre, the Judy Bayley Theatre, and the Artemus W. Ham Concert Hall.

By the time Maxson took over UNLV in 1984, the performing arts center had already become a complex of several buildings. Construction had been crucial to UNLV's offerings in the fine arts. No longer did students work in cramped quarters with inadequate costumes, scenery, lighting, and sound systems, as they had in the 1960s when Jerry Crawford, Paul Harris, and their colleagues struggled daily with the limited resources available. Then, in 1982, President Goodall added the Alta Ham Fine Arts Building to the complex to help UNLV's sculptors, artists, and musicians. Ten years later, Maxson accepted a $2 million donation from the estate of the late Thomas T. Beam. Beam, a jazz devotee, intended the money to enhance UNLV's music programs or to help finance a new music facility. The money sat in an account for almost a decade while UNLV's administration planned the new building. In the late 1990s, President Carol Harter and her provost, Douglas Ferraro, met with Beam's family and secured an additional $4 million. The total amount of $6 million helped finance construction of a 70,000-square-foot facility to house UNLV's music program. The Lee and Thomas Beam Music Center, finished in 2001, added another significant building to the university's fine and performing arts center.

New construction had improved conditions for theater and the fine arts offerings and for courses in other disciplines as well, thanks largely to the efforts of Maxson's predecessors. The new president built upon this foundation by dramatically expanding UNLV's physical plant. His first major project involved a transfer of ownership and some renovation rather than building a new structure. The Las Vegas Convention and Visitors Authority had constructed the Las Vegas Stadium in 1971–72 when Zorn was president. For more than a decade, UNLV used the stadium as the home field for its football team. While there was some talk over the years about UNLV's taking ownership of the facility, nothing came of it until 1984, when discussion began in earnest with the Maxson administration.

That December, UNLV and the Las Vegas Convention and Visitors Authority negotiated for the transfer of what became the Sam Boyd Silver Bowl. Under a complex arrangement worked out by the authority's staff, UNLV would borrow $300,000 in July 1985 and another $600,000 in January 1986, and would make the first $300,000 payment to the Visitors Authority in July 1985. The staff proposal also called for the cities of Las Vegas, North Las Vegas, Henderson, and Boulder City, as well as Clark County, to loan the university $560,000 in recreation grant funds over the next fiscal year. All of the loans would be interest-free. UNLV would then pay the cities and the county $100,000 annually between 1988 and 1992, plus $60,000 more in 1993. The authority would receive $50,000 a year during that period, plus another $90,000 in 1993. A $1.5 million donation from the Boyd family helped the school get the rest of the money to buy the stadium, and for this reason the university later named the Silver Bowl for Sam Boyd. In spring 1985 the cities, the county, the Bureau of Land Management, and UNLV all approved the deal, and the regents agreed to the installation of an artificial playing surface that could be rolled up for concerts and other events. Together, the Thomas & Mack Center and Las Vegas Stadium (renamed the Silver Bowl from 1978 to 1983, the Sam Boyd Silver Bowl from 1984 to 1993, and finally Sam Boyd Stadium, from 1994 to the present) clearly demonstrated how UNLV facilities benefited the larger community. A 1997 study found that between 1984 and 1996, events and related spending at the two venues pumped more than $1.1 billion into the Las Vegas economy.

Maxson was determined to make UNLV a major university, and acquiring a football stadium was just one part of his plan. Although the Maryland Parkway campus began as a commuter school, it had attracted out-of-state students from the beginning. The construction of the original Tonopah Hall in 1973 took UNLV in an important new direction by providing on-campus housing for out-of-state and international students, something every major university had. Between 1970 and 1975, the percentage of out-of-state students at UNLV held steady at about 9 percent, but three years later it grew to 15.5 percent—with Californians accounting for a quarter of it. The sheer number of out-of-state students in the 1980s led some to advocate building more residence halls. In May 1983, O. C. Bobby Daniels, the dean of students, called for constructing a new facility to supplement Tonopah Hall's 250-student capacity. But there was immediate opposition, given the legislature's resistance to more higher education spending. Regent Lilly Fong openly questioned the need, arguing that Tonopah Hall still had empty rooms. In fact, the Goodall administration had even considered reverting to the old policy of requiring all single, out-of-state students under the age of twenty-one to live in Tonopah Hall for at least a year. Fortunately for students, it never happened.

Rising enrollment soon forced the issue. Clearly, the national prominence of the Runnin' Rebels, along with Las Vegas's undeniable lure and UNLV's growing respectability, encouraged a large increase in out-of-state and northern Nevada applicants. In response, Maxson announced in February 1985 that he would build two new residence halls for an additional 750 students. He wanted to locate the new structures in the desert between the Thomas & Mack Center and Brussels Street. By 1986 the spiraling enrollment justified his request, and regents approved the plan. Construction began in 1987 on what became four new residence halls, which opened in 1988 in a community south of University Road. UNLV extended Gym Road from University Road to Tropicana Avenue to provide access to residence hall parking.

Maxson, however, wanted even more student housing. Only weeks after these facilities became operational, he drafted plans to seek $10 million in additional bonds. Because the new residence halls were already filled and the school had a waiting list for more, the president decided to take immediate action. The old Tonopah Hall and the new buildings now accommodated 660 students, but Maxson sought to house at least 1,000 on campus. His reasoning was simple: Many parents preferred not to send their youngsters to school in another city unless they would be living in supervised housing. While no one mentioned it, the need was even more pressing since the city was Las Vegas. Indeed, when the building designers suggested trimming the residence halls with neon lighting to set them off at night, Maxson was quick to nix the idea. He preferred financing the new facility with bonds rather than state funds, because the bonds were like loans that could be paid off with student room and board fees.

In 1989 the regents approved an $11.1 million bond issue that allowed UNLV to build three more residence halls, raising capacity to 1,260 students. Robert Ackerman, who served for fourteen years as vice president for student services at UNLV, oversaw the project. Later, in January 1990, Maxson announced that Bill Boyd, of the Boyd Gaming Corporation, would donate $500,000 toward more than $8.4 million worth of new residence halls. Boyd recognized the importance of UNLV's expanding its student housing beyond the original Tonopah Hall. "It becomes another strong marketing tool," Boyd explained, "to attract students from all over the country and other parts of the world." Boyd clearly saw the advantage of using the dormitories to offset the town's twenty-four-hour, party-time image. "As a parent, I know that families like to have this residence hall option for their student children."[19] In the meantime, Maxson also raised enough money to construct a large new dining commons to accommodate the growing student population. This building opened in 1990.

In an effort to reinforce a sense of community in the new residence hall complex, Maxson also pushed for fraternity housing nearby. In January 1990, regents approved a proposal to build a Greek Row on 25 acres bordering Swenson Street. Each house would cost approximately $500,000, and each fraternity (no sororities expressed interest) would pay rent to cover the cost of the loan. At the time, regents worried about the "Animal House" effect of clustering fraternities so close together. In hindsight, they should have been more concerned about the plan's financing. While four fraternities—Sigma Chi, Alpha Tau Omega, Tau Kappa Epsilon, and Kappa Sigma—expressed early interest in building, none had the cash to do so. With no initial rush to the site, and as support for the idea faded and the high costs of building became more obvious, the project quickly became a minor disaster—eventually delaying construction of UNLV's first parking garage until the twenty-first century.

In planning the grounds around the new residence hall complex and the potential Greek Row, Maxson recognized that the landscaping should be extended farther west to make UNLV's southwestern periphery more appealing. In 1987 the school spent $400,000 to complete the first phase of its efforts to beautify the campus perimeter with lawns and trees. Maxson explained that the intersection of Tropicana and Swenson streets, the main airport exit, was the first priority, in order "to enhance the appearance of the university and the community for the millions of visitors who arrive in Las Vegas at McCarran International . . . each year."[20] The highlight of the project was the Bally's Fountain at the northeast corner of Swenson and Tropicana. It later became the Hilton Fountain when that chain bought out Bally's in 1996 and underwent subsequent name changes. By initiating the beautification process along UNLV's southern and western margins in 1988, Maxson encouraged more donations to continue the work. In April 1989, Las Vegas developer Johnny Ribeiro and his family donated another $500,000 to re-start the landscaping project, which had stalled for lack of money.

Improved landscaping was only part of Maxson's agenda for upgrading the campus. In his 1989 State of the University address, the president announced plans to establish a law school and build a new library. The latter drew more applause than the law school or any of his other initiatives. By 1989 the Dickinson Library's three-story round building of 96,000 square feet and the 91,000-square-foot addition of 1981 were no longer sufficient to hold the increased collections projected for the 1990s. Books in subject areas in the humanities and social sciences had already been taken off the open shelves and put into compact storage, where students and faculty had to turn handles located on the end of each row of book shelves to open an aisle for access.

By June 1988 the Dickinson Library contained more than 1.7 million items, although the book collection lagged far behind what the American Library Association considered average for universities of comparable size. In his State of the University address Maxson noted, "My preference would be to build a new library and take the existing library and have it either as an annex to a library or convert it to offices and classrooms." He estimated the cost of a new facility at $15 million and conceded that it "may not be practical financially."[21] In the end, the president decided to build what became the Lied Library, and by 1993 he estimated its cost at $50 million or more. Before he left UNLV, Maxson began the fund-raising effort. He also began lobbying state legislators for substantial appropriations for the project.

All of these new buildings, especially the residence halls with hundreds of students now crossing University Road, made traffic a serious problem. In April 1990 UNLV finally closed portions of University and Gym roads to safeguard pedestrian traffic between campus buildings and the new residence hall community on the south end of campus. In fall 1994 the university paved over part of Gym Road and created the broad sidewalk in front of today's Harter Classroom Complex and the new student services building to the west.

But this was just one of several projects. Declaring, "We must have more space," Maxson called on regents and legislators in 1988 to fund a $7 million, 50,000-square-foot building to house the College of Health Sciences, which they did. Today's Rod Lee Bigelow Health Sciences Building opened in 1992. In November 1990 UNLV received another boost when the Desert Research Institute announced plans to build a new $50 million headquarters at Flamingo and Swenson. The 66,000-square-foot Southern Nevada Science Center, while not technically part of UNLV, was in the University of Nevada System and contributed further to the research reputation that Maxson was trying to forge for the school. The DRI president, James Taranik, emphasized that UNLV would benefit from having DRI nearby, giving science students easy access to facilities and personnel. The complex, built in four stages, was designed to concentrate most of DRI's technicians and scientists in Las Vegas. "With this new facility," he explained, "our strong contingent of ground-water scientists from DRI's Water Resources Center in Las Vegas will be joined by members of DRI's other four research centers" in the state.[22]

Private donations also supported new construction. In November 1990, Newmont Gold, the state's largest gold producer, gave $1.5 million to UNLV. Normally, Barrick Gold (no relation to Marjorie Barrick) and the other mining firms donated to the Reno campus and its College of Mines. Newmont's gift, the largest in company history, reflected the rising importance of Las Vegas as a power in Nevada higher education, and it no doubt raised concerns at UNR's administrative offices in Morrill Hall. Politics, however, may have played some role in the company's altruism. The donation came on the heels of the 1989 legislature, dominated by southern Nevada legislators, rejecting industry efforts to pass a constitutional amendment capping the mining tax at 2 percent of net proceeds. Instead, lawmakers raised the tax to 5 percent, a revenue-producing measure pushed by Assemblyman Marvin Sedway and other Clark County legislators—an action that the industry was not eager to see become a habit.

Whatever the motivation, UNLV announced that the donation would be used to build an academic advising center that would house programs promoting academic advancement, student development, athletic academic advising, minority student affairs, and student support services. For Vice President Ackerman, who would supervise the project, this was a dream come true. As President Maxson described it, "A centralized academic advising center at the university is much needed at this time." He used the opportunity to assure voters that UNLV was not relying on state money to pay for all its development. Indeed, he told reporters that "academic gifts from the business community have helped us deliver quality education for years." He then emphasized how this trend had intensified during his presidency: "Over the past seven years, they have amounted to some 50 to 60 million dollars."[23]

Private donations continued to finance new construction. In October 1991 Maxson accepted a $4 million pledge from the Donald W. Reynolds Foundation for the new student services building, another Ackerman priority. According to Maxson, Reynolds, founder of the Donrey Media Group, which owned the *Las Vegas Review-Journal* (now part of the Stephens Publishing Group) as well as the Donrey Outdoor Advertising Company (today part of Eller Media), had financed "another step in the maturity of UNLV."[24] According to the foundation's president, Fred Smith, Reynolds, a graduate of the University of Missouri, had long credited education for his success in business and wanted to make a contribution to Las Vegas, which had been so good to him. The building itself would be located just south of the future CBC and, according to Maxson, would house the student development center, financial services, multicultural student affairs, career planning and placement, disabled-student services, and the academic advancement program. The $4 million donation from the Reynolds Foundation for construction was one of the largest gifts to UNLV up to that time.

The university's growing number of new degree programs plus its spiraling enrollment brought calls for even more buildings. As the 1991 legislative session approached and Maxson prepared his budget requests, three construction projects topped his agenda: a $17.7 million classroom building complex (today's Harter Classroom Complex), a $9.3 million structure (the Paul B. Sogg Architecture Building) to house UNLV's proposed architecture program, and a physics-chemistry facility (the Robert L. Bigelow Physics Building).

Maxson's success at program development and building should not obscure the many problems he faced along the way, however. Lack of money always threatened his agenda. In February 1991 he warned that unless the legislature allocated $46.7 million to construct these three new buildings, UNLV would have to cap enrollment. He complained, "Out of the last 12 buildings built at UNLV, the state of Nevada paid for one."[25] Elaine Wynn, outgoing chair of the UNLV Foundation board of trustees, noted that, despite raising $24 million

DIANE AND ROBERT BIGELOW WITH FORMER SECRETARY OF
STATE COLIN POWELL. UNLV FOUNDATION

ELAINE WYNN STANDS BEFORE THE ROSE GARDEN DEDICATED
TO HER MOTHER, LEE PASCAL, NEAR THE CARLSON EDUCATION
BUILDING, 1989. UNLV FOUNDATION

over the past four years, there was not enough money to pay for the new Harter
Classroom Complex, physics, and architecture buildings.

Lack of state funding caused problems across the board at the growing
campus, but new buildings were affected the most, since they were a high-
priced item. Maxson made his point about the danger threatening these capital
projects by emphasizing that state funding was not even enough to pay for personnel. As the exasperated president told reporters, "We're paying staff people
from Foundation money; we're paying accountants and secretaries" with money
that should be going to strengthen programs. Elaine Wynn also made the con-

nection. The lack of state support, Wynn cautioned, was beginning to hamper fund-raising efforts. "The main friends of the university are suggesting: 'We've done enough.' They'll never say no, but it's becoming more difficult to ask them with a clear conscience to build a dining complex."[26]

Wynn's reaction illustrates the growing importance of a strong UNLV Foundation. At this crucial time, the president could rely on a major Strip executive, in this case Steve Wynn's influential wife, to support a university budget position. Maxson's predecessors, although close to Las Vegas's movers and shakers, never enjoyed the kind of leverage in Carson City that Maxson and his successors would have when key university projects needed legislative support. It was important for the university to strengthen its alliances with the local business and resort community precisely at the time when the Las Vegas area's exploding population and influential business leaders were boosting Clark County's power in the state, and Maxson and his successors did just that. The coalition of support that Maxson, Wynn, and others were able to build with local business leaders for his three buildings in the 1991 session resembles the strategy Carol Harter employed in 2001–03 to win approval in Carson City for the science, engineering, and technology building.

Despite the support of Elaine Wynn and other influential Las Vegas executives, it was a tough fight for the president in 1991. A minor slowdown in tourism and the fiscal conservatism of Governor Bob Miller and state lawmakers threatened the new buildings Maxson wanted. When the 1991 legislative session began in February, many wondered whether the state would appropriate its share of the cost for constructing the Harter Classroom Complex and the architecture and physics buildings. In March, Maxson pleaded with the Senate Finance Committee to fund the three projects. "I've got to have an architecture building and a classroom building, or I tell you we come to a grinding halt at UNLV or there will be a *de facto* capping of enrollment." He told them that UNLV's architecture program was now confined to six trailers, and he warned, "We will never get that program accredited in a group of house trailers."[27]

The president jousted with lawmakers, fearing they would adhere to Governor Miller's $495 million budget for higher education, a figure far below the $539 million requested by regents. Maxson knew that all three of his buildings could go up in smoke if conservative lawmakers had their way.

At the same time, he was irked by Miller's rejection of the system's request for a law school at UNLV. In Miller's defense, Senator Bill Raggio (R-Reno) claimed that the state had already been burned by the University of Nevada School of Medicine. "We're led to believe when we start that these things are inexpensive. [But] that's not true." Maxson sidestepped that issue by telling the powerful committee chair: "I want a law school so badly I can taste it. But I'll not put a law school ahead of these critical needs I have now."[28] In the end, the president got all three of his buildings, but the law school had to wait until the Harter administration.

In October 1991 a jubilant Maxson announced the sale of $21.9 million in bonds to erect today's Harter Classroom Complex, composed of lecture halls, classrooms, and faculty offices that finally relieved the space crunch on campus when it opened in 1994. Plans also went forward for a $13 million structure for physics and a $14 million architecture facility. Paul Sogg, who built more than two thousand homes and town houses in addition to shopping centers and warehouses during his forty-year career as a Las Vegas developer, contributed more than $1 million to finance the building that today bears his name. The project, however, faced numerous delays while the courts determined whether a member of the architecture faculty could design the building. As a result, the facility did not open until 1997.

Not all of Maxson's construction projects were buildings. In February 1991 he unveiled plans for an attractive brick plaza, complete with palm trees, tables, and seating in front of the Moyer Student Union. In an emotional ceremony, he announced that the plaza would be named for Valerie Pida, a marketing major and former UNLV cheerleader who was then fighting a determined battle against lymphatic cancer and had endured numerous hospital stays. Although the disease finally took Pida's life, the plaza remains as a lasting memorial to her courageous struggle.

As every student and staff member at any university knows, the construction of new buildings usurps space formerly devoted to parking. Maxson floated the bonds in 1985 to finish paving the Thomas & Mack parking lot and end the facility's pay-as-you-go approach that left most students and other basketball fans in the dust. To accommodate new buildings, however, he also had to close numerous other parking lots. The new residence halls alone eliminated several hundred spaces, as did the Harter Classroom Complex and Reynolds Student Services buildings, which soon occupied most of the Thomas & Mack's east lot. But these were not the only places on campus affected. Construction of the Robert L. Bigelow Physics Building in 1993–94 eliminated 230 spaces. In 1993 alone, new construction cost UNLV 1,300 parking spaces, although Maxson built 1,200 more to help replace them, adding hundreds of spots behind White Hall and Bigelow Health Sciences, as well as on the university's northeast margins, where the UNLV Foundation building stands today. Ultimately, new construction would force UNLV to build vertical parking structures, and while Maxson considered various plans for a garage, the Harter administration built it.

All of this cost money. In October 1989 Maxson hinted that parking fees might be instituted soon for faculty, staff, and some students on campus. The president noted that he had rejected the idea every year since 1984 to avoid raising the cost of attending UNLV, but now he predicted that fees would have to be implemented soon (they came in 1994) to pay for better lighting and the eventual construction of parking garages. Meters and annual charges would be necessary to avoid diverting funds from academic support to parking.

These numerous construction projects, which consumed large portions of UNLV's land, convinced Maxson that it was time to begin planning for a second campus. Of course, there had been talk in 1955–56 of purchasing sites on West Charleston and elsewhere in case Nevada Southern someday needed it. But such optimism seemed a bit excessive at the time. Just three decades later, however, it was necessary. The West Charleston land purchased by the state in 1957 had already been taken by the community college, which opened a big campus there in 1988.

As early as January 1989, Maxson predicted that UNLV someday would have to build a satellite campus in the western part of the valley. Perhaps taking his cue from ASU and ASU West in the Phoenix metropolitan area, the president referred to the new venue as UNLV West. He estimated that UNLV's current "330-acre campus can hold . . . approximately 30,000 students."[29] Even though enrollment at the time was only 14,800, Maxson foresaw the school's continued development into the new century. He told reporters that the new facility would not be an attempt to duplicate the main campus, but instead would be one large building in a parklike setting on an 8-to-10-acre tract. His vision was only partially correct. Today UNLV is developing a multi-campus university with substantial buildings on sites exceeding 750 acres in various parts of the valley.

Continued growth and the effort to make up for past growth were the main forces driving the university's building agenda. But for the Maxson administration, the problem was not just money for new programs and buildings; it was also funding for services and support strained by booming enrollment during a period of budgetary restraint. Higher student populations forced bureaucratic expansion at the school. In March 1989 the president sought more state funds for campus police, counselors, and admissions workers to serve the rapidly growing student population. He told lawmakers, "We simply need more help." He asked for money to hire six more police officers to bring the university force to twenty and "make sure we have two security people on at all times" to help protect 15,000 students.[30] He also requested more admissions personnel to help recruit at Nevada's fifty-three high schools. Finally, he complained about the campus having only two full-time counselors to serve UNLV's entire student body.

In the end, the president received the funding he sought, although critics in the legislature challenged the need for an architecture school, and a law school, and especially an engineering college when UNR already had one. As some pointed out, why not expand UNLV's classroom space, faculty, and bureaucracy enough to handle the increased undergraduate admissions resulting from Las Vegas's development and leave it at that?

Quality was another issue, especially with local critics. To be sure, the president faced skeptics not only in Carson City but also in Las Vegas. Some in the local media openly questioned whether UNLV was really the quality institution that Maxson portrayed to lawmakers and the public. Local newspapers investigated some of UNLV's more obvious shortcomings. Clearly, the school was vulnerable on a number of counts. One lingering problem was high attrition. In June 1990, the dropout rate for freshmen hovered at 40 percent, well above the 29.9 percent national average. Administrators scurried to explain the disparity. As Provost Unrue noted, "We have many commuter students who may attend one semester and then take the next semester off to work."[31] The administration emphasized that as UNLV attracted more "traditional" students and implemented courses to teach incoming freshman study, note-taking, and time management skills, the attrition rate would decline. Of course, those teaching at the time might have added that a number of students came to UNLV to attend a school with a championship-level basketball program and a party atmosphere highly rated by popular magazines. These students, many of whom were from out of state, assumed that academic standards in the classroom would reflect the fun-loving values of Las Vegas. They soon learned otherwise. Very quickly, absenteeism, halfhearted study efforts, and lack of preparation took their toll, and those students left.

While Maxson could proudly repeat the *U.S. News & World Report*'s description of UNLV as an "up and coming school," local critics questioned UNLV's quality and commitment to excellence. In an October 1991 story, *Review-Journal* reporter John Gallant quoted the Northwest Association's 1990 accreditation report noting a "rather shocking lack of support for the rapid growth of faculty, plant, programs, and students that UNLV has experienced since 1980."[32] Of course, the accreditation team hardly factored in the Atlantic City–induced local recession and the national recession of the early 1980s, as well as Nevada's tightfisted approach to spending.

Nevertheless, UNLV was vulnerable to criticism on issues beyond the high freshman dropout rate and funding of support services. In 1991, the school's graduation rate over the past five years was low, just 21 percent. The portion of UNLV's budget dedicated to the library declined from 5.5 percent in 1985–86 to 4.5 percent in 1988–89, although, Gallant conceded, total library appropriations had increased. By many accounts, the library's collections were inadequate to support the growing number of new programs that Maxson encouraged. The percentage of faculty with doctorates also declined from 78 percent in 1982 to 73 percent in 1990, although the number of graduate programs multiplied. Moreover, UNLV's 142-day academic year fell well below the national standard of 150, while the freshman attrition rate was higher. In addition, UNLV continued its policy of not requiring minimum ACT or SAT college entrance test scores for incoming freshmen, while at the same time reducing out-of-state recruiting efforts that, Gallant suggested, would give the school a larger pool of talented applicants.

Clearly, even before the Tarkanian resignation controversy, Maxson faced criticism for UNLV's various flaws. Some even questioned his upbeat touting of the school, viewing it as window dressing and hype. Although the president denied that UNLV was engaged in a calculated national publicity campaign, the school clearly had to do something to enhance its national image. Obviously, *U.S. News & World Report*'s favorable coverage was more the exception than the rule in the national media. Shortly before Maxson's arrival in 1984, CBS News had described UNLV as "a no-name university in Sin City" during a story about the Runnin' Rebels that seemed to target not only Tarkanian but Las Vegas as well. Disliked in the basketball-crazy Bible Belt since the days of Bugsy Siegel and Estes Kefauver, Las Vegas was vulnerable, and CBS News, along with others in the media, knew how to exploit the sanctimonious prejudices of audiences around the country.

Something had to be done to counteract what many on campus considered an unfair characterization of the school. While Maxson hardly claimed that UNLV was, in Gallant's words, "the Harvard of the Colorado," it was no longer Tumbleweed Tech or Sin City Community College. "I've been single-minded in our commitment to advancing the academic reputation of this campus," Maxson insisted, "and I refuse to be distracted."[33] The president recognized that, for all its shortcomings, UNLV had made great strides in the 1980s and early 1990s under Goodall and himself, and, for the sake of the students, there was no reason to let the media plant a misleading image of the school in the public's mind. So he led a decade-long campaign to portray UNLV in positive terms.

Despite the media criticism, virtually everyone recognized that Maxson had begun the process of transforming UNLV into a major university. But the controversy over Jerry Tarkanian's resignation in 1991 ultimately forced the president's departure. Maxson's relationship with the Athletics Department for his entire tenure was mixed at best. While administrators and coaches applauded his decision to subsidize the department annually with Sam Boyd Silver Bowl and Thomas & Mack revenues to reduce its perennial shortfall, other issues caused conflicts.

In March 1986 a rash of embarrassing incidents involving the football team led to the firing of head coach Harvey Hyde. It began when metro police officers arrested two football players outside the Riviera Hotel after tourists accused them of purse snatching. Several weeks later, police took six players into custody for burglary as well as the possession and use of stolen credit cards at the

Boulevard Mall. Although Hyde suspended the players involved and cooperated fully with authorities, Maxson fired him in April. For the president, there were too many questions surrounding the program's recruiting standards in Southern California, and he wanted no more adverse publicity.

Not everyone, however, approved of Maxson's decision to fire Hyde. As athletics director Brad Rothermel has repeatedly noted, Maxson did not inherit a rogue athletics program. Shortly after assuming his post in 1980, Rothermel instituted policies governing players who engaged in criminal behavior. Those arrested for a felony faced immediate suspension from their sport. For players charged with a misdemeanor, the level of punishment rested with the coach. Even though Hyde's players were all arrested for misdemeanors (none were ever convicted), he nevertheless suspended them all. Despite this action, Hyde still lost his job. Rothermel therefore disagreed with Maxson's decision, contending that after the arrests, Hyde had taken all the necessary steps with all of the players on his team to prevent future incidents. Rothermel was impressed by Hyde's dynamism and winning record and did not want to see him leave. But the arrests and subsequent press reports raised serious questions about Hyde's recruiting practices, and many faculty supported Maxson's position that Hyde had to go.

In September 1986 Maxson named former Rebel standout Wayne Nunnely as the interim and then new head coach. At thirty-four, Nunnely became the second black head coach at UNLV (track coach Al McDaniel was the first) and the first African American head football coach at a major university in the West. Though a great honor, it was hardly a tenured job. Maxson cautioned the new hire about "the realities of the coaching profession." To keep his job, Nunnely had to be successful. "If you don't win," the president told him, "you don't sell tickets," and you cannot pay the bills. Coaches had to win, because at UNLV "we do not put a penny of academic money into athletics."[34]

At the time, Nunnely's hiring seemed like a masterstroke that, for the most part, quieted those fans and players angered by Hyde's dismissal. Rothermel, however, was convinced that Hyde's removal was just the beginning. He believed that Maxson ultimately wanted Tarkanian out too, because of his long-standing conflicts with the NCAA. Rothermel did not want to lose the popular coach. The athletics director needed winning coaches in the major sports, especially basketball, for the fan support, donations, and television revenues they brought his department. Maxson, on the other hand, thought his athletics director should play a greater role in reining in the maverick coach.

The Maxson-Tarkanian story has been told and retold in books and articles. More than a decade later, it remains one of the few tragedies in the history of UNLV and the Las Vegas area. The seeds of Tarkanian's problems with the NCAA lay in his January 1973 column for the *Long Beach Independent Press-Telegram,* in which he criticized the regulatory agency for a selective enforcement of policy that often ignored violations of established sports programs while cracking down on smaller and newer ones. Tarkanian used the example of Western Kentucky's basketball team being placed on probation while the state's traditional power, the University of Kentucky, faced no investigation at all. From that time on, the NCAA began scrutinizing Tarkanian more closely. The coach left Long Beach State just days before NCAA investigators launched a probe into his program there and just weeks after his newspaper column appeared. The enforcement committee later found twenty-three violations committed during his tenure. Less than a week after Tarkanian accepted the UNLV job, the NCAA reopened an old investigation into the Las Vegas basketball program under former coach Rolland Todd. In 1976 the NCAA charged the school with ten "major violations" since 1973, including free meals and lodging for players allegedly arranged by a friendly booster and even grade fixing by a UNLV professor.

Tarkanian's claim that the NCAA was engaged in a vindictive campaign to discredit him was true in many respects. An internal UNLV investigation into the affair, supervised by respected Las Vegas attorney Samuel Lionel, determined that the NCAA conducted its probe in a vindictive manner, that it used evidence selectively, and that most of the charges, including grade fixing, could not be substantiated. Despite the NCAA's denials, Tarkanian's contention that the governing body investigated and punished some schools while ignoring others was true, and everybody in college sports knew it. Furthermore, his charge that NCAA investigators denied him the due process usually accorded defendants who were being prosecuted in state and federal courts was also true, although the U.S. Supreme Court in 1988 decided by a 5–4 vote that the NCAA, as a private organization, had the right to do so. In addition to putting UNLV on probation and banning postseason play for two years, the NCAA infractions committee in 1977 also ruled that Tarkanian could not be involved with the UNLV basketball program for two years. This was clearly an excessive penalty and was immediately postponed by an injunction issued by a Nevada court judge, who ordered UNLV to reinstate the coach. Tarkanian's lawyers battled the NCAA in court for more than a decade.

None of this was news to President Maxson when he arrived on campus in 1984. After nearly twenty years in higher administration at schools with sports programs, he, like everyone else, knew that NCAA enforcement could be selective. But he also knew that as a college president he had to work with the NCAA, because it still commanded the respect of most universities, the public, and Congress.

Maxson also recognized Tarkanian's immense contributions to putting UNLV on the national map, drawing many Las Vegans, including wealthy donors, closer to the school, and supporting a chronically underfunded Department of Athletics with millions of dollars in TV revenues. Maxson, like many others, assumed there were some legitimate violations in the basketball program—just as there were at one time or another in virtually every big-time basketball program. He may well have considered the option, as Rothermel has suggested, of removing the legendary coach in 1984, but he made no effort to do so. After all, the Runnin' Rebels were filling the Thomas & Mack with fans, and no one appreciated the value of "Gucci Row" more than Maxson. Like Baepler, he understood the importance of a successful sports program in luring potential donors to the UNLV campus—first to the ball games and later to academics through the vehicle of the UNLV Foundation. As uneasy as Maxson may have been about Tarkanian's ongoing conflict with the NCAA, in the mid-1980s the president understood that Tarkanian was still good for the school; he had incurred no recent NCAA violations, and there was no one who could replace him.

At the same time, Maxson, like all college presidents, wanted no more trouble with the NCAA. Through his aggressive pursuit of new buildings, programs, and donations, he was trying to forge a positive academic image for UNLV as "an up-and-coming" university that attracted "the best and the brightest" students. Obviously, he did not want a barrage of negative publicity offsetting this effort. That is why he fired Harvey Hyde, and that is why his relations with Brad Rothermel were chilly at best. Like all presidents, Maxson expected his athletics director to stop trouble before it started in any of the school's sports programs, especially the major ones. Rothermel, however, questioned Maxson's concern, pointing out that from the late 1970s until 1991, the NCAA levied no sanctions against any UNLV sport, including men's basketball.

But trouble was brewing. A series of incidents in the late 1980s and early 1990s led to the famous confrontation between the coach and the president. In 1988 the U.S. Supreme Court finally upheld the 1977 NCAA demand that Tarkanian leave UNLV's program for two years. The infractions committee took its time before deciding to enforce the ban, but finally acted just as the 1990 team prepared to defend its title. Maxson negotiated a compromise to delay the coach's furlough until 1992, the year after Larry Johnson and the other stars graduated to the NBA.

Even before the court ruling, charges continued to fly that boosters provided players with new cars and other services, but there was no specific proof. All the president wanted was an end to the negative publicity. Three major incidents began the process that divided the faculty, the students, and the Las Vegas community into two camps. The first occurred in 1986, when Tarkanian recruited Lloyd Daniels, an obviously talented player but a weak student (there were even questions about his literacy), who had been kicked out of two high schools over allegations of theft and drug use. One of Tarkanian's assistant coaches even adopted Daniels, who also received a used car and a motorcycle. A UNLV rule that allowed non–high school graduates to enroll provided that they complete some remedial and junior college coursework awarded Daniels admission to the university. Press coverage only renewed faculty concerns about the basketball program. News that Tarkanian had gone to a California juvenile facility to recruit prospect Clifford Allen did little to reduce the pressure on Maxson from elements in the faculty to do something about the basketball program. Then news of Daniels's arrest by North Las Vegas police, who videotaped his purchase of crack cocaine, put even more pressure on the president.

Still, Maxson did not try to fire Tarkanian or Rothermel, although he made it clear that these incidents had to stop. Of course, the president had to recognize that UNLV had admitted Daniels, whom other schools had recruited, and the NCAA had not sanctioned the school for the Daniels affair. For his part, Tarkanian had always prided himself, and rightly so, for taking many young, talented African American players off the streets and putting them in a college setting where they could transform their lives and their careers with his expert coaching. Tarkanian had done this on numerous occasions throughout his career. He had always been willing to take a chance on high-risk players that other schools had passed up. Until 1986 his luck had been good, but it ran out with Daniels. Eventually the furor died down, and over the next five seasons Tarkanian's teams made five postseason tournament appearances, including three Final Fours, and won a national championship.

During this time, Maxson faced continued pressure from many faculty, as well as NCAA officials, to make sure there were no more violations. As historian Richard O. Davies has described it, after the Lloyd Daniels affair, the "Las Vegas media no longer gave Tarkanian the benefit of the doubt. Coverage of the Rebels on television and in the newspaper took on a more critical, distanced, professional tenor. Sportswriters . . . reported sightings of Rebels driving expensive late-model automobiles along Las Vegas streets." As Davies explained, "Maxson was now hearing more and more from community and faculty leaders that something had to be done to improve the image of UNLV's athletic program."[35]

Increasingly anxious to reassure the NCAA and protect the school's revenue-producing basketball program from a "death sentence," some administrators went overboard. The 1991 secret videotaping of a supposed Rebel practice on October 8, 1991, (a week before October 15, when NCAA rules allowed basketball teams to begin practicing), sparked a firestorm of controversy. Faculty, students, Tarkanian supporters, and even some Maxson allies argued convincingly that the secret videotaping threatened everyone's First Amendment rights. Maxson, who did not learn about the taping until it became public more than a week later, was clearly embarrassed and assured everyone that it would not happen again. At the alleged practice, which supposedly occurred during a physical conditioning class in which the players were enrolled, the team did not use a ball, so there was no violation of NCAA rules, although one NCAA official later pointed out that the rule's purpose was to ensure that basketball players at that time of the school year were pursuing their education and not going to practices.

Clearly, the relationship between Maxson and Tarkanian was badly strained by spring 1991. On campus, one got the feeling that another major incident would trigger a showdown. Ironically, the incident was not precipitated by Maxson, or Tarkanian, or the NCAA. On May 26, 1991, the *Review-Journal* published an exposé complete with photographs showing three Rebel players sitting in a hot tub with Richie "The Fixer" Perry, who had been convicted of fixing horse races in 1974 and, more ominously, Boston College basketball games in 1984. Other photographs of Perry at Rebel home games, coupled with Tarkanian's admission that he knew Perry but thought he was a commodities broker (Perry also used an alias), made it impossible for this controversy to blow over as the earlier ones had.

The story rated banner headlines across the nation, more negative publicity for UNLV, and a new and dreaded investigation by the NCAA. Given this set of circumstances, Maxson felt he had no choice but to pressure Tarkanian into resigning, which the coach did on June 7, 1991, effective at the end of the 1991–92 season. As everyone knows, the president briefly eased the concerns of some UNLV students and fans by hiring popular Villanova coach Rollie Massimino, but the latter's failure to match the success of Tarkanian's teams eventually turned the public against him. More immediately, the seemingly amicable agreement regarding Tarkanian's voluntary retirement came apart only weeks later. The coach, who had known nothing about Perry's relationship with the players, eventually reconsidered his position and filed a lawsuit, along with his wife, Lois, against the school. As Tarkanian saw it, his integrity was at stake, and so he resented the summary dismissal from a school for which he had done so much. In the meantime, Tarkanian's supporters launched an effective counterattack in the media and in the courts that ultimately forced Maxson, too, to leave UNLV. It was indeed ironic that Maxson became president of Tarkanian's old school, Long Beach State, where he soon became a popular leader.

In hindsight, both men clearly believed they were right. During their respective careers at UNLV, both had contributed mightily to the school and expected the support of its students, faculty, and the larger Las Vegas community. Certainly Tarkanian's success with the basketball team had given UNLV instant national visibility, promoted contributions to the campus, and generated an intense pride in the university among residents of the metropolitan area. Clearly, nineteen winning seasons in a highly competitive sport required a tremendous effort on his part. With this in mind, Tarkanian objected, as did his supporters, to a president whom they saw as conspiring with the NCAA against him.

Maxson and his supporters on the faculty and in the community saw it differently. Their view was that UNLV's Tumbleweed Tech days were long gone and further trouble with the NCAA had to be avoided at all costs. From the president's standpoint, the negative publicity generated by the basketball team threatened the progress UNLV had made since 1984. But it was not just the negative public image created by the hot tub incident. As Maxson saw it, his efforts in program development, new construction, and fund-raising were all designed to enhance the value of a UNLV degree. Being a college president, he understood that for undergraduates seeking to gain admission to M.A., Ph.D., M.D., and other graduate programs at more prestigious institutions, the value of UNLV's degree was determined by faculty at these admitting schools. If those faculty perceived UNLV negatively, whether it was for an underfunded library, weak faculty, or tolerance of unethical behavior in any department, it could affect the admission of UNLV applicants. Maxson also believed that coaches, whether innocent or not, had to take responsibility for program violations. For these reasons, the president moved against Tarkanian in a decided manner in spring 1991.

Put simply, the loss of both men was a tragedy. Could it have been prevented? Given the course of events and various pressures that came to bear on both of them, probably not. On the one hand, Tarkanian knew what he had to do to recruit, train, and coach a winning team. After nearly two decades of success, he expected more leeway and trust from UNLV's administration. On the other hand, Maxson was determined to assert presidential authority over what he considered an out-of-control basketball program. And he did. In the fifteen or so years since this unfortunate controversy, no UNLV athletics program has ever challenged the president. In 1995 and 2002, President Carol Harter appointed her own athletics director without departmental or booster interference.

In his last two years as president, Maxson faced not only renewed criticism over Tarkanian's ouster but trouble on other fronts as well. In 1992 state legislative leaders formed a subcommittee to investigate a variety of matters relating to UNLV, including the president's use of discretionary funds raised by the UNLV Foundation and the circumstances surrounding Tarkanian's resignation. Regarding the issue of discretionary funds, UNLV Foundation board chair John Goolsby could not provide complete details of these transactions because of incomplete record keeping in the 1980s. However, Goolsby agreed with subcommittee members on the need for new legislation specifically defining the relationship between the foundation and the UNLV president regarding the use of funds. Donors who gave money, some of whom opposed Tarkanian's departure, also raised questions about how their money was spent. While the amount of money in question was not substantial, the controversy resulted in a legislative crackdown on the foundation's accounting practices, especially those relating to presidential use of funds for promoting UNLV.

By fall 1993 Maxson could see the end coming and had quietly begun applying for administrative posts elsewhere. In spring 1994 he accepted an offer from California State University, Long Beach to become its next president and announced his resignation from UNLV, effective following the May graduation.

While Tarkanian's supporters were understandably delighted, others felt differently, among them several regents, many of whom recognized Maxson's contributions to UNLV's development. Regent James Eardley observed, "For a while longer at least, Bob Maxson will be remembered as the guy who took on Tarkanian." Eardley, a former president of Truckee Meadows Community College in Reno, credited Maxson with "being the president who turned UNLV into a full-blown university. My perception of UNLV years ago," he recalled, "was that it was a large, large community college."[36] Regent Shelley Berkley had vigorously criticized Maxson for handling Tarkanian's forced resignation "as poorly as it could have been." But, with the president's departure imminent, she was magnanimous, telling reporters, "We are going to remember Dr. Maxson's time as a time of phenomenal growth and development. Nobody can take away what his energy brought to the UNLV campus."[37]

Maxson himself was circumspect about his departure. "Regarding academics," he said, "I remain convinced that the directions we've taken have been the right directions for this university."[38] Maxson's accomplishments were legion. Under his leadership, UNLV built more than thirty buildings and raised $109 million in private funds. It also created dozens of new programs and degrees, while nearly doubling enrollment. More than anything else, Maxson changed the reputation of UNLV from a jock college to an "up and coming" university.

As the president remarked in his farewell, "UNLV is [today] recognized as a very good academic institution by people in the community who truly understand what should be the focus of the university." "Yes," he acknowledged, "there's a place for athletics, but a university is about so much more than a basketball program."[39] The president understood that by the 1980s, public universities were more "state assisted than state-funded," and he actively worked with the community to supplement state money to build the school. As former UNLV historian Robert Davenport, a faculty member since 1964, put it: "President Maxson did a lot to give this place a sense of pride in itself. . . . There have been greater strides during his ten-year tenure than during any other period."[40] In a 2004 conversation, Carol Harter characterized Maxson's fund-raising efforts as "absolutely necessary" and added that "he established some wonderful relationships with community people that I owe a great deal to."[41]

As the president prepared to depart, a *Review-Journal* editorial noted that "Maxson's infectious exuberance and commitment to educational excellence has helped improve the university's academic climate and drawn national acclaim to the school's achievements." The editor spoke for many when he declared, "Thanks to Maxson, the diplomas for which thousands of UNLV graduates toiled, and to which the children of tens of thousands of Las Vegas residents will eventually aspire, carry more value, more prestige."[42]

CHAPTER SEVEN

Turbulence and Reform

KENNY GUINN

When Bob Maxson left UNLV in May 1994 and headed for Long Beach State, the regents needed to find a capable replacement. The logical choice was John Unrue, a longtime member of the English department. Unrue was a veteran administrator, having served as assistant dean and dean of the College of Arts and Letters in the 1970s and early 1980s before becoming vice president of academic affairs in 1984 and later provost. Unrue's tenure as second in command spanned Bob Maxson's entire presidency, including the go-go 1980s and the turbulent years thereafter. Although the two did not agree on all policy issues, Unrue was a loyal supporter of Maxson, and that ultimately proved to be his undoing.

In the supercharged atmosphere of 1993–94, with Tarkanian supporters jubilant over Maxson's departure and with questions being raised about the president's discretionary fund and other issues, most regents wanted to avoid installing a Maxson ally as interim president. Since Maxson gave notice in March 1994 that he would be leaving after graduation in May, the regents had several months to make a choice. They quickly settled on Kenny Guinn, who willingly offered to take the position for $1 a year.

Guinn was a logical selection. He was well known
in Las Vegas and on campus. His reputation for
decisiveness and sound management appealed to a
majority of the regents, who wanted to rein in what
most considered to be UNLV's overspending and
put an end to the continuing controversy following
Tarkanian's departure. Guinn's rags-to-riches success
story and early career in educational administration
only strengthened his credentials. The son of an
Arkansas sharecropper who moved his family to
California during the Depression, Kenny Guinn grew
up in Exeter, a town of about 5,000 between Fresno
and Bakersfield. As a young boy he picked fruit in
the San Joaquin Valley, and as a teenager he worked
in the garage of Frank List, the father of Kenny's
childhood friend Bob List, another of Nevada's
future governors. Guinn recognized early the value
of schooling and pursued a career in education.
After briefly attending USC, where he played on the
freshman football team, Guinn earned bachelor's
and master's degrees at Fresno State before receiving
a doctorate in education from Utah State.

Guinn moved to Las Vegas in 1964, when he was twenty-eight, and worked
as a planning specialist and coordinator for the Clark County School District. As
part of his training, he briefly took coursework at Nevada Southern, where he
first became acquainted with the campus. After spending two years as a school
planning consultant in California, he returned to Las Vegas in 1967 as an assistant superintendent. He became the Clark County School District's superintendent of schools in 1969 and held that position until 1978.

During his tenure, Guinn presided over a period of rapid development
during which his planning expertise served him well in coping with major decisions with respect to constructing new schools, projecting budgets, revising curricula, and hiring hundreds of new teachers. His most notable accomplishment
was helping to formulate the so-called Sixth Grade Plan in 1971, which racially

integrated Las Vegas's elementary and middle schools. For the previous two years school disturbances and riots had disrupted classes, but Guinn's plan restored calm. Guinn's toughness became apparent early in the 1971 school year when conservative white parents, who did not want their children attending integrated schools, formed an organization called Parents Who Care and attempted to send their kids to alternative sixth-grade schools. Guinn and his colleagues thwarted the move by, among other things, refusing to recognize the alternative schools and forcing the pupils to retake the sixth grade if they wanted to enter the school district's middle and high schools. This broke the back of the Parents Who Care movement in 1971 and brought widespread compliance with the district's integration policies.

J.A. TIBERTI. UNLV FOUNDATION

Guinn's leadership and confidence were obvious. In a bold move, he switched careers at the age of forty-two, becoming an administrative vice president with Nevada Savings and Loan in 1978. The bank subsequently merged with Southwest Gas and became PriMerit Bank. Guinn became the bank's chief operating officer in 1980 and CEO in 1985. Two years later, he became chairman of the board, president, and later CEO of Southwest Gas. He retired as CEO of PriMerit and Southwest Gas in 1992 and 1993, respectively, but continued as board chair of both corporations. In 1998 he was elected governor of Nevada, a position he held for the next eight years.

Guinn's record of civic involvement was also extensive. Among a variety of positions, he chaired the Metropolitan Police Department's Fiscal Affairs Committee as well as the UNLV Foundation's board of trustees. It was not only Guinn's successful career in education and business that attracted the regents' attention but also his long association with UNLV as a fund-raiser and donor. In this capacity, he worked closely with many prominent Las Vegas businessmen such as Parry Thomas and J. A. Tiberti.

Within weeks of assuming his new position, Guinn announced that UNLV's fiscal problems were far worse than the regents suspected. Everyone knew that departments were struggling to pay their bills. The root cause was serious underfunding of the university's operating expenses, which had forced Maxson to use soft money and other financing to supplement operating budgets. Clearly, the blame lay more in Carson City than in the president's office. For at least three decades the state had chronically underfunded UNLV. While there were decent allotments periodically, most of the biennial budgets failed to cover expenses resulting from the school's growth.

Guinn ultimately dealt with this issue in his second term as governor, but in 1994 departmental overspending was the immediate problem. Guinn estimated the projected budget shortfall at $10.5 million. Recognizing that no state agency can legally run a deficit, and cognizant of the political fallout if it was not eliminated, Guinn set out to cut university spending. Although many faculty objected to his unilateral actions taken without much consultation with the faculty senate and other faculty-staff groups, the president realized there was little time for debate. Both the regents and state legislators, concerned about taxpayer and voter reactions, would be more resistant in the next budget season to raising UNLV's appropriations if questions of mismanagement and fiscal irresponsibility plagued the campus.

FRANK AND VICKI FERTITTA WITH BILL BOYD (RIGHT). UNLV
FOUNDATION IMAGE NO. D64833-17

To address this situation, Guinn used his executive powers much as he had at Southwest Gas and the school district. As a first step, he required all departments to operate within their regular budget. He even cracked down on two of the more high-profile programs on campus, the Department of Athletics and the performing arts center, both of which had been spending far more than they were taking in. Reasoning that both institutions were valuable to the university in terms of garnering public support and donations, President Maxson had authorized the diversion of some Thomas & Mack Center and Sam Boyd Silver Bowl revenues to offset the Athletics Department's shortfall. He also subsidized the performing arts center so it would not have to raise ticket prices or charge rent to the locally popular Nevada Symphony Orchestra and Nevada Dance Theatre.

With one stroke of his pen, Guinn changed everything. No program enjoyed untouchable status anymore. In its nineteen years on campus, the Charles Vanda Master Series had incurred a $775,000 debt while attracting performers such as noted violinist Itzhak Perlman and the St. Petersburg Philharmonic. Though Maxson and his predecessors had thought these concerts were worth the cost, Guinn insisted on budget tightening. Given the political climate in the immediate post-Maxson era, he had little choice. "In Performing Arts," Guinn explained, "there were some groups that had never been charged to use campus facilities. That had to be corrected. It is fine for a university to support a performing arts program, but not at the expense of educational programs."[1] Following Guinn's meeting with a sympathetic board of regents, executives of the Nevada Symphony Orchestra and the Nevada Dance Theatre were told they would be charged $900 a day for use of Artemus W. Ham Concert Hall and $300 for the Judy Bayley Theatre. Jim Hopkins, director of the orchestra, glumly predicted, "You may begin hearing a strengthened call for a big, superb hall off the university campus."[2] In response to Guinn's requirements, season ticket prices were raised and a combination of fund-raising and greater appropriations put the performing arts center on a stable footing.

Athletics Department officials also reacted with alarm to Guinn's insistence that they balance their budget without supplemental help from the Thomas & Mack Center and the Sam Boyd Silver Bowl. Faced with high expenses relating to recruiting, scholarships, coaches' salaries, and other items, the department had sought and received help from Maxson, which masked a growing shortfall. Guinn projected that in the fiscal year beginning on July 1, 1994, the Thomas & Mack would pump $900,000 into the department's $10.1 million budget. He ended the subsidy and told athletics director Jim Weaver that his department would have to generate enough money to cover its expenses. As Guinn observed, "Athletics can't continue relying on Thomas & Mack. What if there isn't a Grateful Dead concert one year or an Eagles concert? Or what if the roof of the T&M falls in and there aren't revenues there to fix it?"[3] The interim president was determined to stop what he considered imprudent subsidies.

He was also determined to end another practice common to many of the school's academic departments: borrowing from other funds to artificially enlarge their budgets. While part of the problem lay with the state's inadequate funding in the early 1990s, there was a second issue. After a decade of rapid development, Guinn thought, UNLV officials had overestimated enrollment and hired too many faculty and staff, although the UNLV vice president for finance and administration, Norval Pohl, argued the point with Guinn at an ensuing cabinet meeting. The president agreed that Maxson's regime could not be faulted for this error but insisted on addressing the problem as part of UNLV's current budget shortfall. Noting that 1992–94 enrollment had been expected to grow by 3 percent each year but instead had remained virtually flat, Guinn attacked the problem by declaring a hiring freeze. "When you don't have growth, it brings on difficult times," he explained. Some regents, like Madison Graves, were more direct, charging that the Maxson administration "overhired; they worked off projected income, and the income didn't come in. You and I couldn't run a business like this."[4]

Guinn told reporters that in 1993 UNLV hired twenty-four instructors to accommodate projected enrollment increases that never occurred. In his view, the university failed to budget $1.2 million for legal fees it might have to spend during the next year for the Tarkanian lawsuits and other court cases. Of course, Maxson was an easy target in 1994. After all, he was gone, Rollie Massimino's basketball team—despite winning twenty games—had not gone far in the NCAA tournament, and weak state funding in the face of growth remained the underlying culprit for many of the school's money problems. As regent Carolyn Sparks noted, Governor Bob Miller was at least as much to blame as Bob Maxson. Arguing that for the past two years UNLV had had to cope with $8 million in cuts that Miller had ordered to erase a projected state budget deficit, Sparks correctly observed that "we have seen two years of creative budgeting to keep faculty here, to keep courses open, and to ensure the students had as little disruption possible in their academic lives."[5] While Guinn was right about the need to close the school's budget gap, few department heads at the time would have disputed Sparks's assessment of the larger problem at UNLV.

President Guinn also tackled two more thorny issues in his effort to reduce UNLV's budgetary woes. He negotiated a buyout of Rollie Massimino's contract and settled Jerry and Lois Tarkanian's lawsuit. Maxson's April 1992 agreement with Massimino had awarded the new coach a base salary of $386,000 a year, plus benefits. The total package should have raised eyebrows, and probably did with Tarkanian (whose contract had awarded him $600,000 a year in total compensation, with a base salary of $203,000) and other basketball insiders. But the Las Vegas public and students asked few questions at the time. The real salary, however, was much more. A secret supplemental contract awarded Massimino $375,000 more per year for five years. This included $100,000 a year in retirement funds with interest on his sixty-fifth birthday, an average of $200,000 a year for summer youth programs, and other money. The board of regents approved the deal, although few of the members knew the specifics. The original plan was for the UNLV Foundation to pay the extra money, but board chair John Goolsby objected, so the account was switched to the newly formed Varsity Club, a private corporation.

Guinn acted quickly to void Massimino's supplemental contract in an effort to cut UNLV's shortfall. Support was immediate from the public and most regents in the anti-Maxson atmosphere of 1994. Massimino's failure to make the Runnin' Rebels a national contender further turned the fans against the beleaguered coach. A firestorm of controversy quickly engulfed the campus. In a statement issued from Long Beach State, Maxson defended the supplemental contract. "A group of civic leaders agreed to a payment to Mr. Massimino not as the basketball coach but to serve in a public relations function for the community and the state." The former president explained that the contract had been negotiated by UNLV general counsel Brad Booke and reviewed by Sparks, the board chair. Maxson disputed the need to make the deal overtly public by declaring, "I always viewed the private agreement between coach Massimino and the business leaders as his personal business and not as part of his public university contract."[6] For his part, Booke, who left the university in December 1993, responded that he had gone to Tucson to learn how to draw up such a contract from University of Arizona athletics director Cedric Dempsey, who assured him that such contracts for high-profile coaches were relatively common around the nation—which, of course, they were.

None of this impressed regents in 1994, and they asked Guinn for the specifics of a contract they had approved but most had never seen. Their reactions ranged from embarrassment to outrage. Shelley Berkley denounced the creation of the Varsity Club. "There is no doubt," she insisted, "that the corporation was set up to hide additional compensation to the basketball coach, which was a deliberate attempt by Bob Maxson to circumvent the policy of the Board of Regents." Berkley concluded by claiming, "It's ridiculous that we're signing secret agreements for coaches when we're 80 faculty members short. That $1 million the coach is receiving would go a long way to solve that problem."[7] Regent Berkley's statement reflected the board's anger over the size of Massimino's compensation, but, at the same time, her recognition that UNLV was "80 faculty members short" contradicted Guinn's view that his predecessor had overhired. One might also argue that student enrollment would not have been so flat from 1993 to 1996 if class scheduling and registration processing had been subject to more astute management. After all, Las Vegas's population was booming. Many students no doubt went to the community college or elsewhere because they could not get into classes at UNLV.

The uproar paved the way for Guinn to negotiate a buyout of Massimino's contract. University system counsel Donald Klasic made it even easier by arguing that the supplemental contract was illegal, because Massimino's money was not a private deal for community programs but was related to his university job as coach. Of course, had Massimino been hired in a less supercharged atmosphere to replace a coach who had willingly retired or left for another job, no secret pact would have been made and few would have objected to the supplemental payments, which were relatively common across the country. But the nature of Jerry Tarkanian's forced retirement colored the politics of the time.

For UNLV and its new interim president a buyout was made easier. Massimino found himself in a weak position. At first the embattled coach balked at taking anything less than what he had agreed to. If he had taken the Rebels to a high round of the NCAA tournament, he probably could have rallied enough booster support to get his way. But his two-year 36–21 record at UNLV eroded his position and sealed his fate.

In the end, he and Guinn agreed to a $1.88 million buyout—a hefty amount for a financially strapped school but one with manageable payments spread over several years. In return, Massimino agreed not to sue the Varsity Club or the UNLV Foundation. Regents reluctantly approved the deal by an 8–3 vote. Specifically, Massimino received $350,000 a year until September 1999, paid in monthly installments, as well as $105,500 in retirement benefits, $24,000 for unused vacation days, and a smaller amount for health care and car rentals. According to local newspapers, Guinn saved the school more than $1 million, although the real figure may have been much less, depending on how one does the accounting. Following the settlement with Massimino, Guinn wasted no time finding a new coach. He had to, because Massimino's resignation occurred just a day before the first scheduled practice of the season.

Guinn's choice of a replacement, Seattle SuperSonics assistant coach Tim Grgurich, a former Tarkanian assistant, satisfied Rebels fans. It also aided another Guinn objective: convincing the Tarkanians to drop their suit against UNLV. In September 1993, Jerry and Lois Tarkanian had filed a ten-count, eighty-nine-page lawsuit against several UNLV administrators and regents whose actions, the suit claimed, had caused the coach and his wife emotional distress. The suit further charged that school officials conspired with NCAA investigators to ruin Tarkanian's coaching career. Defendants included Maxson, former UNLV counsel Brad Booke, former interim athletics director Dennis Finfrock, and the board of regents.

Guinn moved quickly to placate the Tarkanians and save the school from possibly paying a large claim. It did not hurt that Guinn had a long and positive relationship with the coach as a donor and fund-raiser for UNLV and its athletics program. Guinn invited the coach and his wife up to the seventh floor of the humanities building, where they had been welcome for almost two decades before the break with Maxson. Deliberations over the suit continued into the summer with representatives of both sides and, in the end, the Tarkanians dropped their suit against the school.

With these matters behind him, Guinn next turned his attention to academics. For the most part, Guinn's relationship with UNLV's faculty, especially in his early months in office, was frosty at best. Preferring more of a collaborative effort, members of the faculty senate and other groups objected to the president's unilateral approach to the budget crisis. Many faculty felt largely bypassed by Guinn's actions regarding spending cuts, and some resented what they considered his efforts to pressure Maxson's provost, John Unrue, to step down. While many students and Las Vegas residents considered Tarkanian's ouster reprehensible, many faculty viewed it as a necessary step toward reasserting UNLV's commitment to academics over athletics. Indeed, hundreds of faculty and staff had filled the Richard Tam Alumni Center for Maxson's farewell reception. After his departure, many resented the attacks against him, and Guinn's efforts to right the university's fiscal ship, with its anti-Maxson overtones, hardly won the new president widespread faculty support. The subsequent resignations of Unrue, Weaver, and Maxson's aide John Irsfeld seemed to many, but by no means all, faculty to be a continuation of Guinn's unilateral efforts to remake the campus. Coupled with this was a common view among faculty that Guinn was just a political appointee and not a real president. To many professors, he was little more than a business executive. Even his years leading the school district, many felt, did not qualify him to run a large university.

Guinn realized that he had an image problem on campus, but nevertheless he believed in the need to change some of the school's top administrators and replace them with his own appointees. Irsfeld returned to the English department in October 1994. Unrue wanted to remain as provost to try and influence his boss and counterbalance Guinn's unilateral style. In his meetings with Guinn, Unrue supported more faculty involvement in the decision-making process with regard to the school's fiscal crisis and other matters. While Guinn and Unrue maintained a cordial, if strained, relationship, the president was determined to select his own provost.

Under Maxson, Unrue had had the power to approve all travel requests from faculty. Using money from UNLV's discretionary accounts, he had authorized

A STUDENT READS HIS NOTES IN FRONT OF THE WILLIAM F. HARRAH COLLEGE OF HOTEL ADMINISTRATION. UNLV OFFICE OF PUBLIC AFFAIRS IMAGE NO. D63480-45

the payment of almost $20,000 for his own travel to Europe to attend confer-
ences and conduct research. Even though Maxson also approved these expenditures for Unrue, anti-Maxson forces in the press and faculty raised questions
about the provost's travel. In October 1994, Unrue finally decided that he had
enough. Guinn's controlling style and the continuing controversy over Unrue's
presence on the seventh floor convinced the latter, that, like Irsfeld, it was time
for him to return to the English department. "The truth is, I found myself
incompatible with much of the present direction," Unrue declared.[8] Maxson's
management style had allowed for much faculty governance and input. Unrue

could not adjust to Guinn's corporate executive approach, and he left shortly after Irsfeld's departure.

From Guinn's perspective, he wanted someone from the faculty who commanded respect and supported his policies. Longtime sociology professor Ron Smith met those criteria. A respected member of the faculty, an accomplished administrator, and then dean of UNLV's Graduate College, Smith would represent faculty concerns in the inner sanctum, and, in return, Guinn would have someone whom the faculty accepted.

Smith's appointment came just in time, because Guinn faced increasing problems with restive faculty members disgruntled by his tendency to bypass them on major decisions. Typical of this group was anthropology professor John Swetnam, who declared, "I am absolutely appalled by this pattern and orchestrated campaign of personal attacks on people prior to their leaving office."[9] A *Rebel Yell* headline read: "Mass Exodus: Who's Next?" Guinn tried to reassure faculty and students. "People need to understand, our entire staff . . . ever since I've been here, we've been doing one thing: trying to work as hard as we can. Every decision we've made so far," the president insisted, "has directed ourselves toward the academic program."[10] Clearing up questions about discretionary funds and balancing the budget ultimately benefited academics. He was right. From the days of William Carlson into the 1990s, faculty and student concerns, while valued, did not determine future appropriations.

How the public, the regents, and especially state legislators viewed the school was the most important component of the process, and Guinn had successfully resolved that image problem. But the president was vulnerable on other matters. Mehran Tamadonfar of political science urged a greater role for the faculty senate, while Terry Miethe of criminal justice and Evelyn Gajowski of English voiced concerns that Guinn had not scheduled a forum to discuss the sweeping changes he was making. Even regent and former Truckee Meadows Community College president James Eardley agreed, conceding that UNLV's faculty "shouldn't be out of the loop entirely."[11]

Guinn did not disagree with these concerns, but his management style never resembled Maxson's or Goodall's. And while he spent the rest of his term meeting with students and faculty, Guinn never converted large numbers of them to his approach. Ron Smith served the university especially well at this time as an advisor and intermediary between the president and the campus community. Len Zane, chair of the Intercollegiate Athletics Council, who was ignored during the Massimino buyout and Jim Weaver's impending resignation, was now assured that the council would be involved in all future oversight of the athletic program. After several meetings with Guinn and Smith, faculty senate chair Jim Stivers told colleagues that "the president is committed to making the administration more responsive to faculty needs and the needs of students."[12] Guinn had come to recognize that UNLV was more a collegial community with a commitment to faculty governance than a corporation run from the top down.

Though Guinn was a controversial and sometimes unpopular figure on campus, his accomplishments were significant. Legislators and regents admired him and were again responsive to UNLV's academic needs. The renewed friendly relations with Tarkanian and the ouster of Massimino, Weaver, and other members of the old regime pleased numerous donors, many of whom supported academics as well as athletics. This reestablished an income stream to the reenergized UNLV Foundation, which was vital in an era when the percentage of state funding for the school was steadily declining.

Guinn was also responsible for beginning talks with school district officials, county commissioners, and airport officials for the purchase of the Paradise Elementary School, at Tropicana and Swenson, with the goal of building a new elementary school on the UNLV campus. Here, Guinn's experience as a former teacher, planner, and district head served the community well.

Although Guinn's relationship with faculty could have been better, his popularity with regents, UNLV supporters, and the public was obvious. As Shelley Berkley observed, Guinn "surpassed all of my expectations." Guinn himself believed that his fiscal reforms "provided the groundwork and certainly the environment for Dr. [Carol] Harter to come in and really get started on what a college president should spend . . . time on." Guinn left, saying, "I don't know what the future holds, but I'll find plenty to do"[13]—and he did, as Nevada's governor.

As it turned out, Guinn's year as president of UNLV was significant for the experience it gave him in recognizing the problem of funding higher education in the Silver State. His time as the school's only non-academic president reinforced what he had come to recognize years earlier as superintendent of Clark County schools: Education and other services in Nevada were badly underfunded, especially since it was a time of rampant growth. In his second term as governor, Guinn would show the same determination he displayed as interim president in convincing legislators and power brokers to raise state taxes so agencies like UNLV would have more money to cope with the demands of a soaring population.

With Carol Harter's appointment as UNLV's new president in February 1995, Guinn looked forward, if ever so briefly, to returning to the relative calm of life outside the public spotlight. Before he left the university, he pleased Rebel Boosters by moving quickly to appoint a new coach to replace Tim Grgurich, who had left the team for health reasons on January 7. Perhaps more time should have been devoted to the selection process, however; in the end Bill Bayno proved to be an unfortunate choice.

As Guinn prepared to leave, many wondered how the incoming president viewed UNLV athletics. Harter, who would not take office until July 1, addressed the issue in response to reporters' questions. In characteristic fashion, she made her position clear: "We want the national attention, but we want it for the right reasons." Harter noted that "the university deserves the attention, as a first-class academic institution," but, she added, "that has been overshadowed by some athletic problems." While she clearly put academics ahead of athletics, she also recognized that the school needed "a very strong athletic program here and a winning program that is also clean and full of integrity."[14] The major battles to firmly establish the dominance of academics over athletics had been fought, and President Harter could concentrate on improving both men's and women's sports while ensuring that operations met all NCAA guidelines.

In his brief tenure, Guinn began to address the underlying fiscal problems in the Athletics Department that the Thomas & Mack subsidies had only masked. With Norval Pohl's help, Guinn established structures and practices that began the process of resolving UNLV's larger budgetary problems. To be sure, these problems were complex and not solved overnight; indeed, the process would continue for several years into Harter's administration. Like Guinn, President Harter would play a major role in reforming the university's accounting and spending practices with the help of Pohl and others.

Guinn served for only a year as UNLV's president, but he made his share of contributions. For all the controversy and resistance that his policies triggered, his accomplishments helped ease the transition from the divisive conflicts of Maxson's last year to the new era of university development that Carol Harter envisioned.

CHAPTER EIGHT

The March to Excellence

CAROL HARTER

The selection of Carol C. Harter as UNLV's seventh president marked the dawn of a new age at the school. A native of Brooklyn, Harter received her bachelor's, master's, and Ph.D. degrees in English from the State University of New York at Binghamton. She taught English and American literature before serving in various administrative capacities, including ombudsman, vice president and dean of students, and vice president for administration, at Ohio University, and then assumed her first presidency at the 5,400-student campus of SUNY-Geneseo. On February 15, 1995, the board of regents selected her as the president of UNLV. With the Tarkanian controversy ended and the school's fiscal crisis in the process of resolution, Harter had the opportunity to lead the campus to new levels of development. She would take full advantage of that opportunity.

In her first State of the University address, the new president wasted no time declaring her major goal: "I hope to assist us to become a nationally, even internationally acclaimed university recognized for the excellence of our faculty, programs, and students." She also told a cheering crowd of four hundred that UNLV must "reaffirm its commitment to student community and athletic success

168

without compromises to its integrity." Recognizing that "UNLV may be in a unique position nationally in that it is this major city's only university, its island of intellectual, artistic and cultural opportunity," Harter emphasized the need for comprehensive planning, serving students more effectively, encouraging quality research, and promoting diversity and technology.[1]

PRESIDENT CAROL HARTER, 1995–2006. SPECIAL COLLECTIONS, UNLV LIBRARIES 0062-1434

She quickly set about implementing her agenda. During her first year, Harter rallied more than two hundred people from on and off campus to work for months on UNLV's strategic plan, which was later embodied in the 1996 publication *UNLV, Premier Urban University: A Public Agenda for the Decade 1996–2005*. The project sparked much enthusiasm among faculty and students. As English professor and former graduate dean Joseph McCullough noted, "I have never seen as much campus involvement under any president before Dr. Harter." McCullough, a UNLV faculty member for twenty-seven years at the time, insisted that "far from being insensitive to faculty and student concerns . . . she has done everything possible to engage all members of the university community in meaningful self-examination, dialogue, and planning."[2]

Equally enthusiastic was student body president Aaron Rosenthal, who asserted, "In one year, she has brought the focus away from secret basketball contracts and put it on academic integrity. That's important to everyone enrolled here because UNLV is something we're all going to carry on our diplomas for the rest of our lives." Regent Shelley Berkley, a former UNLV student body president who staunchly supported Harter's appointment, observed that the new president "had the skills that UNLV most lacked—internal management and academic planning. She does those things very well."[3]

President Harter and her new provost, Douglas Ferraro, a psychologist who joined the school in March 1996, both worked on the project to reorganize UNLV's academic structure. One of their major goals was to reduce the number of independent colleges, a trend that accreditation teams had criticized as early as 1970. Harter appointed a committee of faculty and administrators to study UNLV's organizational structure. The group submitted its recommendations in May 1996. In its report, the committee rejected efforts to convert the Greenspun School of Communications into a college. It also proposed abolishing the College of Human Performance and Development and the College of Architecture, Construction Management, and Planning and transferring their courses into other colleges as schools or departments. Ferraro called the reorganization effort "a very exciting initiative that should provide a major step forward in the academic quality of the university." This marked the beginning of a lengthy process whose final outcome, Ferraro predicted, "will improve academic, administrative and budgetary efficiency" to better serve UNLV students.[4]

In the end, the committee's proposals resulted in the creation of the College of Urban Affairs, designed to streamline bureaucratic operations and reduce costs. In August 1996 the regents approved disbanding the College of Architecture and the College of Human Performance and Development and placing them both in Fine Arts. They also rejected efforts to make the Greenspun School a stand-alone operation, instead including it in the College of Urban Affairs. Smaller independent programs also joined existing departments, although not always willingly. Moving Dr. Craig Walton's graduate program in ethics and policy studies from its autonomous status within the College of Liberal Arts into the political science department frayed a few nerves on both sides, but it thrived there until Walton's retirement in 2004. For the most part, the various marriages succeeded. Ferraro put a positive spin on the reforms by declaring, "We are already finding that new relationships among the reorganized units have begun to generate promising collaborative initiatives."[5]

Of course, there were skeptics, among them Walton, who was hardly enthusiastic about the new president's management style. "The whole question of shared governance is up in the air. That has been a disappointment," he said. But the curricular and administrative structure needed reform, as accreditation teams had repeatedly pointed out. Harter responded that opposition was inevitable. "Change is at the root of it all, and some people are more resistant to change than others."[6]

Still, the first few years were bumpy. Numerous faculty and administrators balked at more than a few minor reforms. Opponents criticized the president for her no-nonsense management style, her sometimes distant manner, and her perceived inaccessibility to many faculty. In Harter's second year, regent Madison Graves even suggested that she spend more time getting to know faculty and students. Veteran faculty and administrators who had grown used to smiling, easily accessible, and highly visible presidents like Baepler, Goodall, and Maxson—even Kenny Guinn was a handshaker on campus—adjusted poorly to a president with a different kind of personality.

In the first two years of her presidency, Harter somewhat resembled Roman Zorn, who was hardworking and busy attending vital functions, with little time for strolling through the student union to gladhand faculty and students. As Harter explained, "I will be as visible as my life allows me to be. I cannot be everywhere." And she was right. UNLV, beset by years of strife and disunity, was not the same place it had been. By the mid-1990s it was no longer a medium-sized school on the edge of a small city. It had become an emerging research university in the heart of America's fastest-growing metropolis, and the UNLV presidency had evolved into a big job. In addition, Harter inherited a management and budgetary system that required overhauling and modernization, a process that consumed much of her time during the first few years of her presidency. As a result, she was not that visible on campus, a circumstance that contrasted sharply with Bob Maxson's public presence and did little to help her image. Harter recognized the advantages of spending less time in the office, but her determination to straighten out the myriad problems she saw with UNLV's administration took priority. As she declared, "If you're trying to manage finances and programming change and reorganization as well, you might not be in the student union as often as you'd like. Hey, I'd like nothing better than to be sitting over there drinking Cokes with students."[7]

The transition took time. Many of Maxson's administrators and deans left, replaced by other men as well as a refreshing number of capable women, including deans Carolyn Sabo of health sciences and Martha Watson of urban affairs. Harter chose Dr. Rebecca Mills, who initially headed the planning process and served as senior advisor to the president, for the position of vice president for student life. Dr. Margaret Rees became associate provost for academic budget, and Dr. Penny Amy, interim graduate dean and later director of the Shadow

Lane campus. Harter also appointed Dr. Juanita Fain, the first African American and female cabinet member, as vice president for administration and later UNLV's first chief of staff. In short, the president brought in a new management team that was loyal to her and willing to bring UNLV into line with her vision of what the university could become. These and other new administrators implemented many of the management reforms in budgeting, personnel, registration processing, development, and other operations that UNLV needed if it was to progress to the next level.

The new administration tackled a variety of problems. Along with Provost Ferraro, Harter devised enrollment strategies to adjust to the growing popularity of the Community College of Southern Nevada and the new private college chains like the University of Phoenix, which had contributed to UNLV's enrollment slowdown in the mid-1990s. Harter and Ferraro urged departments to offer more courses in the evenings and late afternoons and to beef up their distance-learning commitments. Harter and Ferraro also challenged complacency and recalcitrance at all levels, even removing a library dean whose commitment to his off-campus consulting business interfered with his UNLV position.

Of course, the strong use of presidential power carried some liabilities. Harter's early years were marked by a strained relationship with some elements of the faculty. By the late 1990s, however, the testy period had largely ended. The departure of Ferraro as provost in August 2000 further improved the climate. Though an effective administrator and a brilliant budget analyst, Ferraro lacked the personal skills needed to promote and reinforce positive relations between the president and the faculty. Harter's selection of Dr. Raymond Alden, dean of the College of Sciences, as her new provost was a fortunate choice. Alden, too, was a talented administrator who shared Harter's vision and enthusiasm, and he enjoyed great popularity with faculty and student leaders.

As the new century dawned, it became clear to many that Harter's presidency ranked with UNLV's best. As regent Jill Derby, who had chaired the presidential search, said of Harter in 1997, "Her presidency has not been without controversy. But a certain amount of that is inevitable when you're brought in as a change agent. UNLV needed a strong, courageous leader and we got one. She has taken the challenge we gave her and handled herself beautifully."[8] Not the supporter of the status quo and hardly the "jock president" that so many feared would be selected in the wake of UNLV's basketball fiasco, Harter was a strong leader—the university's first woman president and someone capable of taking UNLV to the new levels that many faculty talked about but were largely unprepared for.

A clear sign of the respect that Harter enjoyed in the larger community was her ability to raise large sums of money for the school. Even more than in the Maxson years, Las Vegas individuals and businesses opened their checkbooks and contributed millions to UNLV. Academics benefited from the gift giving, but so did athletics. The hiring of former USC and Los Angeles Rams football coach John Robinson in 1999 delighted fans and resulted in a sharp increase in attendance and contributions. In 2001, the family of Las Vegas developer Ernie Becker donated $1 million to the UNLV football program. Robinson, the new athletics director, used part of this money to replace the grass at Rebel Park, his on-campus practice facility, with FieldTurf. After receiving the gift, Harter renamed the facility to honor two longtime supporters of the athletics program, calling it the Ernie Becker, Sr. Football Fields at Bill "Wildcat" Morris Rebel Park.

Fund-raising was crucial to upgrading UNLV's athletics program. President Harter recognized the pressure on both men's and women's sports following Department of Athletics budget deficits of the early and mid-1990s and moved to ease the burden on the school's coaches. In August 2003 she chose Mike Hamrick as UNLV's new athletics director. After eight seasons in that position at East Carolina, Hamrick had become a skilled administrator as well as a productive fund-raiser. This was crucial because Harter wanted to relieve individual coaches of the responsibility of having to raise money to support their teams. This practice had begun in the wake of Bob Maxson's departure when Kenny Guinn attacked UNLV's $10 million shortfall by forcing across-the-board spending cuts. When he ended the Department of Athletics' supplemental payments from the Thomas & Mack Center, the coaches had to cut their spending *and* raise funds for their sport. For the most part, the coaches did not like the role of pressing boosters for money. As baseball coach Buddy Gouldsmith remarked,

"It is every coach's hope" to have an athletics director active in raising funds.[9] Hamrick's appointment raised hopes that the department could now attract enough donations to restore needed scholarships for many of UNLV's teams.

Harter not only hired Hamrick to reinforce the new image of UNLV athletics, but she also played an active role in restoring the program's credibility with NCAA officials. Part of that effort involved heading off new sanctions. Unfortunately, UNLV's basketball problems with the NCAA did not end with the Tarkanian era. In 2001, President Harter and athletics director Charles Cavagnaro traveled to Chicago to meet with the NCAA appeals committee in an effort to reverse the postseason ban levied against the program for violations involving Bill Bayno's recruitment of Lamar Odom in 1997. Harter insisted that it was important for the school to support the team's efforts to compete in the Mountain West Conference's tournament for a shot at the NCAA finals.

The president and Cavagnaro met with the committee for three hours. "My main thrust to the committee," Harter told reporters, "was to please see us in a different light than in the past." Having already fired Bayno, Harter assured the committee, "We are determined to do things the proper way and not to hurt innocent people." She was committed to helping the six seniors on the team, "who had no choice in this."[10] In the end, the committee agreed not to ban UNLV from television, which generated revenues that were vital to the athletics department. However, the school went on probation again, losing scholarships and the ability to compete in postseason play for one year. The probation period finally ended in December 2004.

While former presidents like Maxson, Goodall, and Baepler all enjoyed the respect of NCAA officials, Harter went a step further: She helped the NCAA govern collegiate sports by serving on the NCAA's Division I board of directors. This board, composed of eighteen university presidents, is the NCAA's major governing body, setting policy and dealing with financial matters involving Division I athletics programs. Harter held this position when UNLV was a member of the Western Athletic Conference (WAC). Then in September 1999, the member schools selected her as the first board representative from the Mountain West Conference, which she helped form.

During the summer and early fall of 1998, UNLV and seven other WAC members—Air Force, BYU, Colorado State, San Diego State, New Mexico, Utah, and

Wyoming—left the WAC to create their own conference. It was a bold move at the time, but the advantages were numerous. Not only would there be less travel for the athletes, but revenues would be greater, since each school would get a larger share of the money. And there would be more money, because, collectively, the eight schools were stronger than the overall WAC in the major men's sports, football and basketball. This would mean more television exposure for the campuses and more revenue. Finally, Air Force, Utah, Colorado State, and the other new conference members were also stronger academic institutions overall than many members of the WAC.

Besides bringing new direction to UNLV athletics by raising funds, representing the school in the NCAA, supporting the basketball team in an appeals hearing, and helping to create a new conference, Harter also asserted the power of the presidency over the athletics program. Clearly, Maxson and Guinn had made progress in the decades-long effort to bring all UNLV sports under total presidential control, but Harter completed the process. Even the boosters had to recognize the new power relationship. In 2004, for instance, there was strong support among some of the Rebel Boosters to replace basketball coach Charles Spoonhour with a local favorite, Reggie Theus, and other names were also bandied about. But in the end it was the president's choice, and Lon Kruger got the job.

Of course, while President Harter helped UNLV athletics, she did even more for academic programs. Between 1995 and July 2006, UNLV created 105 new degree programs, 22 of them at the doctoral level and 3 at the professional level. The president's success at fund-raising was crucial to curricular development. By July 1, 2006, the Harter administration and the UNLV Foundation had raised more than $525 million in gifts and pledges. The money went for both programs and schools. Take, for instance, the Law School. Harter first struggled to get the school opened and then encouraged donors to consider expanding programs within it. For years, plans for the school had faced serious obstacles. The idea of a law school at UNLV dated from Donald Moyer's presidency, but it was Donald Baepler who began an earnest campaign to drum up support from regents, legislators, and local attorneys. While regents considered the school premature in the 1970s, the idea never died. For the next two decades, Clark County legislators and regents, still miffed that the Reno campus had gained a

medical school in the 1970s, blocked UNR's occasional efforts to buy the struggling Old College School of Law in Reno, a small private institution. In the early 1990s, the Maxson administration again pushed for creation of a law school at UNLV. But lack of money, the need for a new library, the Tarkanian controversy, and other factors delayed action.

The Harter administration built upon renewed momentum and enthusiasm and, with regent support, again pushed lawmakers to fund the school. Clearly, the idea's time had come. Las Vegas was no longer the 1970s city of 400,000; it had become a booming metropolis of more than 1 million, with a growing service economy. Legal expertise was in greater demand than ever before. In June 1996 President Harter articulated the major arguments for a law school to an approving board of regents. She reminded them that Nevada and Alaska were the only states that did not have a public law school. Nevadans were spending more than $11 million annually for legal education in other states. Except for a few graduates of what was then called the School of Law at Old College in Reno, none of Nevada's 4,400 attorneys had been trained in the state. Population and economic growth projections indicated that Nevada would need at least another 1,900 practicing attorneys by 2010. A UNLV law school would also help to create a first-class law library, which southern Nevada lacked. Moreover, the school would be an invaluable resource for clinical assistance to the state's court system and a resource for continuing legal education for Nevada's bar and judiciary, as well as for paralegal and law enforcement personnel.

Fund-raising for the proposed law school began in the mid-1990s. In August 1996 Kenny Guinn and Carol Harter announced that $7 million had already been pledged, including $5 million from attorney William Boyd, head of Boyd Gaming (who added $25 million more in February 2005). Other major donors were gaming industry leaders Jackie Gaughan, Michael Gaughan, Warren Nelson, the Marnell Family, attorney and media magnate James Rogers, and Sam Lionel, the cofounder of the state's largest law firm, and his wife, Pat.

FACING PAGE:

MIKE AND CAROL HARTER WITH FORMER SECRETARY OF STATE
COLIN POWELL AND ELAINE AND STEVE WYNN AT A UNLV
FOUNDATION DINNER IN 1999. UNLV FOUNDATION

BOTTOM: BEVERLY AND JAMES ROGERS WITH COLIN POWELL
UNLV FOUNDATION

The need was clearly there, but state money was not. In 1997, with higher
education budget appropriations kept tight by Governor Bob Miller's administration, Harter appealed to legislators for additional money to open the Boyd
School of Law. The president warned that she might be unable to raise the additional $902,000 in matching funds required by Miller's proposed budget. The
governor had recommended that the state pay a portion of the school's two-year
costs by funding $3.6 million of the $4.5 million operating budget requested by
the board of regents. Miller wanted donors to supply the remaining 20 percent
as a "challenge grant."

Harter objected to the plan, arguing that UNLV had already raised $7.2 mil-
lion for non-operational items. She indicated that donors preferred to fund
scholarships, not lightbulbs and desks. While she assured senate majority
leader Bill Raggio and other members of the Senate Ways and Means Committee that "we'll do everything possible to obtain the matching funds," Harter
nevertheless expressed the hope that "you'll see fit to fund it."[11]

She also dismissed suggestions that the additional money come from higher fees, contending that the proposed tuition of $7,000 was already high enough. The president expressed concerns about pushing the figure any higher. Indeed, she told legislators that the tuition was already far more than the resident rate of $4,009 at Arizona State and $4,524 at the University of Utah. In the end, Harter raised additional funds, the legislature covered the remaining shortage, and the Law School opened for classes in fall 1997.

Within a year, James Rogers, who had practiced law in Nevada for more than twenty years and made a fortune as an attorney and as a founding member of Community Bank of Nevada, Nevada First Bank, and the Sunbelt Broadcasting Company, pledged an additional $28.5 million beyond an earlier gift. Payable in increments over the next twenty years, much of the money was intended to cover operating expenses. A major reason that Rogers (who later became chancellor of the university system) made this pledge was to help stabilize the fledgling school's finances for the near future.

The long-awaited opening of the William S. Boyd School of Law, with an experienced and aggressive dean, Richard Morgan, whom Harter recruited from Arizona State University, prompted a new wave of enthusiasm and gift giving to expand its programs. In September 2001, the Thomas and Mack families, who had generously donated to the campus throughout its five-decade history, gave another $2 million. This donation, supplemented by an annual state appropriation, established the Thomas and Mack Legal Clinic, the Boyd School of Law's program for training attorneys by providing legal assistance for needy southern Nevadans. All of these efforts rapidly improved the school's quality. By 2004, just seven years after the school opened its doors, *U.S. News & World Report* ranked the institution as the eighty-second-best law school in America.

The administration faced similar problems in trying to open a dental school. In June 1999 Harter announced that "we may be able to open the [dental] school [in fall 2000] if everything falls the way we're hoping it will."[12] She immediately earmarked some discretionary funds to meet the costs of opening the school. Despite strong support from UNLV alumnus and state senator Ray Rawson, lack of revenue sources caused repeated delays. In 1999 the legislature approved part of the funding plan when it agreed to use state Medicaid funds to support the school. The deal called for faculty dentists and senior students to care for 40,000 indigent patients annually in return for the Medicaid reimbursements. Lawmakers endorsed the idea after learning that the state and federal governments spent $13 million a year for indigent dental care. Following intense lobbying by Harter, Rawson, local dentists, and others, the school finally opened in 2001. Three years later, Senator Harry Reid helped ease the school's budget concerns by securing a $1 million federal grant to purchase badly needed dental equipment.

Harter also moved to expand dental program offerings. With the help of the UNLV Foundation and the dean of the School of Dental Medicine, Pat Ferrillo, she lined up an impressive series of donors. In fall 2003, for example, the Orthodontic Education Company offered a gift of up to $100 million spread over thirty years to underwrite the new advanced education program in orthodontics at UNLV's dental school. After informing regents that "only 280 orthodontists are produced in the United States every year," Harter presented her proposal to the board for its consideration.[13] Explaining that there was only one orthodontist for every 58,000 people in Nevada, compared to one for every 32,000 people nationwide, she offered a compelling argument for studying the program's feasibility.

President Harter not only encouraged donations to fund new schools and centers on campus but also invited deans and faculty to create new programs that helped the city. UNLV's new architecture program dovetailed nicely with Las Vegas's role as the fastest-growing metropolitan area in the nation and home to half a dozen new megaresorts, many of which boasted impressive architectural designs. Add the valley's numerous master-planned communities, as well as its office parks, shopping centers, residences, and a seemingly endless building boom, and the need for more architects was obvious.

The architecture school's debut in 1997 was the culmination of strenuous lobbying and fund-raising efforts by the Maxson administration, though the Harter administration actually opened the school. With faculty help, Harter immediately set about expanding the curriculum to encourage more high-quality applicants and to satisfy the managerial needs of local builders. In fall 1999 UNLV added a complementary degree, a master's of science in construction management. As program director John Gambatese explained, "There are people out there who have been working in construction for a number of years and have gone as far as they can with a bachelor's degree. This program can help them come back to school and move forward in their careers." The new initiative symbolized the university's growing value to a sprawling metropolitan area, as opposed to the small city where Nevada Southern had developed. At the time, NSU had appealed primarily to local teachers, with programs designed to further careers through advanced training. This new program in construction reached out to a different segment of the community by training midlevel supervisors in Las Vegas's booming construction industry. The degree also benefited local building firms. As Gambatese explained, "I recruited out of the master's of construction program at Arizona State before. . . . Now, instead of having to send employees to Phoenix or Los Angeles for a master's degree, they can get it right here."[14]

The construction management master's was not the only new program that UNLV offered in the fall of 1999. The university's Department of Health and Physical Education unveiled an interdisciplinary master's degree in health promotions. The goal was to produce graduates trained to assist residents in protecting health by teaching people to avoid risk factors for diseases and to change unhealthy behaviors. Noting that "research is showing that poor health does increase insurance costs," department chair Charles Regin cited a practical example. "In the last month, there's been a lot of *angst* about health-care costs, particularly prescriptions." With national health insurance resurrected as a major issue by Bill Clinton's administration, with health care costs becoming a growing burden on Medicare and Medicaid, and with spiraling state employee health care budgets, this program was timely. Professor Warren McNab further observed, "We're always talking about issues relating to people, whether it's about HIV, mental health, obesity, or diabetes." He concluded that the new program "will help the community as well as the state by providing professionals in health promotion."[15]

In addition to health promotions, the Harter administration also approved a new master's of science degree in physical therapy education. Harvey Wallmann, director of the program, asserted that if accredited, the degree would be the first of its kind in Nevada. In a fast-growing city that hosted several retirement communities and numerous rehabilitation facilities run by NovaCare, HealthSouth, and other national chains, this was a natural area for UNLV's expansion. As Wallmann declared, "We already know there is a tremendous de-

(FROM LEFT): CLAUDINE WILLIAMS, CAROL HARTER, AND KITTY
RODMAN. UNLV OFFICE OF PUBLIC AFFAIRS IMAGE NO. D64537

mand in Nevada—and in southern Nevada in particular—for this program."[16]
Wallmann's program had received an early boost from Kitty Rodman's generous grant to fund equipment, leading President Harter to name the program's
center for her.

New programs appeared in virtually every college, encouraged by Harter's
planning criterion that UNLV grow selectively in areas that served regional
needs. In 1997, for instance, the hotel college began offering a degree in
culinary arts management. This program focused on food operations rather
than accounting or other aspects of hotel administration. Professor John Stefanelli called the new degree "a radical idea that combines the best of business
management and the best of culinary tactile" arts. Stefanelli went on to explain
that "at the very least, a graduate should be able to leave with some entry-level
management position" such as restaurant manager, hotel kitchen manager, or
assistant manager in a local eatery or chain.[17]

In fall 1998, the College of Liberal Arts added the new major of cultural studies to its interdisciplinary bachelor of arts program. As the director, sociology
professor Simon Gottschalk, told reporters, "many of the world's universities
are implementing these types of programs. Universities in Australia, Great Brit-

ain, Canada, Hong Kong, Japan, Israel, and elsewhere recognize the importance of cultural studies and know that through these programs, their students can learn tolerance and foster respect for other cultures."[18]

With the turn of the century, more new programs were introduced. Given the proximity of the Las Vegas Strip and its need for personnel trained in advanced technologies for staging shows, UNLV's new cross-disciplinary program in entertainment engineering was a natural. Actually, the idea for developing such a degree at the campus was first suggested in a January 1968 development plan, but the proposal quickly fell by the wayside as Nevada Southern struggled to offer even basic subjects. Reintroduced in the Harter era, the program was even more timely, given the use of sophisticated computerized light design, animatronics, and robotic control systems for the hydraulic stages and platforms used in many Las Vegas extravaganzas.

Besides the creation of new schools and programs, Harter also encouraged the development of numerous institutes and research centers. In addition to research programs for studying the effects of thermonuclear explosions and the dangers of radioactive waste at Yucca Mountain, the president also supported the establishment of the Institute for Security Studies in 2003 in the wake of the 9/11 attacks. As she described it, the institute would address a range of homeland security concerns—"from the applied science of creating new security technologies to combat terrorism to the psychological study of the human toll of emergency service industry work."[19] As part of this effort, UNLV created an executive master's of science degree in emergency crisis management to supply trained leaders for a new industry that will unfortunately be part of everyone's life for the foreseeable future.

As the first woman president of UNLV, Harter not only attracted more women to the campus at all levels but also encouraged efforts that promoted the study of gender, women's issues, and equal rights. One of the most visible new initiatives in this area was the Women's Research Institute of Nevada, founded in 2000 by history professor Joanne Goodwin. The institute's mission was "to expand the existing body of knowledge on a variety of subjects related to women" by encouraging "high quality research on women."[20] The institute not only created a database identifying Nevada researchers with a description of their work on gender but also awarded internships for talented graduate and undergraduate women to provide them with valuable experience and prepare them for careers. Taken together, all of these new programs, schools, institutes, and centers supported by the Harter administration have promoted the long-term process of making UNLV a "premier urban university" by redefining it as a nationally known research center rather than just "an up and coming university."

In its first decade, the Harter administration worked to strengthen every college in the university through donations, increased state appropriations, new faculty, and higher salaries. Harter also replaced several deans in an effort to generate fresh ideas and a renewed sense of commitment. The business college was a case in point. With the arrival of Dean Richard Flaherty in 1999, plans immediately went forward to strengthen the M.B.A. degree and to launch a new executive M.B.A. program. The latter was designed to allow working professionals to return to school and earn their master's degree. As Flaherty pointed out, "We aren't starting this from scratch; there is a plan in place." Clearly, Las Vegas had grown large enough to guarantee the enrollment. "There should be tremendous demand for working professionals who don't have an M.B.A. in their background, and we expect companies will be willing to sponsor their employees' tuition."[21]

Flaherty symbolized the enthusiastic dedication to quality growth that Harter envisioned. An accounting professor at Arizona State University for twenty-one years, he came to Las Vegas for the same reasons that had lured him to ASU in 1978. "UNLV in 1999 reminds me of what first brought me to Arizona State. . . . It's part of a growing community and it's a changing university."[22] He enjoyed the challenge of building a stronger business college, an opportunity that was not available at many American colleges by century's end. Strengthening and expanding UNLV's M.B.A. program, using his expertise in accounting to improve that major, and raising funds in a city whose economy was booming all appealed to him. Indeed, a vibrant metropolis, a university with aspirations of becoming a first-rate research institution, and an administration dedicated to achieving these goals drew a large number of talented administrators and young faculty to the campus as the twentieth century ended and the twenty-first began.

Thanks to Flaherty's efforts, the business college added many new instructors and courses over the next few years, which encouraged faculty to identify appropriate areas into which their college could expand. Sometimes the approach was interdisciplinary and involved old units working with new ones. This was the case in 2004 when UNLV added a new wrinkle to its business curriculum by announcing plans to offer a dual M.B.A. in law and dentistry. This degree drew on the expertise of faculty in the business college, the Law School, and the dental school. As Professor Nasser Daneshvary, associate dean and director of UNLV's M.B.A. programs, explained, "Some lawyers and dentists are brilliant professionals, but do not necessarily have academic training and education to manage people." Richard Morgan, dean of the Boyd School of Law, emphasized that many new lawyers who want to enter the field of corporate law need more coursework in business than a law school can provide. He predicted that this new degree would be valuable, because today "there are a lot of people with a corporate background and a law background in the upper ranks of big corporations."[23]

A series of national accreditations reinforced the growing academic quality of UNLV's new programs. In 1997, for instance, the National Architecture Accrediting Board endorsed UNLV's architecture school through 2003. This was a major boost for a program that had struggled for several years with no adequate facility because of construction snags and legal problems. Accreditation was vital to the school's development. Anticipation of accreditation helped increase enrollments at the undergraduate and graduate levels by 35 percent and 50 percent, respectively. As faculty members explained, many prospective students had hesitated to apply earlier, because it was impossible to be licensed as an architect without a degree from a nationally accredited school.

For the most part, the Harter administration collaborated smoothly with the colleges on the curricular process. Occasionally, however, intransigence at the college level called for action. The College of Education was a prime example. The program dated from Nevada Southern's earliest days, when Las Vegas teachers complained about having to spend their summers on the Reno campus taking required coursework. In 1957, Las Vegas's population of nearly 100,000 had been the major reason for creating an education program on the Maryland

Parkway campus, but over the years, growth became the education college's greatest nemesis, as faculty struggled to produce enough teachers to serve the community's mushrooming student population.

Just as it had in earlier decades, Las Vegas's frantic development in the 1980s and 1990s strained local school budgets and created a teacher shortage. The problem became acute with the construction of large master-planned communities such as Green Valley and Summerlin as well as job-creating mega-resorts like MGM Mirage, Excalibur, Luxor, MGM Grand, and Bellagio. Just as the need for local teacher training won public support for creating Nevada Southern in the 1950s, many of the same pressures helped create Nevada State College in Henderson as the new century began. UNLV did what it could to supply the Clark County School District with qualified instructors, but frequent class cancellations, limited evening classes, and other roadblocks that the tradition-bound college had created over the years held down the number of graduates. As one disgusted observer, Skip Wenda, head of the Nevada Department of Education Teacher Licensing Office, complained: "It's a bureaucracy. You either learn to deal with it or you go to a private college and pay to have them deal with it for you."[24]

Harter and Provost Ferraro set out to eliminate the major bottlenecks, some of which dated back three decades or more. After consulting with their spouses, both of whom possessed education degrees, Harter and Ferraro pushed the college to offer additional courses and make required courses more available to majors. Other reforms included a new program that allowed prospective instructors to be licensed while they were completing their master's degrees. The faculty also began preparations for a fast-track master's degree aimed at helping students with other majors to qualify as teachers at the same time.

These and other reforms resulted in more education degrees. In 2001 UNLV graduated about 600 teachers compared to just 366 in 1996. But it was still not enough. Despite calls for "crash courses" to produce more instructors, Harter and college officials refused to sacrifice quality and instead insisted on maintaining curricular rigor. In fact, the president surprised many by supporting the creation of Nevada State College in Henderson, portraying it not as a rival but rather as a needed supplement to the university, especially in the field of teacher training.

Of course, new programs and colleges required new buildings, and Harter, like her predecessors, struggled with state officials to get sufficient appropriations for enough new buildings to cover spiraling enrollment, new schools, and new programs. In her first decade as president, UNLV undertook twenty-four major capital construction projects totaling more than $240 million. Private gifts accounted for more than 63 percent of the funding for these projects. Harter and Maxson together more than tripled the number of buildings on campus, and both raised millions to do it. While Maxson's fund-raising and building efforts were impressive by any standard, Harter eventually surpassed them. She had to, as the amount of state support for new construction dipped below 40 percent.

In some cases the two presidents' efforts overlapped, with Maxson starting a project and Harter finishing it. This was true of the Paul B. Sogg Architecture Building, which opened in August 1997. The 76,000-square-foot structure, designed by Swisher and Hall, featured a library (a prerequisite for accreditation), numerous classrooms and faculty offices, 20,000 square feet of loft for studio space, and laboratories for building architectural models. As Lisa Lutton, a senior in the architecture program, remarked, "Having everyone in the same open space will be great. We were all isolated in trailers before. Now we'll get to interact with students at all levels."[25] Even before the building opened, eager faculty scheduled visits throughout the fall semester to recruit even more undergraduate and graduate applicants following the architecture school's accreditation. In 2003–04, the Harter administration enlarged the building to provide more work space.

Athletics also benefited from the fund-raising efforts of Harter and others. In 1996, UNLV completed work on the new Lied Athletic Complex, an $8.5 million facility that finally liberated many of the school's sports programs from their spartan quarters in the old McDermott Physical Education Complex. "The Lied" had been the dream of former athletics director Jim Weaver in 1993. He worked to finance the project completely by donations, most notably $4 million through Christina Hixson, executor of the Lied Foundation Trust, which also helped fund the new library. When it opened in 1996, the 65,000-square-foot facility contained locker rooms for all fifteen sports in which UNLV competed, a spacious weight room, a fully equipped sports medicine center with a hydrotherapy

CHRISTINA HIXSON WITH LEE IACCOCA. UNLV FOUNDATION

pool and drug-testing areas, training facilities, and a 328-seat auditorium. It also housed offices and meeting rooms for every coach except those in the men's and women's basketball programs, which remained in the Thomas & Mack Center.

The project's value lay in centralizing operations and recruiting. Baseball coach Fred Dallimore stressed the importance of bringing the programs together under one roof. "Right now the coaches are at the Thomas & Mack, the players dress over at McDermott, we play at Wilson, we lift weights at MPEC. We're all screwed up right now." But, he predicted, "this is going to solidify a station where everybody's going to dress, your equipment and everything is going to be there." The new center's value as a recruiting tool was also apparent. As football coach Jeff Horton remarked, "It's hard to say exactly how many, but I know we've lost kids just because of the facilities. . . . If you're at Nebraska or Notre Dame it doesn't matter. But when you're here it does matter." Horton recognized that the Lied now gave him a new "carrot to dangle" in front of prospective recruits. "When we brought the kids in here this year," he explained, "they were impressed. . . . Next year when recruits come in and see it actually operational, that's just a really big, big selling point."[26]

Construction of the Cox Pavilion was another milestone for the athletics program and UNLV. In May 1999, Cox Communications and the Thomas & Mack Center jointly announced that the cable company and the university would partner to build a multipurpose venue connected to the Thomas & Mack Center. This facility would host smaller events such as corporate parties, university addresses, academic conferences, small trade shows, and concerts, in addition to women's basketball and volleyball games. Thanks to a $5 million gift from Cox Communications, the building opened in May 2001. The two-story, 40,000-

LOOKING SOUTHWEST. AT TOP IS PART OF THE THOMAS & MACK PARKING LOT; AT TOP RIGHT IS COX PAVILION UNDER CONSTRUCTION. RESIDENCE HALLS LINE THE PARKING LOT, AND THE NEW ADDITION TO TONOPAH HALL AT BOTTOM IS NEARLY COMPLETED, 2001. UNLV ATHLETICS DEPARTMENT

square-foot structure contained men's and women's locker rooms, lounges, and a seating capacity of 2,500–3,500. Former women's volleyball coach Deitre Collins was clearly delighted. "I can't even begin to compare the Lied gym to the Cox Pavilion. For where we want to go, those big-time athletes need to feel like they're in a big place. This gets them much closer to that."[27]

The pavilion also allowed UNLV to compete with the Mandalay Bay Events Center, the MGM Grand Garden, and even smaller venues like the Joint, at the nearby Hard Rock Hotel. It was obvious that the Cox Pavilion not only would benefit students but also would draw more community residents to the campus and contribute to revenues. As facilities director Pat Christenson commented, "The uniqueness of this venue is its 3,000 seats versus 1,800, and I'd like to think it's more of a community venue than . . . a tourist venue."[28]

In addition to securing construction of the Cox Pavilion, Harter also pushed for a much-needed expansion and modernization of Sam Boyd Stadium. In February 1999 work began on the $16.1 million project after several delays caused by conflicts over contractors' bids. The stadium opened in time for the football season, giving new head coach John Robinson more seats for fans and increased ticket sales for the athletics department that he would soon head.

Of course, Harter's building agenda also emphasized academics. In her first year, the president built upon the historic relationship between Las Vegas's gaming industry and the campus, whose roots lay in the 1960s when industry executives first approached campus officials about creating a hotel program. The Harter administration's first contribution to this process involved constructing a suitable home for UNLV's fledgling International Gaming Institute. Anchor Gaming founder Stan Fulton donated $6.7 million, which financed construction of the $5 million International Gaming Institute on the corner of Swenson and Flamingo and provided an additional $1.7 million in scholarship endowment money for UNLV's honors program.

Las Vegas was clearly the best location for the gaming center. As Vincent Eade, managing director of the university's gaming institute, explained, "This gift is the culmination of a three-year dream. It enables the UNLV International Gaming Institute to establish a presence unlike any other educational institution involved in gaming education." Physics professor Len Zane, director of UNLV's honors program, was equally pleased. "It's wonderful to know that in the future we will be able to offer scholarships to many more of the top students applying for the Honors Program."[29]

In addition to a gaming institute, Harter also helped the hotel college. In 2005 President Harter and Dean Stuart Mann announced plans to build a new facility for the William F. Harrah College of Hotel Administration. Though the hotel college had spent more than twenty years in Frank and Estella Beam Hall, it was obvious that that building was better suited to house the business school and other traditional academic programs than to accommodate the special needs of the hotel college. The new complex, called INNovation Village, will be located on the northwestern edge of the campus. Anchored by the Stan Fulton Building, this facilty will contain classrooms, meeting rooms, and a small, deluxe hotel where students and faculty can test the newest ideas and technology in the resort industry. When completed, INNovation Village will become the leading hospitality research facility in the world.

The education college also benefited from the generosity of donors. In October 1996 UNLV moved a step closer to helping education faculty members realize their dream of providing majors with on-campus training with real teachers and economically disadvantaged students when it approved moving the Paradise Elementary School to a new facility on campus. Under the terms of the proposed deal, McCarran International Airport would pay $8.5 million for the project, $6.5 million of it to be used to buy the current school and its 10-acre parcel on the corner of Tropicana and Swenson to reduce the traffic to and from the school along the airport's main exit road. The airport offered another $1 million if school district trustees surrendered their right to ask the airport to soundproof Cannon Middle School on Russell Road near Eastern Avenue as well as the Southern Nevada Vocational Technical Center on Mountain Vista, which were both underneath McCarran's main landing pattern.

With Clark County's approval, officials scheduled construction to begin in the summer of 2000. Carolyn Edwards, principal of the forty-eight-year-old school, called it "thrilling news." "What has made me so happy about this partnership is the profound effect it will have on a very at-risk population of students. They will have the best of everything." Expressing the school district's view was area superintendent Maurice Flores, who declared: "It's a cooperative effort that is a win-win situation for everyone. . . . We intend it to be a model

TOP: WILLIAM G. BENNETT PROFESSIONAL DEVELOPMENT
CENTER, PART OF THE COLLEGE OF EDUCATION. BENNETT WAS
A LONGTIME CHIEF EXECUTIVE AT CIRCUS CIRCUS ENTERPRISES
AND THE MANDALAY RESORT GROUP AND LATER OWNED THE
SAHARA HOTEL. UNLV OFFICE OF PUBLIC AFFAIRS IMAGE NO.
D63480-14

BOTTOM: CAROL HARTER AND, TO HER RIGHT, LYNN BENNETT,
REGENT THALIA DONDERO, AND LOCAL CHILDREN CUT THE
CEREMONIAL OPENING RIBBON FOR THE LYNN BENNETT EARLY
CHILDHOOD DEVELOPMENT CENTER AS REGENT MARK ALDEN
(LEFT) AND DEAN GENE HALL (FAR RIGHT) LOOK ON, 1999.
UNLV FOUNDATION IMAGE NO. D64084-30

for other universities and schools to follow."[30] What set the university-based school apart from "lab schools" elsewhere was its emphasis on traditionally low-achieving students from relatively poor families.

But there was more. In spring 2000, UNLV opened the William G. Bennett Professional Development Center next to the new Paradise Elementary School on campus. Bennett, owner of the Sahara Hotel and a developer of Circus Circus, the Excalibur, and the Luxor, made the building possible with a $2.7 million pledge in 1996. Three years later, he donated another $5 million to build the Lynn Bennett Early Childhood Development Center, a state-of-the-art preschool named for his wife. "This new gift," Harter explained, "will help us build the third phase of a project that began with moving the Paradise Elementary School into a new building at the UNLV campus in 1998." "These three facilities will provide a professional practice education program that we believe will become a national model." Echoing the president's enthusiasm, dean of education Gene Hall said: "We are excited about the opportunity to develop a model space for the educational environments of young children . . . and we hope it will become a site that educators around the country will want to visit."[31] By the early twenty-first century, it was obvious that a new education center was developing on UNLV's northwestern edge.

Besides these projects, the university also prepared to spend $16.5 million on new residence halls for the existing complex on the south side of the campus, as well as $15 million to convert the James Dickinson Library into a permanent home for the Boyd School of Law, $6.3 million for a parking garage, and $13.5 million for construction of the Cox Pavilion. Despite the progress, Harter cautioned faculty and students that "our needs keep moving ahead of our ability to meet them. We need lots of things in lots of places."[32]

Unfortunately, not every project went as smoothly as these. President Harter's solution to finding inexpensive space for more than a hundred staff members housed mostly in the old Westfall Business Services building seemed like a stroke of genius at the time. Her intention was to save the costs of constructing a new building by purchasing an 80,000-square-foot metallic, modular building that the Boeing Corporation no longer needed. The university would refit it and move it to a vacant section of the Thomas & Mack parking lot near Swenson Street.

TONOPAH RESIDENCE ADDITION, SHOWN UNDER CONSTRUC-
TION IN 2000, ADDED 433 BEDS TO TONOPAH HALL'S OLD
COUNT OF 215. WHEN THE ADDITION WAS COMPLETED, THE
OLD AND NEW BUILDINGS WERE CONNECTED AND WERE
NAMED THE TONOPAH RESIDENCE COMPLEX. SPECIAL
COLLECTIONS, UNLV LIBRARIES 0062-1814

The notorious "Bubba Building" arrived in ninety-six pieces from Seattle in 1999. Financed by a twelve-year loan, to be paid off by student fees, total costs for the two-story structure were initially $5 million. But a series of unforeseen design, construction, and environmental problems, including dirty ductwork creating dangerous mold, caliche impeding sewer line work, fire code violations, and litigation, all slowed progress. The apparent stroke of genius had almost become a white elephant by the time the newly named Campus Services Building finally opened in 2002. Since its debut, however, it has functioned admirably. The experience only demonstrates that university building, much like city building, is never a smooth process; there are always unforeseen bumps and bottlenecks along the way.

The university's first parking garage further illustrates the point. In 1997 President Harter reassured students, "We're pretty much committed to a parking garage. It's just a matter of how large it will be, exactly where it will be built and what kind of access there will be."[33] Students had protested earlier in 1996 when it appeared that their parking fee revenues were not being used to build a garage. They had begun paying for parking in fall 1995, and President Guinn had assured them that the funds would go for the garage. Unfortunately, however, the money had to be used for making $760,000 in payments on the idle construction bonds for a Greek Row that the Maxson administration had planned to erect. Shortly after UNLV obligated itself, student services vice president Robert Ackerman had decided there was not enough revenue to build the costly project, and it was left to the Harter administration to make the payments until UNLV could be released from its obligation.

Finally, in 1997, Harter began planning on the garage, which she hoped might be finished by late 1998. The $12.6 million structure, delayed several times and shrouded in controversy, contained 1,600 spaces, 1,272 of which were for students. With the mushrooming growth in enrollment and buildings on the finite campus, UNLV was running out of horizontal parking lots and had to begin imitating what resorts on the Strip and downtown had been doing for decades: build vertically. Incredibly, the state refused to contribute to the garage, although it was just as vital a structure as any university building. Student and faculty-staff parking fees largely financed the four-story garage, which opened

in 2001. It was larger than Maxson had planned, and it greatly relieved parking congestion at the campus's north end. In 2006 it was enlarged to six stories.

While the Bubba Building and the parking garage brought more than their share of headaches, UNLV's new library was delayed by a different set of problems. Much of the early money came from Maxson's and Guinn's lobbying, while Harter accounted for the later funding. Construction had begun in March 1998, but delays resulted from numerous changes in the original plans. Just like the 1981 addition to the Dickinson Library, the midlevel floors were not designed to hold large numbers of books. Unlike the 1981 fiasco, however, here the mistake was caught in time by librarians and builders, and the third and fourth floors were reinforced. Fire prevention issues, subcontractors' liens, and substantial conflicts over design, construction, and oversight all delayed progress.

But the wait was worth it. On January 8, 2001, the 301,000-square-foot building opened its doors and was an immediate success. Ninety-six workstations
filled an "informal commons" just down the steps from a soaring entrance.
The Lied Library was as modern as any in the country. As the library's Internet
specialist, Kay Tuma, explained, the new facility exploited the latest trends in
electronic data processing. Information files brimming with search indexes and
millions of online journals, books, and documents gave UNLV students "a whole
new way of doing research."[34] Moreover, the library's state-of-the-art robotic
book retrieval system created even more space for computers by keeping old
journals, government documents, and other little-used items out of the way in
compact storage.

The building's final cost was $58 million. Of this total, $15 million came
from the Lied Foundation Trust on condition that the structure be named for
the foundation's founder, real estate entrepreneur Ernest W. Lied. James Dickinson, for whom UNLV's first library had been named following his untimely
death in 1965, continued to be honored, as President Harter designated the
large plaza in front of the new library for him. For its part, the state also helped
to finance construction, pumping in $32.8 million initially and another $9.8
million later for furnishings, equipment, and a parking lot.

This, however, was not the only big project on campus. Also in 2001, the
president dedicated the $8 million Lee and Thomas Beam Music Center. This
37,000-square-foot building housed a music library equipped with thousands
of recordings, a three-hundred-seat recital hall, a recording studio, rehearsal
rooms, and teaching studios. Funded mainly by a large donation from the
Beam family, the facility's recital hall was designed for small ensemble performances, and the state-of-the-art studio gave students a place where they
could record their own music. As Jeffrey Koep, dean of UNLV's College of
Fine Arts, commented, "Tom Beam loved music, and he wanted to share
that with others."[35]

Work proceeded on other projects as well. Just north of the new music complex, a smaller, but just as significant, structure, the $4.3 million UNLV Founda-
tion Building gradually took shape. The 23,000-square-foot structure, designed
by Tate and Snyder Architects, opened in April 2000. This project, initiated and
funded by the foundation's board of trustees, allowed the foundation to escape

(BACK, FROM LEFT): FORMER UNLV COACH BILL IRELAND,
CAROL AND MIKE HARTER, JEAN IRELAND, AND DONNA BEAM.
(FRONT): ARTURO RANDO GILLOT AND JIMMA LEE BEAM. UNLV
FOUNDATION

its cramped quarters in the Richard Tam Alumni Building. This was important, because the agency needed more room for its expanded staff. As UNLV's chief fund-raising arm, the foundation also required larger offices and meeting quarters for the negotiations it conducted with prospective donors.

Of course, President Harter sometimes faced an uphill struggle in constructing the buildings that were vital to her ambitious agenda. While everyone outwardly applauded her goal of making UNLV a premier urban university, numerous factors threatened state funding for the buildings needed to accomplish that goal. In April 2000, for example, she announced plans for a $75 million science, engineering, and technology building. At 190,000 square feet, the structure would bring UNLV close to the average of science and engineering space found at similar institutions. The proposed facility, she explained, would include all of the laboratory and classroom facilities critical to the school's future as a doctorate-granting institution in these important subject areas. In 2001 the legislature gave UNLV planning money for the project.

In 2003, when the president moved forward to secure the state's share of construction costs, support was lacking in Carson City. Despite ranking second on the regents' priority list, not only did the project face stiff opposition from other system projects like UNR's $66 million library, but the building and the facilities it would house were expensive. Even with $15 million generated by renting some UNLV property to the Environmental Protection Agency and another $10 million in private donations and other sources, the state's share was a whopping $50 million. Given the demands being made on state coffers by school districts, relief programs, and growth in general, some regents openly doubted whether the project had any chance even in a Clark County-dominated legislature.

With tourist revenues lagging in the wake of the 9/11 terrorist attacks, the state public works board delayed the building. Citing a lack of available bonding capacity for other, much-needed state buildings and the likelihood that UNLV could not begin construction until 2005, the board voted the project off the governor's budget for the 2003–05 biennium. President Harter was understandably annoyed, telling reporters that she was "totally shocked and disappointed." Recognizing how inflation would raise costs if the building were delayed much longer, she declared: "Not funding this project is incredibly short-sighted," and she vowed to work with business and community leaders to get it back on Guinn's list.[36]

The benefits were obvious, not only for the school's students and faculty but for Las Vegas itself. For a city desperately in need of diversifying an economy threatened by the nationalization of casino gambling, a project that would attract high-tech and biotechnology firms had been the top priority of the board of regents and even the public works board's staff. Harter refused to concede defeat, and after a vigorous lobbying effort by the president with help from the Las Vegas business community, legislators funded the building. It should open in time for UNLV's 50th anniversary in 2007.

The effort to raise funds, create new programs, and construct new buildings all revolved around a central issue: inadequate state funding. In her 2003 State of the University address, Harter pointed to the lack of state support in the face of Las Vegas's continued development. After the largest tax increase in Nevada history, she acknowledged her gratitude to Governor Guinn and state legislators "for this enhanced funding," but reminded her audience that "even at '04 levels, the percentage of state funding is still well below the 55 percent we received in 1995, the first year of my presidency." She and other UNLV fund-raisers had to work harder than ever to create large sources of private and internal financing for "virtually all activities that go beyond core teaching and administrative functions."[37]

For UNLV, the problem was not just a lack of legislative appropriations; it was also the school's share of the total system pie. For decades the Reno campus had received far more money than its Las Vegas counterpart. In the early years, Carlson, Moyer, Zorn, Baepler, and Goodall were never fully satisfied with their budgets, but they recognized the dominance of the older and larger university. As early as 1977, however, UNLV's enrollment surpassed UNR's, powered largely by the rapid urbanization of the Las Vegas metropolitan area. By the mid-1980s, Clark County regents, pushed by President Maxson and influential community leaders, began to question the continued inequities, especially in the face of surging enrollment, projections of future growth, and perennially tight budgets. Interim president Kenny Guinn also wanted more money for a university budget that he struggled to keep in the black. Carol Harter was even more insistent. By the mid-1990s, UNLV was a much larger school than Reno in terms of students, staff, and faculty. Harter recognized that the dream of becoming a premier urban university rested on the assumption that state funding would be adequate.

But this was not the case. Despite the 1965 reapportionment of the state legislature and the 1971 shift to southern domination on the board of regents, appropriations continued to favor UNR. In 1999 Harter told reporters, "We take two steps forward and one step back. We continue to struggle." In 1998 UNR received $3,160 more per student in state funding than UNLV. In 1999 the figure dropped only slightly, to $3,024. Moreover, the debut of Governor Guinn's Millennium Scholarship Program, which used monies from the national tobacco company settlement with the states to finance a free college education for every Nevada high school graduate with a grade average of A or B, was expected to further dilute UNLV's slight gains in funding. As regent Steve Sisolak remarked, "I'm concerned that we're going to get so far behind, it's going to be difficult, if not impossible, to fix. We need help in southern Nevada."[38]

Not everyone in the state agreed. UNR president Joseph Crowley and interim system chancellor Thomas Anderes disputed the $3,000 gap between the two campuses while trying to justify UNR's advantage. They argued that UNR had older buildings and more buildings to maintain, different and more expensive programs in agriculture, mining, forestry, medicine, and other subject areas that western land grant colleges were obligated to offer, higher graduate degree productivity, and higher income from research-related projects.

Harter and southern regents dismissed these claims. Ultimately, the board of regents authorized a study of the problem by MGT of America, which found that UNLV was underfunded by $7.6 million. In response, the 1999 legislature appropriated an extra $115 per student, or $1.86 million, to UNLV with plans to address the equity issue even more in the 2001 session. Nevertheless, the glaring disparity in funding remained a problem. In fall 1999, UNLV reported 16,156 full-time students compared to UNR's 9,500, but per-student state funding remained out of balance, at $8,131 and $11,155, respectively. And the disparity continued into 2007.

On a related front, everyone understood that part of the key to maintaining UNLV's state appropriations was to increase enrollment in the face of competition from the community college, the budding state college in Henderson, and the small private colleges in town. In the late 1990s, the Harter administration instituted a variety of strategies to increase student recruitment, but it also acted to retain students already on the campus who were struggling with their grades. Compounding the retention problem was the administration's determination to make UNLV a premier urban university, a commitment to quality that required higher admission and academic standards.

Harter's major response to the retention issue was creation of the University College. In her 2003 State of the University address at the Judy Bayley Theatre, the president declared that regent approval in 2001 of more-stringent standards for admission to UNLV and UNR promoted UNLV's goal of becoming a major research university by 2010. However, Las Vegas regent Linda Howard, who voted against the measure to raise the minimum GPA for admission from 2.5 to 2.75 by 2006 (and, in December 2005, successfully opposed raising the GPA to 3.0 by 2007), complained that too few resources were being made available for students, including minorities, who would have trouble making the grade.

Although the regents in 2006 finally raised the GPA to 3.0, creating the University College was a partial response to Howard's concerns, which Office of Minority Affairs director Wayne Nunnely and others had also expressed during Maxson's tenure.

The Zorn administration had established a University College in 1971, but it was abolished in the 1980s. The Harter version was more multifunctional. Its mission was to help students with no specific major or many academic interests, including transfer students and those with lower grades who were struggling to enter existing programs. The interdisciplinary, undergraduate program would require a minimum 2.0 grade point average. The new degree, Provost Alden explained, would be offered through the University College. Alden told regents that he expected more than 2,000 students in the program by the fifth year. Not only was the plan intended to maintain enrollment and reduce attrition, but it clearly benefited the hundreds of students UNLV lost each year when their GPAs fell below 2.5 and they could not get into programs. As Alden pointed out, most UNLV colleges required at least a 2.5, and some higher. In addition, since President Harter planned to raise UNLV's admission requirements soon, the minimum grade point average probably would exclude many students who were struggling academically.

Initially, some regents, as well as many faculty, were skeptical of the plan. Regent Sisolak was somewhat concerned about the lower grade point average, saying, "I don't want it to be a second-rate degree." But he liked the degree's flexibility. "A certain number of students don't just want a major in finance, for example. Maybe they also want some sociology or math. This degree gives them a lot more flexibility." Anne Hein, director of UNLV's student development center slated to advise these students, agreed with Sisolak: "We see that a lot of students like learning and like different subject areas, but they don't just want to focus on one."[39] Clearly, the new college would benefit these groups and, just as clearly, help many students who have trouble adjusting to the academic rigor of university training or who for any number of good reasons—divorce, loss of employment, or illness—see their grades drop. Zorn's University College had been designed to provide entry-level students with more institutional help than upperclassmen; it was a temporary incubator. But Harter's college, which opened in fall 2004, went much further.

With efforts under way to address four of UNLV's leading challenges—maintaining high enrollment, increasing retention, improving academic quality, and increasing donations and state appropriations—the Harter administration remained on course for achieving its major goal. In a September 2004 speech to the campus and Las Vegas communities, the president reiterated her determination to make UNLV a premier urban university regionally and nationally and predicted that the school would become a Doctoral/Research Extensive University, as then defined by the Carnegie Foundation for the Advancement of Teaching, within five to seven years. Harter understood that reaching this goal would require a number of prerequisites, including a major capital campaign to raise funds to endow chairs in a dozen or more areas through which UNLV could "create internationally recognized centers of excellence." She also reiterated her intention of constructing the science, engineering, and technology building, Greenspun Hall for the Greenspun College of Urban Affairs, and other needed buildings, while also developing additional programs within the dentistry, law, and architecture schools. Locally, her goal was to make UNLV an "indisputable resource" and a "partner in economic development and diversification, health care, fine and creative arts, highly competitive athletics and community development."[40]

From its inception, the Harter administration embraced planning as the means to the end of advancing UNLV's national academic stature. To emphasize the need for continuous planning, the campus created the University Planning Council, chaired by a member of the president's staff. The basic goals embodied in the academic master plan of 1998 and its various updates, as well as the comprehensive campus master plan of 2003, came from two planning documents outlining UNLV's new strategic plan: "The University of Nevada, Las Vegas Premier Urban University: A Public Agenda for the Decade 1996–2005" (1996) and "The University of Nevada, Las Vegas, The Engaged Research University: Extending the Agenda, 2002–2007" (2002). The list of major goals included being more student-focused, hiring more quality faculty, promoting research, and serving the community.

During its first decade, the Harter administration made significant progress toward meeting these objectives. For example, between 2000 and 2005, UNLV hired more than five hundred new faculty with terminal degrees and solid scholarly track records. The administration also boosted the number of faculty research awards and grants, hired grant writers to help obtain even more funding, created dozens of new research centers within the colleges, and reformed the merit system to encourage more research. It also made the honors program a college in 1997 and boosted its scholarship endowment from $30,000 to $2.5 million. The program, which counted fewer than 40 students in 1986, boasted 580 by 2005.

The administration also generated millions in funds for UNLV. Although some of the money was already in the pipeline before 1995, UNLV Foundation records credit the Harter administration with raising $447 million in cash, gifts, and pledges during its first decade, compared to $109 million by the Maxson administration during its nearly ten years in office. Harter also raised millions for research, nearly quadrupling UNLV's external dollars from grants and other sources, from $19 million to $73 million in her first decade as president. Of this amount, $46.7 million went for research. In 2005 extramural funding soared to $95 million, with $69.3 million going for research. In 2004 the top three federal agencies providing direct research support to UNLV were the U.S. Department of Energy, $18.9 million; the National Science Foundation, $2.1 million; and the U.S. Department of Agriculture, $1.9 million, with the Department of Defense and the Department of Education not far behind. To reinforce its premier urban university mission, UNLV joined the Coalition of Urban and Metropolitan Universities, an organization of sixty universities located in urban areas of more than 250,000 people.

Besides hiring quality faculty and raising millions in supplemental private funds, other goals of the strategic plan facilitated this march toward excellence. Of particular significance were the strides UNLV made after 1996 in becoming more student-focused and growing selectively to serve the region and achieve distinction.

From the beginning, President Harter particularly emphasized the importance of being student-centered. Aside from her administration's pumping more money into student services to address a greater variety of student needs, several projects epitomized her commitment and UNLV's progress in this direction. Completion of the massive south wing of what is now the Tonopah Residence Complex in 2003 and the Dayton Complex near Tropicana in 2004 contributed hundreds more rooms for dormitory students. In the early twenty-first century, the Harter administration initiated two more projects that will benefit UNLV's greatly expanded student body. When it originally opened in 1968, the Moyer Student Union was a facility designed to serve an enrollment of about 15,000. In the early 1990s, the Maxson administration renovated and modernized the building and constructed a separate dining commons nearby. By 2000, however, with UNLV's student population approaching 25,000, the school obviously needed a larger structure.

In 2001 the Harter administration announced plans to build a new 135,000-square-foot student union and a 184,000-square-foot recreation center near the Cox Pavilion. The president's staff—principally Rebecca Mills—helped organize the Rebel Renovation Committee and secured funding to hire a consulting group that drafted plans. After nearly a year and a half of meeting with all concerned parties, Harter proposed raising student fees to pay the $91 million cost. In August 2003 the board of regents approved the so-called Rebel Renovation Project and the fee increase. Both buildings should be fully completed in time for UNLV's 50th anniversary in fall 2007.

Since the Harter administration took over in 1995, it has championed a wide variety of new programs, schools, and construction projects to build upon the work of its predecessors and pursue an expensive and challenging goal: to "grow selectively, serve the region, and achieve distinction."[41] Of course, this goal did not begin with Harter; its roots lie deep in the school's past. Earlier presidents, like Bob Maxson, recognized that someday UNLV might require multiple campuses for expanded research facilities. At the same time, Maxson campaigned for law and architecture schools to supply the growing Las Vegas community with more professionals trained in these skills. Donald Moyer had first embraced the community service goal in the mid-1960s when he worked to establish a hotel college and make Nevada Southern a strong science research school. Fifteen years later, Leonard Goodall created UNLV's engineering school to help Las Vegas diversify its economy.

With the wide range of academic programs and new schools it launched, the Harter administration took this historical commitment to new levels. Motivating Harter's efforts was her dream of making UNLV a "premier urban university." In a 2004 conversation, she explained that this dream was not a recent revelation but stemmed from her experience of growing up in New York City, where she saw how "modern metropolitan universities can help develop their cities." Her father graduated with a finance degree from New York University, an urban campus set in Greenwich Village—one of many inspirations for her Midtown UNLV project. While Harter's career initially took her to small towns like Athens, Ohio, and Geneseo, New York, the UNLV job notice "jumped out" at her because the school was based in America's fastest-growing metropolitan area and, thanks to the Runnin' Rebels, UNLV was known around the world. For these reasons, "growing up in New York made me feel comfortable here." Las Vegas provided an "opportunistic" environment for building. Indeed, UNLV was not the traditional elite campus she had encountered in the East—it was more transformable. As she explained, "All of the great schools, the greater they are, the more nuanced they are." But at UNLV, "You are really moving whole levels at a time. . . . The very creative nature of that keeps me going."

Significant change and progress certainly marked the first five years of her presidency, but the movement of "whole levels at a time" became even more obvious in the new century.[42] Two of the major pillars supporting Harter's effort to make UNLV a Doctoral/Research Extensive University by 2010 were the acquisition of new campuses in the valley and their development as research centers in health care and science/technology as well as educational centers serving community needs. While the Paradise campus was a small, though useful, by-product of the deal to build the new Paradise Elementary School at UNLV and enhance the education of local teachers, obtaining and developing the Shadow Lane and North Las Vegas campuses required much creative thinking and was firmly rooted in Harter's planning process.

In the case of Shadow Lane, her administration sought not only to promote research but also to serve the community. In 2001 UNLV acquired this 18-acre site as a home for its new dental school. In October 2004 UNLV officially opened its first regional campus, next to University Medical Center on Shadow Lane, in the heart of Las Vegas's medical district, with the new 110,000-square-foot dental facility. By 2005 the dental school was training more than 200 students, treating virtually all of Clark County's Medicaid recipients, and offering low-cost dental care to any community residents who sought it. By April 2005 the school's dental clinics had already treated more than 60,000 patients. The

Shadow Lane campus's three buildings also housed other operations, including UNLV's Forensics and Biotechnology Center, with its prospects of establishing research partnerships with the Nevada Cancer Institute. At full build-out, the 18-acre campus will provide a minimum of 420,000 square feet for advanced training and research.

Shadow Lane symbolized the administration's commitment to serve the community by providing health services and by training desperately needed health professionals. To accomplish this, Harter chose to create not a college but rather the Division of Health Sciences to house numerous departments offering degree programs as well as units like the School of Dental Medicine and the School of Health and Human Sciences. In an effort to meet the growing local and national demand for more nurses, Harter elevated the old nursing program to the College of Nursing in the division and instituted a Ph.D. program in 2004 to train more nursing professors. By that year, nursing enrollments had more than doubled, just as several new hospitals opened to serve Las Vegas's booming population.

Also in 2004, the Harter administration established the School of Public Health in the Division of Health Sciences. This school, led by interim dean Mary Guinan, a physician and scientist specializing in inner-city health promotion, offered graduate coursework in such areas as environmental and occupational health, health care administration, health promotion, and epidemiology. The new school also hosted research units, including the Indian Research and Education Center and the Nevada Institute for Children's Research and Policy. In the 2005 legislative session, Harter even collaborated with the University of Nevada, Reno to obtain funding for a joint pharmacy school to benefit Nevada residents. Although it was not funded, the program remains a likely prospect for the future.

In the twenty-first century, these new initiatives dwarfed the old nursing and radiology offerings of the past, allowing UNLV to extend itself directly into the Las Vegas community. But there was more. The Harter administration's health care initiatives, concentrated at Shadow Lane and in the Bigelow Health Sciences Building on the main campus, were more visible in terms of direct benefits to the community than the advanced research programs planned for the new science, engineering, and technology building and UNLV's proposed research campus west of the Strip. In 2003 Senator Harry Reid helped the university acquire 115 acres from Clark County for a research park. This site, located in the southwestern part of the valley near the Beltway and Durango, will be managed by the University Research Foundation. Established in 2002 as an arm of the UNLV Foundation, the research foundation helps the university obtain and manage highly specialized federal research grants while also providing a home for public/private collaborations and partnerships. According to preliminary plans, the UNLV Harry Reid Research and Technology Park will house both university and private research activities, many of which will benefit the community—albeit less visibly than UNLV's health care initiatives do.

By contrast, UNLV's new 640-acre campus in North Las Vegas will serve the public in a more traditional way by providing a convenient classroom venue for residents in the northeast valley. Unlike the southwest technology park and Shadow Lane, UNLV will develop this campus in partnership with other units in the university system, offering programs that best serve the needs of North Las Vegas. According to the master plan that UNLV is preparing, the proposed higher education center will include academic offerings by the university, the community college, and Nevada State College. A feasibility study to determine the needs of the burgeoning city of North Las Vegas will help decide what academic, athletic, and research programs ultimately find a home on the new campus.

Finally, UNLV opened its first international campus in Singapore in fall 2006, with the William F. Harrah College of Hotel Administration offering the first degree programs there.

While all of these initiatives and accomplishments are impressive, perhaps the event that best symbolized UNLV's march toward excellence was the appointment in 2000 of Wole Soyinka, the first black African to win the coveted Nobel Prize for Literature. Soyinka, a member of the Yoruba people, founded the national theater in Nigeria following his graduation in 1958 from the University of Leeds in England. A distinguished novelist, essayist, and playwright whose work fuses Western elements with subject matter and techniques rooted in Yoruba folklore and religion, the Nobel laureate was a member of Emory University's faculty when UNLV invited him to campus.

Recognizing the advantages of luring Soyinka to UNLV, Harter worked with

Glenn Schaeffer, the president and CFO of Mandalay Bay Resort Group, to
create a funding structure that could be used to attract Soyinka and others to
Las Vegas. Schaeffer, a distinguished hotel executive by any standard, was also
trained in the literary arts. He had graduated summa cum laude in English literature from UC-Irvine and later received a master's degree and an M.F.A. from
the renowned Iowa Writers' Workshop.

Schaeffer and Harter collaborated with others to create the International
Institute of Modern Letters (IIML), with joint headquarters at UNLV and Victoria
University in Wellington, New Zealand. The institute's purpose was to support
both established and emerging writers worldwide and to help persecuted writers prevail against censorship. Schaeffer, Harter, and others created the Elias
Ghanem Chair of Creative Writing in the UNLV Department of English for Soyinka; in this position he could not only mentor students in the university's own
writing program but also have a part in the institute's global activities.

With her own training in literature, President Harter played a crucial role in
recruiting Soyinka. In a recent conversation, she recalled, "In this case, my expertise did help the situation; normally it does not. I appreciated the Laureate's

writing." By inviting Soyinka to campus and awarding him an honorary doctorate, UNLV "laid the foundation." "We stole him from Emory University," with the help of Schaeffer's philanthropy.[43]

In summer 2005, Carol Harter became the longest-serving president in school history, surpassing the mark set by Robert Maxson. At that time, Harter indicated that she would retire as president in 2008, at the end of her current contract. But it was not her decision to make. It was becoming increasingly obvious that new university system chancellor James Rogers (who had been given the power by the regents to fire any campus president) wanted new presidents at both UNR and UNLV. John Lilley's problems with faculty and others in Reno had grown to the point that he had to find a new job, which he did, leaving UNR on December 31, 2005, to become president of his alma mater, Baylor University. But Harter was a relatively popular figure on her campus. After a somewhat rocky start in 1995–96, she attracted growing support among faculty and staff as she moved UNLV toward the status of a Doctoral/Research Extensive University. Even though the Carnegie Foundation had changed that classification and raised the criteria, Harter remained confident that UNLV could reach this elusive goal by 2010 or so.

So a news leak on January 27, 2006, that she would resign as president by June 30 caught many people off guard. Certainly it was no secret that her relationship with Rogers was strained; after all, they were both strong personalities, and they disagreed about several key issues. These included the president's supposed micromanagement of university operations and fund-raising as well as her reluctance to create a minority affairs office. And conflict surely would have arisen over Harter's reworking of an old Donald Moyer idea, broached to reporters that March, to have separate governing boards for the two university campuses and possibly separating the two universities from the rest of Nevada's higher education system. Such a reform would have given UNLV the autonomy it had long sought for pursuing its own growth agenda. The chancellor and most of the modern-day regents, with their system-oriented approach, surely would have viewed this threat to their power much the same as their 1960s predecessors had when they frustrated Moyer until he resigned. Still, Harter's resignation seemed ill-timed, coming as it did in the midst of new program initiatives and a major fund-raising campaign. Initially, the formal announcements were accompanied by smiling faces and statements that President Harter was leaving UNLV voluntarily to help the UNLV Foundation and engage in other fund-raising activities benefiting the school. But it was soon obvious that she had been forced out by the chancellor, who, over the next few weeks, willingly took most of the heat from angry faculty, donors, and community members. But just as clearly, the board of regents, with the notable exceptions of Linda Howard, UNR professor Howard Rosenberg, and Thalia Dondero, supported Harter's ouster.

Harter's popularity at UNLV, however, was evidenced by the huge turnout in early February for her formal resignation announcement to the campus community at the Foundation Building. In many ways the assembly resembled the large gathering twelve years earlier for Bob Maxson's farewell. Over the next few months, Harter's future plans shifted somewhat. She would remain at UNLV and possibly even resume teaching someday in the Department of English. But her immediate task was to establish the Black Mountain Institute as a vehicle for bringing high-profile authors to campus and encouraging them to write articles about major issues in language that would engage the public. In April 2006, America's only living Nobel laureate, Jane Morrison, came to UNLV and delivered a public lecture and appeared at a dinner that kicked off the new institute's fund-raising effort. To be sure, the earlier International Institute of Modern Letters that Harter had begun with Glenn Schaeffer and Wole Soyinka served as an inspiration and model for this new organization. Once again, Soyinka participated, awarding the new institute instant stature by joining its board of directors. Over the next few months, Harter and Soyinka attracted other talented people to the board, including Harriet Fulbright and Henry Louis Gates, the director of Harvard University's W. E. B. Du Bois Institute for African and African American Research.

The creation of another prestigious entity at UNLV marked the culmination of a presidency full of accomplishments. It seemed only fitting that in recognition of President Harter's numerous contributions to UNLV, the board of regents renamed the sprawling CBC Building the Harter Classroom Complex (HCC) at a public ceremony on May 11, 2006. In championing these myriad initiatives undertaken between 1995 and 2006, the Harter administration pursued its mission of redefining UNLV as an "engaged university" in research, teaching, the arts, and community outreach. Like her predecessors, Carol Harter attempted to shape events by aggressively pursuing an ambitious agenda that included not only new programs, new buildings, and strategic planning but also the implementation of an improved management system—reforms that finally brought order to university spending, personnel, development, and many other school operations. Helped mightily by Las Vegas's growing prominence, influence, and affluence, President Harter took UNLV to new levels of excellence, a crucial prerequisite to her ultimate goal of placing UNLV in the exclusive company of America's premier urban universities.

CHAPTER NINE

Student Life

During the first three years of Las Vegas's extension program, when enrollment still numbered less than a hundred, students mostly concentrated on their classwork. Of course, faculty and students exhibited a certain esprit de corps as they roughed it in the often cold dressing rooms of Las Vegas High. Over time, however, a sense of community emerged, along with a separate identity from the high school.

Student government at Nevada Southern began while the school was still based at Las Vegas High. In October 1954 the entire student body met to elect a "freshman class president." In the first-ever student election they chose Tom Krause as president and Jim Norris as vice president. Krause pledged to draw up a constitution for what became the Confederated Students of Nevada Southern or CSNS (today CSUN) "by revising the constitution of the University of Nevada." The students recognized that with a student government they could organize more social activities to bring their little community together at times other than between classes. So, as part of his campaign, Krause also promised that "during the year will be planned many social activities, including a formal Christmas Ball at which a queen will be chosen."[1]

In the early 1950s the entire student body met to conduct business. For example, they met in fall 1954 to select two representatives, Sunny Boone and Bart Jacka, to ride the bus up to Reno to attend the university homecoming. The students wanted Boone and Jacka to wear Nevada Southern's school colors. The entire student body therefore met to decide what the school's colors should be. Three sets were nominated—turquoise and yellow, sage green and gold, and turquoise and black—but there was no consensus. The familiar scarlet and gray colors of the old Confederacy came in the next year when CSNS adopted the Rebel name and mascot. Later, in fall 1954, students elected a seven-member "Student Council," which began planning social events, scheduling elections, and collecting dues to defray the cost of "government." Once students and university officials approved the CSNS constitution, which provided for a formal senate and other offices, the council and meetings of the full student body ended.

At first, CSNS officers served for a year. Even when Nevada Southern moved to its Maryland Parkway campus in 1957, Arlene Henson Oakes, the first woman student body president, served for a year. But beginning in 1958 and into the 1960s, there was a separate president for each fall and spring semester, because the students were constantly leaving to finish their degree at Reno or to transfer to some out-of-state college. Ernie Cranmer, Bob Schnider, and Pat Whipple all served as CSNS presidents in the campus's early years, leading the effort to enhance student life.

The student government quickly became an important institution at Nevada Southern. In fall 1954, only three of the school's 310 students had scholarships; CSNS would lobby hard over the next few years to increase that number. At the first-ever regents' meeting in Las Vegas, in October 1954, Nevada Southern students, encouraged by their infant government, turned out en masse to persuade the reluctant board to give the school its own campus. The students even sponsored a reception after the meeting in Las Vegas High's auditorium (with James Dickinson and his wife providing the punch and cookies) to mingle with the regents informally and press the case for a campus.

The students began their newspaper at about the same time they started their government. In September 1954 they held a contest to choose the name for the occasional mimeographed sheet they planned to circulate. Mrs. Rita

Moore, a student, won the contest for her entry, the *nevso News*. By spring 1955, the name had been changed to the more familiar *Rebel Yell*, with Lydia Malcom as the first editor. The monthly publication helped reinforce Nevada Southern's identity in students' minds. For example, the regents had originally called the Las Vegas program "The University of Nevada Southern Regional Division," but the students soon popularized the shortened name, Nevada Southern. The first-ever edition of the *Rebel Yell*, which appeared on April 20, 1955, used the terms "rebel" and "Nevada Southern."

The new student government functioned as the hub of student activities while promoting the young institution's sense of community. Las Vegas was still a small town of 30,000 or so then, and most of the students knew one another from high school. Galas like the first-ever winter dance, the "Sno-Ball," helped maintain the bonds of community. It became an annual event in the school's first decade. In 1956 students ran the second annual Sno-Ball (later spelled Snow-Ball), which was announced in the *Rebel Yell* and held at a local country club. The same was true of the "Confederate Cotillion" gala, which began in 1954 and usually took place at a Strip hotel. And there was an annual Christmas party, a St. Valentine's Day dance, and soirées on other holidays during the school year. Students also sponsored a float each year in the city's big Helldorado Parade, and on several occasions Nevada Southern coeds won the coveted title of Helldorado Queen.

Students in the extension program at Las Vegas considered themselves an integral part of the University of Nevada, even though it was 450 miles away. In November 1956, thirty (no longer just two) Nevada Southern students, calling themselves "delegates," took a bus to Reno for the homecoming celebration. Later, on January 8–10, 1966, csns sponsored the first-ever Nevada Southern Homecoming on the Maryland Parkway campus in conjunction with a basketball game against its archrival, the University of Nevada.

Fraternities also came quickly. In fall 1954 a group of male students proposed creating the school's first fraternity, Wi Tappa Kg, but it never really formed. Then, in November 1956, even before the Maryland Parkway campus opened, the *Rebel Yell* announced that one senator would introduce a proposal in the student senate to form a "social fraternity." The ultimate goal was "to form clubs for the purpose of drawing desirable fraternities and sororities to

Nevada Southern."[2] Students wanted to establish the kind of institutions that bound the school community closer together.

Nevada Southern's first real fraternity was THPO, chartered on March 15, 1958, with Don Nelson as president. The second was the Intercollegiate Knights, headed initially by Don Caldwell. The first sorority was Iotta Kappa Phi, and Nu Sigma Epsilon followed shortly thereafter. But these groups limited their membership. However, female students at Nevada Southern soon created an organization they could all join. In 1958 they established the Associated Women Students, with Pat Whipple as the first president. It was really Donald Moyer who pushed the effort to get national fraternities and sororities to establish chapters at the Las Vegas campus, and in the mid- to late 1960s a number of major ones did. Movie legend John Wayne actually attended the Sigma Chi installation ceremony on the Maryland Parkway campus as the official representative of his old chapter at USC. By the 1968–69 school year, there were a dozen fraternities, sororities, and related organizations on campus.

Of course, these were not the only student groups. There was, for example, a biology club, led in the early 1960s by student body president and future dentist and state senator Ray Rawson, who, almost forty years later, would spearhead the drive for UNLV's dental school. A psychology club and a Model United Nations joined political organizations like the Young Democrats and later the Young Republicans.

Religion also played a role on campus. From NSU's earliest days, local religious leaders worked to establish organizations to help students cope with a variety of problems relating to campus life, secular education, and Las Vegas's hedonistic culture. Nevada Southern's Catholic students formed the Newman Club in 1961 with Father Leo McFadden as director; the first student president was Mike Tobin. In that same year, Mormon students established the Deseret Club. The first president of this group was Lyle Johnson, with future school board member Howard Hollingsworth functioning as an advisor. Later, church authorities switched the format from a club to an "institute," with a paid staff and institutional programs for Mormon students. As the college grew larger, students practicing other religions also formed organizations. By the late 1960s and early 1970s, the campus had the Baha'i Club, the Baptist Student Union, the Christian Science Club, and the Muslim Student Union, as well as the

Latter-day Saint Student Association, and the B'nai Sholom for the school's Jewish students.

The Catholics and Mormons organized first and built substantial facilities just off campus. In the early 1960s, members of the Deseret Club and the New-man Club usually scheduled meetings in a room on or near the campus. But as the student body rapidly expanded, both churches obviously needed a building in which to conduct their meetings and services. The Mormons acted first, purchasing three acres of land "behind the Gym" (just west of today's Lied Library) on Harmon Avenue and constructing their first building, a 3,700-square-foot facility (today's University Hall) in 1964.

1963 STUDENT BODY PRESIDENT, LATER STATE SENATOR, AND DRIVING FORCE BEHIND UNLV'S DENTAL SCHOOL, RAY RAWSON IN HIS SENIOR YEAR AT NEVADA SOUTHERN. *EPILOGUE,* 1963

The Catholic bishop in Reno also wanted to erect a Newman Club facility near campus, but the Diocese of Reno (the Las Vegas Diocese was not formed until 1996) did not have the money. Fortunately, the Von Tobel family, whose lumber and hardware business dated from Las Vegas's earliest days, made a generous donation. According to Ed Von Tobel, his devoutly Catholic brother Jake convinced his brothers to buy three acres for the club adjacent to the Mormons' site and deed it to Bishop Robert Dwyer, which they did in 1963.

The regents, however, did not want the clubs taking up valuable land that Nevada Southern might need for future expansion westward beyond the 1960 science and technology building (today's Lilly Fong Geoscience) and the Gym (now the Marjorie Barrick Museum of Natural History). As the Mormon build-ing suddenly went up, regents scurried in an attempt to prevent the Catholics from building also. During an April 1964 meeting, the regents, after a lengthy discussion, decided that it would be unwise to acquire the Catholics' land through condemnation proceedings while leaving the Mormons undisturbed. Several years later, at the urging of President Roman Zorn, the regents agreed to a land exchange in which both churches gave up their properties on Harmon in return for smaller, 1.5-acre sites on University Road, plus cash. Portions of the new parcels were on state land that the regents controlled, and the rest were holdings of the university's land foundation. In the summer and fall of 1972, President Zorn completed the deal to move both church organizations from Harmon to University Road. The Mormons built a new structure first because they had received more than $245,000 from the sale of their old building and land. In 1974 they opened their present LDS Institute, which the church modernized and expanded at century's end.

The Catholics, after getting the Von Tobel family's approval for the land swap, acquired their present lot just south of the Mormons' facility. Since the old Catholic site had no building, the bishop received less than $70,000 in cash, not enough money to construct a home for the Newman Club. The eventual building would not be a traditional Newman Club but more of an ecumenical facility. During the 1960s, students and priests at the Newman Club had gradually affiliated themselves with Protestant groups on campus. Clearly the ecumenical effects of Vatican II, as well as the moral questions raised by the civil rights movement, the Vietnam War, and other contemporary issues influenced this process.

In the late 1960s, the groups formed an informal organization called the Center for Religion, Life, and Peace, which met at the United Methodist church across Maryland Parkway from the campus. The early center consisted of Catholic students and their counterparts from the six (and, briefly, nine) mainline Protestant groups—the Lutherans, Presbyterians, Episcopalians, Congregationalists, Methodists, and American (not Southern) Baptists. The Reverend Jerome Blankinship was the early chaplain for the Protestants, followed by a succession of dedicated chaplains in the 1970s and 1980s, including the Reverends Gretchen Stamos and Ellie Shapton. Leading the Catholics was a succession of priests, such as Father Bob Simpson and Father Caesar Caviligia.

By the early 1970s, the center obviously needed a building. The Catholics had the site for it, but money was a problem. The goal was to provide an ecumenical facility where students and community members could socialize and discuss ideas relating to religion and everyday issues. At the urging of Reverend Blankinship and Father Walter Nowak, the new Catholic chaplain, former student Jim Bilbray, by then an attorney who had served as a regent, organized a meeting at the Golden Nugget of interested businessmen, including Art Marshall (of today's Marshall Rousso clothing stores) to devise a fund-raising strategy to finance a building. Marshall recruited prominent Jewish business leaders and resort executives. A committee chaired by developer Irwin Molasky, with help from resort executives Alvin Benedict, Billy Weinberger of Caesars Palace, and others raised funds for the $250,000 building. Molasky, Benedict, Jake Von Tobel, Blankinship, Rabbi Philip Schnairson, and Father Walter Nowak presided at the groundbreaking ceremony on February 27, 1974. With construction under way, UNLV opened Brussels Street to provide access off University Road.

Nowak and Blankinship reserved space in the building for a Jewish group of some kind, but none came immediately. In 1968 Jewish organizers formed a B'nai Sholom group, which attracted some students. By 1972 the UNLV catalog indicated the presence of a B'nai B'rith Hillel, but it was a relatively small group. The construction of a home for the Center for Religion, Life, and Peace inspired action. In 1974 members of the B'nai B'rith continued to sponsor what some students informally called the Jewish Student Union. In 1976 the Combined Jewish Appeal funded the Jewish Student Union's move into an office at the center. Because the B'nai B'rith was not financing the student group's operation, the Combined Jewish Appeal and its leader, Jerry Countess, took control. To prevent a rift with their counterparts in the B'nai B'rith, Countess contacted Hillel's national headquarters and asked if he could rename the group Hillel. Hillel officials agreed. Hillel: The Foundation for Jewish Campus Life, founded in 1923 at the University of Illinois, Champaign-Urbana, already had hundreds of campus chapters in the United States and abroad, but its leaders still considered UNLV and its relatively small Jewish student body too small for a formal chapter in 1975, though they let UNLV's students use the name anyway.

The Combined Jewish Appeal, later renamed the Jewish Federation, contributed its religion's share to the center's budget. In these early years, the federation staffed its Hillel office with a number of capable volunteers, including library technician Marta Sorkin, who managed the place for most of the 1980s. Only in the 1990s did Hillel finally establish a formal chapter at UNLV and assume control of the program. But it remains a student-led program, as it always has been. The activities, such as holiday celebrations, Torah readings, and trips, are conceived, planned, and implemented by student leaders under the supervision of paid Hillel staff.

Father Nowak, who had been a founding faculty member of Bishop Gorman

High School in 1954 and left town in the early 1960s to finish his doctorate in chemistry, had returned in the late 1960s to run the Newman Club. After helping to organize the effort to construct the center's new home, he managed the facility until his death in 1989. Nowak also taught chemistry and physics classes at UNLV for years, which made it even easier for students to relate to him and the center. He and Blankinship created a programming entity called the United Campus Ministry that signed a twenty-year, $1-a-year lease with the Diocese of Reno in 1975. But in 1995, just as the lease ran out, Pope John Paul II decided to split Nevada into two dioceses. In 1996 the newly installed bishop of Las Vegas, Daniel Walsh, announced plans to end the ecumenical ministry and create an enlarged Newman Club and perhaps even a parish on the site. As of 2005, negotiations were continuing with the Protestants and Hillel concerning the issue. The rapid development of UNLV over the past quarter of a century has complicated matters, since there is no more land on campus for these groups to build facilities of their own.

While organizations, both secular and religious, played a vital role in establishing a sense of community, so did student efforts to construct more buildings on the campus. From the beginning they were totally involved in this process. The purchase of land on Maryland Parkway for a campus in 1955 delighted students and their parents, many of whom attended the cornerstone-laying ceremony for the school's first building, on March 17, 1957. That fall, after the campus opened, the *Rebel Yell* reported that regents had designated Nevada Southern as a "college of the University of Nevada." The independent-minded rebels, however, had already begun referring to their school as a "university," even though it did not officially become one until 1965. Still, the *Rebel Yell* and Las Vegas newspapers often used the NSU acronym in 1950s stories about the school.

Although many residents followed the events on Maryland Parkway in the local newspapers and took pride in their new school, it would be a mistake to assume that all Las Vegans knew exactly where the campus was. Even several years after classes began, some residents still were unsure about the location of Nevada Southern. In one humorous incident, visitors from the Reno campus hopped into a Las Vegas cab and told the driver to take them to the "Rebel Hangout." As the student newspaper reported, "The cabbie immediately deposited them at the Colonial House Rebel Room, a popular cocktail lounge on the Strip."[3]

Building the campus soon became a priority, as enrollment swelled and classes in Maude Frazier Hall and later Archie C. Grant Hall quickly became crowded. Regents talked of building a gymnasium and in 1958 began planning for a "Science and Technology Building" (today's Lilly Fong Geoscience), but students knew these plans required funding by the governor and the state legislature. Political activism on campus in the 1950s never approached the fervor of the late 1960s and early 1970s, but gubernatorial and local legislative candidates frequently visited the young school and pledged their support.

This was the case when regent Grant Sawyer, who had backed Nevada Southern on numerous occasions, ran for governor in 1958. His campaign garnered widespread support on the Las Vegas campus and in the student newspaper. Even though Sawyer came from northern Nevada, everyone knew he would help the Las Vegas school. Much has been made, and rightly so, of northern Nevada officials' blocking or slowing the process of NSU/UNLV's development, but many northerners, like Sawyer, also helped the infant school. This group included regents, politicians, professors such as Eleanor Bushnell, who came down from the main campus to help start the political science program, and coaches like McGill natives Bill Ireland and Michael "Chub" Drakulich (the latter was born in Kimberly but grew up in McGill).

As administrators, faculty, and friends of Nevada Southern struggled to expand the new campus, students sought to enhance the sense of community in a variety of ways. First, they increased the number of annual events beyond the old Sno-Ball and other socials of the Las Vegas High era. With a campus of their own, student leaders expanded their yearly program to bring the school's community closer together. "University Day" began in March 1958. Sponsored by the THPO, the celebration featured a tug-of-war, cross-country races, a bonfire, and other contests pitting sophomores against freshmen.

THPO's plan was to boost campus morale by creating an event that would involve the entire Las Vegas community, which University Day did in the school's early years. Indeed, local politicians often participated in University Days (it became plural after 1960) and other events to show their support for the school. In 1962, for instance, Las Vegas mayor and gubernatorial candidate Oran Gragson attended the University Days behind the science and technology building, where the bonfire-building, egg-throwing, tug-of-war, and other contests took place. There were also booths for the Newman Club, fraternities, and other student organizations. In July 1967 Nevada Southern students challenged civic leaders to a tug-of-war. Holding the community's side of the rope were city commissioners Wes Howery, a resort executive, and prominent insurance broker Phil Mirabelli. Joining them were Sheriff Ralph Lamb, his brother and county commissioner Darwin Lamb, and state senator (and future U.S. senator) Chic Hecht, as well as assemblyman Frank Young and Clark County public administrator Phil Cummings.

Nevada Southern students also reached out to their community in other ways. The school's early theater or drama "department" (it was a "program" until the mid-1960s), led by Drs. Lauren Brink, Paul Harris, and later Jerry Crawford, played an important role in making the new school a cultural center for students and residents. As Crawford pointed out in a recent reminiscence, "In such a city as Las Vegas, theater was a natural discipline/art form for focus."[4] Beginning in 1959, students and faculty staged their plays at the 100-seat Little Theatre in room 125 of Grant Hall, until the Judy Bayley Theatre opened in 1972. In February 1960, for example, the school's drama students produced *She Stoops to Conquer*, which drew enthusiastic audiences. Nevada Southern offered several productions each year, posted on the college marquee along Maryland Parkway, which daily confirmed to residents the value of having a college in their town. In addition, a "Sunday Afternoon Music Matinee" on campus during the regular school year provided weekly entertainment for interested students and residents.

A variety of events and institutions bound members of the campus community closer together. Politics was one such activity. Elections for CSNS offices politicized the electorate, as students reviewed the issues in the *Rebel Yell*, printed fliers, and campaigned for friends. By 1960, Clark County even loaned CSNS some of its voting machines to facilitate the counting.

The *Rebel Yell* was a key source of information and cohesion. The newspaper regularly announced cheerleader tryouts, political club meetings, and even basketball practices, which all students were invited to attend. In fact, athletics functioned as another unifying activity. Although Nevada Southern had only a few teams to root for in the 1950s, there was plenty of intramural play within the student body. In February 1963, school officials announced that the athletic field (today the site of the Central Desert Complex) in front of the Gym would be finished in a few weeks. It subsequently hosted plenty of informal competition.

By the early 1960s, the campus took on a more conventional appearance and students found more rules being enforced. In March 1963, for instance, the superintendent of buildings announced that sidewalks connecting the Gym and the science building (Lilly Fong Geoscience) with Frazier and Grant halls would soon be finished. "When the sidewalks are completed," he warned, "there will be no excuses for students walking on the lawns. Tickets will be given to students caught walking on the lawns."[5]

Three years earlier, enrollment had grown sufficiently to warrant construction of the first student bookstore across Maryland Parkway. The on-campus bookstore did not arrive until 1968, when the student union opened. Nevertheless, students in 1960 were delighted. As one put it, "We no longer have to journey downtown for our books and supplies."[6] Even though they lacked a formal student union, Nevada Southern students had a gathering place. Between classes, they stepped out of the rear doorway of Maude Frazier Hall (the only building on campus in 1957) and onto a partly shaded patio, a roughly 50-by-50-foot area where students could relax. The Service League of Las Vegas furnished the space with chairs, tables, and some greenery. As the 1958 yearbook noted, "The colorful furniture was added with gay umbrellas and . . . some landscaping . . . to provide an informal gathering place for the students to study, discuss, and relax." Even after Maude Frazier Hall was converted to offices and large new buildings opened on campus for course offerings, students continued to head over to "the Patio" after class to play chess, strum the guitar, and converse. After the student union opened in 1968, President Zorn covered over the Patio on the west side of Maude Frazier Hall to provide more room for the registrar's office and its files.

As the 1960s wore on, CSNS began to expand the range of events being offered. Long before the opening of the Artemus W. Ham Concert Hall in 1976, students sponsored concerts in the Gym, often featuring well-known rock groups from the 1960s. In 1963 CSNS staged its largest show ever, drawing

3,000 students and residents for Peter, Paul, and Mary, whose hit song "Blowin' in the Wind" became a standard of the civil rights movement. The successful concert was a significant milestone for the student body. As the *Rebel Yell* asserted, "It proved that students here can work together harmoniously," and "that Nevada Southern is ready . . . for further events in the future to enrich the culture of its students and the general public."[7]

The school and student government also sponsored lectures almost twenty years before Marjorie Barrick endowed her prestigious namesake lecture series. CSNS regularly scheduled distinguished speakers to appear on campus. In November 1963, for example, novelist T. H. White spoke to a large audience. Almost from the beginning, the tiny campus in Las Vegas attracted prominent figures to its infant lecture series. In 1964, distinguished *New York Times* correspondent Harrison Salisbury appeared. NBC news anchor Chet Huntley, renowned anthropologist Margaret Mead, and other notables spoke on a makeshift stage in the Gym years before the student union ballroom became available. Later on that stage, in the 1970s, the students sponsored such distinguished speakers as Ralph Nader, Dick Gregory, and Germaine Greer.

In the 1960s students across the nation became immersed in national politics, and those at Nevada Southern were no exception. Although many went to meetings and protests sponsored by the local NAACP, others traveled out of state to learn more about the movement. In March 1964 Angela Davis spoke at Nevada Southern. Inspired by her rhetoric and other events, several students and faculty attended a civil rights conference at Pomona College in Claremont, California; others marched in Dixie and in troubled cities across the country to protest racial injustice.

Civil rights was a burning issue nationally and locally. In October 1964 President Lyndon Johnson addressed a rally at the Las Vegas Convention Center that included Nevada Southern students, many of whom were members of the Young Democrats. Several weeks later, the president won a mock election on

FACING PAGE:

TOP: PETER, PAUL, AND MARY CONCERT AT THE GYM, 1963. *EPILOGUE,* 1964

BOTTOM: NOTED ANTHROPOLOGIST MARGARET MEAD DELIVERS A LECTURE IN THE GYM, 1964. *EPILOGUE,* 1964

campus against his Republican opponent, Senator Barry Goldwater. But student support for the chief executive waned a year later when he committed American troops to widespread fighting in Vietnam. By 1965 President Johnson's escalating war finally sparked the first unrest on campus, as it did that same year at UC-Berkeley and dozens of other schools.

However, at Nevada Southern, at least initially, the faculty rather than the students pushed the issue. In November three professors circulated an antiwar petition among the faculty demanding a public debate on Johnson's policies. Later, history instructor Gary Roberts and Dr. Charles Sheldon, chair of the Division of Social Sciences, led a protest against administrative warnings not to violate the university code by veering off their courses' subject matter to discuss the war and other issues in class. In true C. Wright Mills fashion, Sheldon warned against using the university to "train students to be contented members of the establishment."[8] The political science professor ultimately resigned in disgust after the 1967 commencement. However, the school's Young Republicans immediately announced their staunch support of the war. CSNS president Tom Hribar was less emotional. He recognized the dissidents' right to conduct a debate, but he reaffirmed the student government's support of the president and its "Loot from Las Vegas" campaign to fund gifts for troops overseas.

This policy would soon change. A year later, CSNS sponsored a lecture by Frank Emspak, chair of the National Coordinating Committee to End the War in Vietnam. Debate over the war intensified following the election of Richard Nixon. The *Rebel Yell,* which in 1968 had condemned President Johnson for ending college draft deferrals, kept up a barrage of criticism in columns and cartoons denouncing President Nixon's war policies. In response to Nixon's decision to invade Cambodia in May 1970, the *Rebel Yell* urged students to "send your congressman a telegram for peace."[9]

Other issues also triggered protests in the 1960s. While Nevada Southern hardly approached the fever-pitch levels of protest evidenced at Berkeley, Harvard, and other radical campuses of the times, the local student body was not quiescent. Numerous issues attracted their attention. In March 1963, for example, students protested the effort by Las Vegas city attorney Sid Whitmore and a committee of concerned citizens to ban Henry Miller's best-selling *Tropic of Cancer* from bookstores and newsstands. In that same year, citing various

U.S. Supreme Court decisions limiting censorship, students also objected to the committee's efforts to exclude several magazines featuring nude women from local newsstands. In the end the censorship effort disintegrated, and Las Vegas continued its march toward the permissive secular culture that complemented its last-frontier image.

One issue, however, unified all students on the Las Vegas campus in the 1960s and 1970s. Student criticism relating to Vietnam and civil rights, though intense, paled in comparison to the consistently militant attacks on northern lawmakers, regents, and university officials for their foot-dragging approach to Nevada Southern's development. Despite some concern about the regents' reluctance in 1954 to build a campus and establish a full-fledged college in Las Vegas, there were no major attacks in the student newspaper or demonstrations. Governor Grant Sawyer (1958–66) eased concerns by supporting most of Nevada Southern's funding requests. In 1963 students applauded state support for a social science building, a dormitory, and a dining commons. At a special 1966 session of the state legislature, the governor successfully pushed funding for construction of what became Tonopah Hall and the Moyer Student Union.

By the mid-1960s, however, a series of issues symbolized growing student frustration over delays in building the campus. Discontent periodically yielded to anger. A typical example was the April 1965 student protest led by CSNS president Bill Daley at the site of today's Tonopah Hall. Students were furious at the three-year delay in starting construction. Some saw it as a conspiracy by the main campus to deprive Nevada Southern of out-of-state students and keep the place a commuter college. "They had the money for this dorm two years ago," Daley thundered, "and it does not look like they broke ground yesterday."[10] The vice president for financial affairs at the Reno campus, Neil Humphrey, acknowledged that the university again missed a promised deadline, but he attributed the delay to the failure of a federal housing loan agency to approve bonds for the project. The students, however, would not be put off. In May 1965 acting student body president Tom Hribar told regents that "students here are convinced that Nevada Southern has been receiving unfair and unjust treatment." Referring to the three-year wait for a dormitory and dining complex, he warned the board that "we have 1,500 students ready to march on the 'Strip' to protest this delay."[11]

NEVADA SOUTHERN STUDENTS REGISTERING FOR CLASSES AT
A MAKESHIFT TABLE, 1963. *EPILOGUE*, 1964

Nevada Southern students were proud of their school but impatient with the slow pace of its development, which they alternately blamed on the regents and on Reno campus officials. The *Rebel Yell* consistently led the charge. A 1965 column took University of Nevada president Charles Armstrong to task for his statement that Reno's programs first needed to be "finished" before they could be extended to Las Vegas. The editor characterized this as part of "the tradition of stalling funds for this campus." The priorities seemed obvious to the newspaper and its readers. "What this paper would like to know," the editor asked, "is how the northern shams can call a new football stadium, a chime system, and an intracampus TV setup essential when this campus is now in a desperate need of some landscaping, an addition to the science building, more space in the library, dorms, a dining facility, parking space, [and] a fine arts complex."[12]

Clearly, Las Vegas's need for a larger share of the university budget was a clarion call to students. In March 1965 four Nevada Southern students lobbied state legislators for more money. The *Review-Journal* characterized the effort as "a dismal failure." But, in a more hopeful vein, the newspaper noted that "perhaps our campus crusaders now have the knowledge of politics that will make the next move 'checkmate.' Let's hope so."[13]

An unfortunate snafu intensified the anger. In spring 1964 Nevada Southern graduated its first class, the so-called Centennial Class. But the joy, pride, and hoopla surrounding the first commencement slowly turned to cynicism as the summer and then autumn passed without any diplomas arriving from Reno. By December it had almost become a joke. An obviously embarrassed William Carlson tried to explain the delay, blaming it on the University of Nevada's need to print the degrees with a new boilerplate devoid of all references to the Reno campus and its mascot. But the damage had been done. Nevada Southern supporters viewed the incident as just another northern plot, and that conviction did little to ease tensions. The diplomas finally arrived in May 1965, a year late.

Tired of what they considered second-rate treatment, Nevada Southern students were determined to obtain the same facilities their counterparts in Reno had. In his 1965 campaign for the CSNS presidency, Tom Hribar called for a "vigorous drive for a student union" at Nevada Southern and "continued pressure on the Legislature, Board of Regents, and university officials for more favorable allocations to the NSU campus." Following his election, Hribar sought to form a "regent coalition" to secure more funding, but until 1971 northerners still constituted a majority of the board.[14] While some were more sympathetic to Nevada Southern's plight than others, budget allocations continued to favor the Reno campus. Still, there was progress. In November 1965 regents installed Donald Moyer as the Las Vegas campus's "chancellor," and his dedicated effort to increase funding and win total independence from the university at Reno would please Hribar and the students.

The frustration of Nevada Southern's students over what they considered Reno's excessive share of university programs and construction became apparent in October 1966 when CSNS announced plans to reapportion the board of regents. Inspired by Flora Dungan's successful 1965 action to force the reapportionment of the state legislature, which ultimately gave the more populated southern Nevada control, the students reasoned that the one-man, one-vote rule should also apply to the board, which was still controlled by northern Nevada.

CSNS president Jack Abell and Don Amair, president of the Young Democrats chapter on campus, led the movement to persuade Dungan, who was then running for an assembly seat, to ask the federal court to extend its ruling to Nevada's regents. Of course, both Moyer and Clark County's regents were publicly cool to the idea. Nevertheless, Abell pushed forward, telling the press: "Unlike university administrators with jobs to protect, and Regents from Southern Nevada who are interested in protecting their nebulous board harmony, students here are ready to take a stand on this issue which is vital to the welfare of the university."[15]

Concerned faculty members met with students to talk them out of the action. Dr. John Wright, founding member of the history department and a Nevada Southern professor since 1956, advised them to leave the reform to those not directly connected to Nevada Southern. Wright and his colleagues were blunt: If the effort failed and the board remained firmly in northern hands, retribution might result in budget cuts and other actions detrimental to the Las Vegas campus, its faculty, and its students. Clearly, they were right: The 1962 *Baker* v. *Carr* decision and similar rulings doomed the north's future control of the board. In 1971 the state legislature, now firmly in southern hands, redistricted the board according to population, and southern Nevada finally gained control. Even though student leaders temporarily backed off on their reapportionment plan in 1965, the issue died slowly. In 1966 Republican gubernatorial candidate Paul Laxalt opposed reapportioning the regents and instead favored giving the Las Vegas and Reno campuses separate budgets. CSNS leaders, however, were unimpressed by this proposal and petitioned the state legislature unsuccessfully to reapportion the board.

The regents also faced opposition from the Las Vegas educational community. The Clark County School District's board of trustees expressed its disappointment with the lack of graduate programs for local teachers at the Las Vegas campus. In the tradition of Maude Frazier, trustee Helen Cannon charged that "the problem of an inadequate university is common knowledge. The thing we are facing is a university president who refuses to recognize our needs." Fellow trustee Clare Woodbury was even more to the point: "The day NSU will grow and be recognized as it should be, is the day we have a reapportionment of the Board of Regents and get more southern support."[16]

Governor Sawyer was more sympathetic than some regents to Nevada Southern's plight. In December 1965 he toured the campus with Moyer to discuss the school's needs. At Sawyer's invitation, student leaders attended a luncheon later that day at the Desert Inn to air their views. In fall 1966, Sawyer published campaign advertisements in the *Rebel Yell* promising students that, if reelected, he would fight for more money for Nevada Southern. But Paul Laxalt won the election. The new governor immediately antagonized students on the Maryland Parkway campus by preparing an austere budget, one designed to, as he put it, "hold the line" on spending. In a rare miscue, the governor suggested to a reporter that his budget would not be enough to fund more growth at the Las Vegas campus. He tried to backtrack a few weeks later, but it was too little too late.

Many Nevada Southern students interpreted Laxalt's "hold the line" budget to mean that he would be little more than a conservative supporter of the Reno campus and an obstacle to the improvement of higher education in the state. Under Governor Sawyer, a friend of the campus, Nevada Southern had enjoyed eight relatively good years of growth; now the school would face a different regime. Laxalt's actions were a call to arms for student activists, who began to organize protests.

In February 1967 CSNS president Jack Abell, Mike Sloan, and others established SHAME (Students Helping to Assist and Maintain Education), an organization designed to lobby state legislators in the upcoming session. SHAME leaders also planned student boycotts of classes and scheduled

GOVERNOR PAUL LAXALT HANGING IN EFFIGY FROM ARCHIE GRANT HALL IN PLAIN VIEW OF PASSING MOTORISTS ON MARYLAND PARKWAY, 1967. *EPILOGUE*, 1967

meetings to dramatize the education crisis at Nevada Southern. They kicked off their campaign in grand style by hanging Governor Laxalt in effigy from Archie C. Grant Hall for all the students and motorists on Maryland Parkway to see. Abell also announced a campaign aimed at recalling several regents. While *Rebel Yell* editor Terry Lindberg's refusal to support the recall put the damper on that effort, he did endorse reapportionment of the board. "We're tired," Lindberg declared, "of always getting the 'short end of the stick' at Nevada Southern simply because of a mal-apportioned board, sympathetic to a homestanding Reno campus forever scheming to undercut and override NSU."[17] The editor particularly railed against the proposal to build a medical school on the Reno campus while Nevada Southern needed money for classrooms and other basic facilities. Lindberg complained in vain, "The northern regents had the power to railroad the issue through, while the southern regents—with fewer members and even fewer guts—were afraid to stand up and protest the obvious injustice."[18]

In April 1967 student leaders denounced Governor Laxalt for appointing Art Smith and Tom Bell as two new regents from southern Nevada after the reapportioned legislature enlarged the board and gave Clark County five of eleven members. Editor Lindberg pointed out that neither man had been on the list of candidates that students had compiled for the positions. He also charged that the governor had sent his brother, University of Nevada Press editor and occasional Reno professor Robert Laxalt, down to Las Vegas to persuade the men to serve. A year later, with strong student support, Nevada Southern alumnus and future congressman James Bilbray won a regent seat and became an influential voice on the board in behalf of his alma mater.

Students on the Maryland Parkway campus kept up the barrage of rhetoric and protest, and slowly the tide began to turn. Although in 1967 the newly reapportioned legislature was generous to Nevada Southern, students refused to credit Laxalt, whose original budget proposals they considered austere. Instead, they showered their affection upon southern Nevada's legislative delegation. In May CSNS leaders even organized a motorcade to honor those lawmakers who had supported the school's budget requests. The little parade began at the Greyhound bus station on Fremont Street and proceeded up Las Vegas Boulevard and the Strip to Flamingo Road and then to Maryland Parkway, with cheering residents occasionally lining the sidewalks. At Nevada Southern's front entrance, students staged a rally featuring the school's band and cheerleaders.

It was bad enough that some Nevada Southern departments had to turn away students for classes in 1966 and 1967, but when Governor Laxalt made a surprise appearance at a board of regents meeting in January 1968 to tell officials from both campuses that he would not approve additional funds for the current biennium, he incurred the wrath of Las Vegas students. In their view, Laxalt's conservative message that Nevadans should expect less from government and be more self-reliant posed a direct threat to the Las Vegas campus. As one senior, Tony Martin, wrote, continued low faculty salaries "raises serious doubts about the quality of instructors at Nevada Southern in the future." That's why many students supported the efforts of Moyer, Crawford, Zorn, and Baepler to raise salaries to the levels of comparable schools in the region. Students recognized the danger of underfunding higher education. As Martin pointed out, "Nevada [in 1968] spends only ten percent of its budget on education, less than Mississippi, and next to last in the nation."[19]

In his book on the history of the University of Nevada, James Hulse argues persuasively that Governor Laxalt tried to heal the strained relationship between the two campuses and that he supported increasing the university's bonding capacity to allow both schools to expand. But Laxalt's conservative budgets, devotion to low taxes, and support for expanding programs on the main campus, often at the expense of Nevada Southern's needs, antagonized students in Las Vegas. For Martin and others, it was a disgrace that a state whose resort economy was booming invested so little in the education of its youth. As the students on Maryland Parkway saw it, Laxalt's policies were a greater menace to Nevada Southern's progress than the university in Reno because, as Martin put it, "when you're fighting for meager funds from the state, there is bound to be bullying of the smaller, less powerful campus in a two-campus system."[20]

In spring 1968 activists formed STRUD (Students to Remove Upstate Domination) in support of Chancellor Moyer's efforts to pry Nevada Southern away from northern control. In addition to planning an "autonomy demonstration" at the state Republican Party convention, the group encouraged the student body to help draft a proposal again asking state

CONGRESSMAN, REGENT, ALUMNI PRESIDENT, AND NSU GRADUATE JAMES BILBRAY. SPECIAL COLLECTIONS, UNLV LIBRARIES 0062-1806

STUDENTS PROTEST BEFORE A REGENTS' MEETING IN THE
STUDENT UNION, DECEMBER 1968. *EPILOGUE*, 1968

legislators to reapportion the board of regents. They also wanted lawmakers to create separate university administrations for the state's Las Vegas and Reno campuses.

Reno's efforts to get a medical school only intensified the conflict and strengthened STRUD's hand. Nevada Southern students could not understand how the regents and university officials could spare any money for such an expensive facility when the Las Vegas campus still needed classrooms. Later, in February 1969, Nevada Southern alumni, including regent James Bilbray, blasted the efforts of the university's former vice president for fiscal affairs and now chancellor, Neil Humphrey, to obtain funding for a medical school in Reno.

Both campuses, however, supported passage of Question 2 in the 1968 general election, as did Governor Laxalt. The proposition would have increased Nevada's bonding capacity to allow more money for the construction of state facilities, including university buildings. But Nevada voters rejected the question and, in a wave of conservative feeling, helped elect Richard Nixon president. Student activists viewed the Republican victory and the defeat of Question 2 as support for more spending cuts.

On election night in November 1968, James Bilbray defeated Paul McDermott for a regent's seat. After McDermott resigned the next day, Governor Laxalt immediately appointed Bilbray to take his seat. Bilbray wasted no time before antagonizing his colleagues on the board. In his first meeting, he moved, but failed get a second, to remove Neil Humphrey as chancellor of the university. Next he complained publicly that the regents typically held two meetings—the first was a private one at someone's house where the real discussion of agenda

IN 1968 NEVADA SOUTHERN STUDENTS SUPPORTED ALUMNUS AND REGENT JAMES BILBRAY AND OPERATION LAZARUS, AS THESE SIGNS HANGING FROM THE STUDENT UNION INDICATE. *EPILOGUE,* 1969

items took place, and the second was the public meeting in which the board moved swiftly and politely through the agenda. While his objection raised eyebrows in the north, it received sympathetic treatment in the *Review-Journal* and the *Sun*.

By the time regents came to Las Vegas for their December 13 meeting at the Moyer Student Union, the atmosphere was electric. Governor Laxalt, who was scheduled to discuss higher education funding in the next biennium, wisely sent his budget director instead. More than 200 students attended the meeting, in which regents did little to calm the mood on campus. Besides agreeing to formally consider the proposed medical school for the Reno campus at their next meeting, regents also discussed the need to scale back the size of NSU's performing arts center for lack of money and rejected a proposal by the school's male dormitory students to allow women visitors in their rooms at any hour of the day. None of these actions pleased students in the gallery. Outside, activists hanged Governor Laxalt (for the second time in two years) and the regents in effigy from the second floor of the student union. And protesters, seeking to raise faculty salaries to discourage the annual resignations of talented professors, marched in front of the building and in the lobby.

While student activists regarded most of the regents as adversaries, they considered Governor Laxalt their chief villain. In December the *Rebel Yell* openly mocked him, referring to the governor as "Uncle Wiggly" for what students considered his shifting stands on higher education—seeming to support Nevada Southern when in Las Vegas, but acting differently when in Carson City. As one columnist remarked, "Compared to the north, he treats us like Mohicans." Students later picketed the governor when he visited the campus, holding placards on the stairs of the student union as Laxalt walked up to speak in the ballroom. Three months later, the newspaper's headlines read, "Uncle Wiggly Cuts UNLV Budget," after the governor, concerned about a potential state deficit, trimmed his higher education budget with across-the-board cuts.[21]

They also staged new protests. Having joined SHAME, STRUD, and SPA (Students for Political Action) to protest the lack of funding, Nevada Southern's students employed another tactic. They erected a shantytown of oil drums, scrap board, and lumber, and sympathetic professors taught classes there for a week. Built on the site of today's Frank and Estella Beam Hall and called "Education

EDUCATION CITY, PART OF THE OPERATION LAZARUS PROTEST
ON THE SITE OF TODAY'S FRANK AND ESTELLA BEAM HALL,
1969. *EPILOGUE*, 1969

City" by some students and "Tumbleweed Tech" by others, the place boasted
numerous protest placards with such messages as "Thank You, Voters" and
"Does This Mean Our Wants Are More Than Our Needs?" As historian Robert
Daven-port noted, the students also established "Operation Lazarus." In a
parody of the biblical story in which Lazarus begged for crumbs off the rich
man's table, in this campaign NSU students, sometimes clad in rags, begged
state legislators, who ostensibly represented the interests of Nevada's elite, to
increase funding for NSU during the 1969 legislative session. Supporting the
students in these efforts were a number of professors, including historian John
Wright, who was incensed by the defeat of Question 2 and the actions of the
regents. In a meeting with students, the normally reserved Wright surprised
activists when he denounced the draft, the Vietnam War, and the university administration, and urged students to stage a sit-down protest. It was in the midst

of this tumult that the northern-dominated board of regents agreed to rename
Nevada Southern UNLV—at the same January 11, 1969, meeting in which they
voted to seek state authorization and funding for the controversial medical
school in Reno.

In the 1960s, civil rights marches, antiwar protests, and the struggle against
northern domination reinforced an activist spirit among students on the Maryland Parkway campus that extended to other issues, such as faculty termina-
tions for nonpublication, forced residence in the dormitory, and even higher
book prices. In February 1968 the student newspaper denounced the school's
bookstore for charging students "an exorbitant amount for necessary texts" and
instituting draconian policies that mandated no returns or refunds.[22] Students

NSU'S MARQUEE INVITES THE LAS VEGAS COMMUNITY TO THE
STUDENTS' EDUCATION CITY PROTEST. *EPILOGUE,* 1969

fought these measures by threatening boycotts, and eventually the store manager capitulated.

At times, students also challenged campus administrators. For example, African American students in Tonopah Hall objected to what they regarded as harassment in the residence hall. In particular, they resented unscheduled inspections of their quarters by Mrs. Louis Macintosh, the officious dormitory manager, who was fond of spot-checking rooms for cleanliness. Complaints also increased about living arrangements for black athletes from out of state, who, having been recruited by Nevada Southern's football and other athletic programs, had to live in the residence hall, but often on separate floors. In November 1968 interim president Baepler attempted to resolve some of these issues by agreeing to suspend the inspections and by allowing athletes to live together on the third floor.

White students also clashed with the administration over the school's housing regulations. In 1969 Bruce Adams and other activists objected to a rule that required students under the age of twenty-one not residing with their parents or relatives to live in Tonopah Hall. Students argued that some unattached men and women preferred to live off campus in nearby apartments. In one incident, assistant dean Paul Schofield spoke with friends of a coed who told him that she was living off campus. Schofield confirmed this with her landlord and threatened her with expulsion if she did not move into Tonopah Hall. Adams met with Vice President Baepler to complain: "You are still using the paternalistic attitude that this university's been operating under since it started." And he demanded, "It's time we changed."[23]

Baepler was adamant, telling Adams that Schofield, who was in charge of "student affairs" and therefore Tonopah Hall, was "just doing his job."[24] The vice president explained that because UNLV was paying off its dormitory construction bonds with student room and board fees, he had to fill Tonopah Hall with students. School administrators had no intention of changing the rules: Out-of-state students had to pay off the residence hall built to house them. However, Baepler conceded that administrators would respect student rights. He later urged a liberalization of the school's code of conduct and a relaxation of rules respecting the complete separation of male and female students in the dormitories. "The authoritarian role," Baepler told regents, "must give way to one of cooperation and service."[25]

To deal with residence hall problems, students had earlier organized men's and women's dormitory associations, each with its own president and governing board elected by those living in Tonopah Hall. Baepler worked with these organizations and CSUN to liberalize some of the school's housing policies. For their part, students drafted a ten-page set of guidelines and established a seven-member student board to resolve conflicts in Tonopah Hall.

Of course, the 1960s at Nevada Southern were not all about protests and complaints. Students also had much to cheer about, because they eventually got all the buildings they sought. Trailers had always been part of Nevada Southern's landscape, and in September 1967 students returned to find ten more trailers, seven for the school's thirty-three new faculty and three housing science laboratories. Faculty looked forward to the construction of new buildings, because the trailer accommodations were "pretty grim," with partitioned desk space. In the new buildings, like Wright Hall, professors at last got their own private offices with bookcases and filing cabinets while dozens of new classrooms eased crowding.

Aside from finally getting a residence hall (Tonopah), students also got a student union. In spring 1966 Chancellor Moyer urged construction of the student facility: "At present, there is no single place on campus that students can claim as strictly their own. They need a common meeting place and other facilities strictly for students and designed to enhance life here."[26] President Armstrong also agreed that the time had come, and the board of regents agreed as well. In September the first drawings of the proposed building appeared in the *Rebel Yell,* and in 1968 the facility opened, finally liberating students from the blistering heat and the dusty, cramped quarters of the patio behind Maude Frazier Hall.

Clearly, Nevada Southern's development owed a lot to the men and women enrolled there. In these early decades, students did not just go to class; they were a political force that helped build the school. They pressured regents in ways that administrators and even community leaders could not, to construct buildings, to get an increased share of budgets, and even to shape policy on the Las Vegas campus. Students demanded services, sponsored debates, ran concerts, threatened the bookstore, obtained and then managed their own student union, worked and fought with administrators, and formed political organizations, religious clubs, fraternities, sororities, honor societies, and dozens of other groups to enhance the sense of community on campus.

Even former students got involved. When James Bilbray campaigned for a seat on the board of regents, alumni enlisted the support of current students to run a campaign that ended in victory. Students also worked to create today's alumni association. In May 1965 Nevada Southern graduates Bilbray, Bob Schnider, and future state treasurer Stan Colton, all former CSNS presidents, announced plans to establish an alumni association. Bilbray, the 1959 student body president and by 1965 a deputy district attorney for Clark County, had pushed the idea and drafted the necessary documents, with help from later district court judge Addeliar "Dell" Guy. At the first meeting attended by Colton, Pat Whipple (NSU's second female student body president), and other former CSNS officers, the members elected Bilbray president. He served from 1965 to 1968, after which Ben Knowles (1968–70), Stan Colton (1970–72), and Dave Stevenson (1972–74) held the office.

In 1973 President Baepler appointed tennis coach Fred Albrecht as executive director of alumni relations, a position he held for more than three decades. Under his guidance the association expanded its activities. Also in 1973, when future state senator Bob Coffin became the association's president, the board of directors voted to award $50 book scholarships. Despite the young organization's relative lack of funds, the awards began in fall 1974. In 1978 alumni association president Nancy Galyean and the board decided to establish annual awards to recognize meritorious faculty, alumni, and members of the community whose achievements merited honor. Bilbray won the first Outstanding Alumnus Award and history professor John Wright won the first Outstanding Faculty Award. In an effort to influence policy, the association encouraged some of its members to run for office. Along with Bilbray, who later served three terms in the U.S. House of Representatives, congresswoman and former regent Shelley Berkley, and state senators Bob Coffin and Ray Rawson were just a few of the alumni who won elective office and helped the school.

As the 1970s began, the politics of state support for UNLV continued to motivate alumni and students, as did the Vietnam War and civil rights. By the late 1960s, as the crusading Donald Moyer gave way to Baepler and then Zorn, antiwar, pro–civil rights, and anti-regent passions became more intense. For the most part the school's presidents handled it well. The Vietnam War controversies lingered until American troops left that country in 1973. In April 1971 the *Yell* (formerly the *Rebel Yell*) printed a full-page advertisement urging students everywhere to boycott classes on May 1 to commemorate the first anniversary of those shot by National Guardsmen at Kent State and later by police at Jackson State College in Mississippi. Earlier, in March, the newspaper reported a peaceful march down the Strip to expose the plight of the poor in Las Vegas. UNLV students participated in the procession, which was led by civil rights activist Ralph Abernathy and actress Jane Fonda.

But the war gradually overtook civil rights as the major issue on campus in the early 1970s, even though many UNLV students either supported the war or had no opinion about it. There was certainly no lack of speakers on the campus. In October 1971 future U.S. senator John Kerry spoke at an antiwar rally at UNLV attended by then student body president Shelley Levine (later Congresswoman Shelley Berkley) and hundreds of students. Years later, in 2004, Berkley and Kerry would again meet at a rally near the campus during the senator's presidential campaign.

In 1972 antiwar activist and renowned baby doctor Benjamin Spock attacked the war while *National Review* publisher William Rusher supported it. Most speakers, however, opposed the conflict, including Democratic vice presidential candidate Sargent Shriver, Senator Wayne Morse of Oregon, and Daniel Ellsberg, the central figure in the Pentagon Papers controversy of 1971.

The school newspaper kept students informed about speakers, protests, and related issues, including occasional regent efforts to police student protests. In particular, the paper monitored regent discussions in 1970–71 about toughening the university's code of conduct for students in the wake of "major disturbances" on the Reno campus. For the most part, university regents, like many older Americans, supported the Vietnam War and opposed what they considered unpatriotic student activism.

While most of the regent-student conflict on this issue centered at UNR, the regents managed to inflame many UNLV students in 1971 when, at the height of antiwar feeling, the board discussed establishing an ROTC program on the Las

STUDENT BODY PRESIDENT SHELLEY LEVINE BERKLEY
DELIVERS A SPEECH AT UNLV 'S COMMENCEMENT, 1972.
SHELLEY BERKLEY

Vegas campus. Although southern Nevada regents Bilbray and Helen Thompson voted against it, Paul McDermott did not, and the measure passed. The *Yell* editor could hardly restrain his anger. "Some of us still retain the mental scars of the events of May 4, 1970 [at Kent State], and if that wasn't enough to make your blood curdle, then how about the military surveillance programs of students [and] professors?"[27] After much debate and lobbying, regents wisely postponed their ROTC plans for UNLV until the Vietnam War ended. The passage of time slowly healed the wounds. UNLV's program finally began long after the war's 1973 cease-fire. Years later, in 2005, the Harter administration, after seven years of effort, brought an Air Force ROTC unit to UNLV, which seemed appropriate for a metropolis that had hosted one of the service's largest bases for sixty years.

Civil rights was another popular issue on campus in the 1970s. Students activists like Bruce Adams marched to protest local discrimination against minorities in housing, education, and jobs, occasionally risking arrest. At the same time, the increasingly radical civil rights movement and the 1968 assassinations of Martin Luther King Jr. and Robert Kennedy combined to increase black student militancy across the nation and at UNLV. Unlike the University of Alabama, Ole Miss, and many other segregated public universities, Nevada Southern had always been open to all students, but it was not immune from controversy. Minority students, for instance, objected to the school's traditional Confederate mascot, Beauregard the Rebel Wolf, although the school's colors—gray matched the Confederate uniform and scarlet the Confederate flag—drew less attention.

In November 1970, African American student activist Bert Babero Jr., the son of a UNLV faculty member, wrote a column in the *Rebel Yell* that questioned UNLV's Rebel nickname and identity. While acknowledging that students adopted it in the mid-1950s "to be simply symbolic of the separation of the students of southern Nevada from the students at northern Nevada and the formation of a separate university," Babero argued that the Las Vegas campus had accomplished that goal. Moreover, when white students first decided upon the mascot, "Black opinion was a subject of little concern to most non-Blacks."[28] After all, Rosa Parks's courageous refusal to sit in the back of a Montgomery bus and Martin Luther King's decision to head that city's bus boycott had occurred in late 1955 and early 1956, just as regents were formalizing plans for building the Maryland Parkway campus.

At the time, he conceded, civil rights was not the pressing issue that it became after 1957. Confederate Cotillions, the Rebel Wolf insignia, and other vague references to the Old South passed without much notice among the Nevada Southern students at Las Vegas High and later on the Maryland Parkway campus. But, as Babero noted, times had changed. Explaining that for African Americans the term *Rebel* bore racist connotations, he insisted that "to expect black people to love and glorify the Confederacy, to wear a Confederate flag or applaud a Confederate wolf defies all logic. It's like asking a Jew to wear a swastika."[29]

His column inspired numerous letters to the editor and much debate on campus, including calls for changing the name of the *Rebel Yell,* which the newspaper did a month later, becoming the *Yell* in the December 11, 1970, issue. In April 1971 the editor commemorated the newspaper's sixteenth year of "continuous service" by reprinting an April 1955 column from the first edition in which the founding editor, Lydia Malcom, explained the rationale for choosing the newspaper's name. "We feel that *Rebel Yell* is an appropriate name," she declared, "because Nevada Southern students are often called Rebels."[30] But the Confederate mascot lingered.

In September 1973 the student newspaper supported efforts to drop the Rebel name and urged the adoption of a new mascot for the school. As the editor recognized, "The year is 1973. Plenty has happened to the country in the last eighteen years . . . much has taken place at the Southern Regional Division. For one thing, the school has a different name—UNLV. It is no longer a step-child, but a strong autonomous university." Aside from UNLV, only the University of Mississippi still used the rebel mascot. To reinforce his point, the editor even invoked the prospect of Jerry Tarkanian making UNLV a nationally ranked team. Now, declared the editor, UNLV's "athletic teams—basketball in particular—are about to carry its name throughout the households of America. . . . The Rebels in Nevada are about to become famous." But, he added, "the name—today—no longer rings true. The 'Rebel' belongs to a different era." The logic was inescapable; "Beauregard, decked out in his gray symbolism," had to go. "We believe," the editor insisted, that "it is time [that] the university and its athletic mascot reflect a national image which is meaningful to our era and not insulting to our black brothers and sisters."[31] Jerry Tarkanian personally supported a change of mascots, as the Confederate Beauregard made it increasingly difficult for him to recruit good African American athletes to UNLV.

With President Baepler's encouragement, the CSUN Senate voted to amend its constitution and change the government's name from the "Confederated Students of the University of Nevada" to the "Consolidated Students of the University of Nevada." In 1976 the students voted to eliminate the wolfish-looking Beauregard mascot from all of their events, although the image is still embedded in the hardwood floor of the original Gym (today's Marjorie Barrick Museum). The school's new mascot evolved from a Revolutionary War, musket-bearing rebel soldier in the 1970s to the long-mustached cartoon Rebel known as "Hey Reb" in the 1980s. Today the musket is gone along with all the trappings of 1776.

There was also strong support for dropping the Rebel name. In January 1971 the student senate put the issue to a vote of all the students in a special-initiative

1974-75 • 1977-82

1976

1983-96

1997-PR

UNLV MASCOTS, 1957–2006. UNLV ATHLETICS
DEPARTMENT

election, and they voted 446–246 to retain the Rebel name. But pressure built to change it. By September 1973 virtually everyone had a suggestion for a better nickname. Tarkanian favored the "Stars"; football coach Ron Meyer argued for the "Big Horn Rams"; athletics director Bill Ireland preferred "Rebel Express"; and alumni director Fred Albrecht favored the "Nuggets." Others championed the "A-Bombs," the "Silver Streakers," the "Sand Burners," the "Superstars," the "Elk Stags," and the "Heaters." But none won the hearts of the entire campus community.

Although UNLV dropped its Confederate mascot, the school's colors and the Rebel nickname endured. After all, "rebel" stood for much more than a supporter of the Civil War against the Union. In the 1960s especially, it symbolized those who rejected convention, tradition, racism, and even the Vietnam War. Most of all, in southern Nevada it stood for those who had opposed northern domination in the state legislature and unwanted dependency upon Reno. The word was simply too generic to refer only to the Confederacy, and African American students, content with changing the *Yell*'s title, the school's mascot, CSUN's name, and other trappings of the Old South, were amenable to leaving the "rebel" issue and the school colors alone.

While civil rights continued to be a widely discussed issue on campus, growing enforcement of the Civil Rights Act of 1964, the Voting Rights Act of 1965, and the integration of Las Vegas schools in 1971, along with passage that same year of Nevada's open housing law to end residential segregation, helped ease concerns. However, African American students continued to press for more minority-oriented courses and instructors and complained about crowding in Tonopah Hall and other policies that they considered discriminatory. In the early 1970s, African American students formed the Black Student Union, a sponsored CSUN organization. Under the leadership of future Las Vegas attorney and district court judge Lee Gates, the group was very active on campus. It organized a series of events geared to minority students, including book displays, lectures, and cultural exhibits, especially in February during Black History Month, to commemorate the contributions of African Americans to the United States.

Although they were initially less active than their African American counterparts, UNLV's Hispanic students began to organize as well. In 1973 they formed La Raza of UNLV, which met once a week on campus. Its purpose was "to create self awareness among the Spanish-speaking students within the community and university."[32] The organization operated out of the student union and sponsored lectures, exhibits, speakers, and other programs highlighting the accomplishments of Cesar Chavez, as well as other public leaders, artists, and craftsmen.

Women also became more of a force on campus in the 1970s. In August 1973 concerned students organized a chapter of the National Organization for Women (NOW), which began scheduling gender-equity workshops and monthly meetings. Later, it supported the effort to put the Equal Rights Amendment on Nevada's ballot. In 1978 the issue appeared as an advisory question, but the student effort fell short as Nevada voters rejected the measure by a decisive 2–1 margin.

Increasingly, women students at UNLV asked for classes emphasizing the role of women in politics and history beyond the usual coverage of gender in sociology and psychology courses. They also requested better school services for married and single mothers trying to attend classes. Several CSUN actions on behalf of women antedated the local NOW chapter. In spring 1971, two years before the U.S. Supreme Court upheld the right of abortion in *Roe* v. *Wade,* CSUN established a birth control and abortion information center in the student union. That fall, CSUN borrowed $3,000 to create a day-care center for married students with children across Maryland Parkway at the United Methodist church. In fall 1973 CSUN responded by moving its day-care center to the first floor of Tonopah Hall. Several years later, the facility moved to a more permanent home, behind the William D. Carlson Education Building, where primary school majors could earn college credit supervising and teaching the children.

Many of these reforms can be attributed to female student senators. Certainly the accession of Shelley (Levine) Berkley to the CSUN presidency in 1971 helped implement some of these changes benefiting women and other minority students. In April 1971 Levine ran for vice president in the CSUN student elections. She adopted a liberal platform that included "giving the minorities on campus a larger voice in policy."[33] Levine had some political experience, having already served on UNLV's Intercollegiate Athletics Council. Ever an advocate of more democracy, she championed the cause of encouraging more students to participate in planning CSUN-sponsored concerts and lectures. Although Levine did not receive an endorsement from the school newspaper, she won the vice presidential election. Shortly thereafter, she became student body president when UNLV suspended the duly elected president, Ron Kent, for academic reasons.

By the late 1970s the major battles were over. American troops had long since departed Vietnam. Thanks to the passage of civil rights legislation, racial discrimination, though still alive and well, was no longer the burning issue it had been. And UNLV, while certainly not funded on a par with UNR, had nevertheless become a full-fledged university with money to finance enough new construction, faculty hiring, and programmatic expansion to satisfy students.

Moreover, a new generation of students came to campus in the late 1970s and 1980s, bred in modest comfort and coming of age in the Reagan era, a time that was more prosperous and conservative than previous decades. In an article on student life at UNLV, alumnus and now director of UNLV-TV Laurie Fruth called the decade from 1978 to 1988 "the Party Years." Gone were the old Sno-Ball galas and cotillions of NSU's early days; the sheer size of UNLV's student body and its diverse interests made university-wide dances impractical in the 1980s. Indeed, the school's yearbook, *Epilogue,* went from a print format to a video in the late 1980s before ceasing publication altogether. But as Fruth explained, new events in the late 1970s and early 1980s, like Oktoberfest and Mardi Gras, brought large numbers of students together. Oktoberfest, held in the fall, featured beer-chugging contests in front of the student union, as well as the entertaining antics of the Fox. Mardi Gras, in the spring, was a throwback to the old University Days celebration with pie-eating, lip-syncing competitions, and the more risqué wet T-shirt, hot-legs, and best-body contests. In addition, CSUN annually commandeered the parking lot east of the student union for its carnival rides.

By the mid-1980s, however, enthusiasm for these activities had begun to wane. A variety of factors, including the growing influence of the national women's movement, led faculty and students to raise questions about the sexist aspects of the wet T-shirt contests and other hijinks. At the same time, administrators and faculty became increasingly concerned about the widespread use of alcohol and the hedonistic behavior that these events encouraged. In 1988

UNLV adopted new policies that strictly limited the consumption of alcohol on campus.

By the late 1980s Oktoberfest had begun to give way to Unityfest, a one-day festival that celebrated diverse cultures, foods, and traditions. In the 1990s, the Spring Fling, which replaced the old Mardi Gras, and an occasional rock concert on a Friday or Saturday night became the new events that brought students together. As Fruth has noted, Homecoming, with its floats and elected kings and queens, was the only event that survived—helped along after 1980 by tailgate parties in the Silver Bowl parking lot.

In these later decades, students still became members of fraternities and sororities and voted in CSUN elections. Like their predecessors of earlier decades, they joined a dizzying variety of clubs and organizations and continued to follow world events. They staged drives to raise awareness for such issues as AIDS and starvation in Third World countries, protested harassment by campus police at century's end, packed a service honoring the victims of the September 11 attacks, and raised thousands of dollars for tsunami victims in 2004–05. But the enormous size of the student body and the growth of night classes made it increasingly difficult to organize large numbers of students as CSUN had in earlier decades.

In 2002, however, the Harter administration took steps to remedy the problem by proposing a massive expansion of student facilities—much to the delight of CSUN officials. In 2003–05, numerous CSUN leaders and ordinary student volunteers worked tirelessly on various committees with architects, school administrators, and others to construct a greatly enlarged student union and a new recreational center for themselves and the generations of students to come. The groundbreaking ceremony, attended by President Harter, former president Moyer, former student body president Shelley Berkley, current CSUN president Henry Schuck, and hundreds of students and staff, took place on March 30, 2005. Scheduled to open in 2007 (part of the new student union opened in August 2006) and financed largely by the fees of all UNLV students, these new buildings undoubtedly will promote more mass interaction and a sense of community as the campus begins its next fifty years.

CHAPTER TEN

Donors and Foundations

Students may not immediately appreciate the pivotal role that donors have played in shaping UNLV's development over the past fifty years. After all, it is a public university supported by millions of dollars from Nevada's higher education budget. Certainly, public funds maintain the campus, provide for utilities, hire professors, and buy books for the library. But private money has also been vital.

The school's buildings and programs are the most obvious manifestation of donor generosity through the years. While some facilities, like Archie C. Grant Hall, have been erected almost totally with state funds, many others owe their existence partly or completely to philanthropy. These include Thomas T. Beam Engineering, the Lied Library, the Stan Fulton Building (housing the International Gaming Institute), the Donald Reynolds Student Services Building, and the Earl E. Wilson Baseball Stadium. Aside from buildings, private funds have also built an endowment for the William S. Boyd School of Law, the Greenspun College of Urban Affairs, the Jean Nidetch Women's Center, the William F. Harrah College of Hotel Administration, the Howard R. Hughes College of Engineering, and other institutions within the university.

From its earliest days, Nevada Southern benefited greatly from private giving. In the beginning donations were usually small, sometimes just $10 or maybe a few books for the library. The donors were, for the most part, ordinary Las Vegans. As William Carlson once noted, the Strip resorts and downtown casinos gave relatively little even after the campus opened in 1957. Not until the hotel program's debut in the mid-1960s did Las Vegas's gaming industry begin making major contributions. That was not true of the regular business community. From the beginning, Archie Grant and others who profited from Las Vegas's resort and defense industries gave their time, expertise, and money to help the fledgling school.

As early as 1955, the Las Vegas business community used the foundation concept as a tool to raise funds privately. In that year, Grant and others formed the Nevada Southern Campus Fund to purchase land from Estelle Wilbourn and her husband after state legislators required it as a condition for financing the campus's first building. Ten years later, President Donald Moyer recognized the importance of establishing a land foundation to acquire property around the existing campus to allow for future expansion. As President Leonard Goodall declared in his 1982 State of the University address, "Urban-based campuses often find themselves land-locked long before their period of growth and expansion is over." Then, in a tip of the hat to Moyer, Goodall acknowledged that "thanks to those who had the vision and foresight to create the Land Foundation, UNLV was saved from that fate."[1]

Goodall established today's UNLV Foundation. Impressed by the success of the school's land foundation and having seen how such organizations generated money in colleges across the country, he issued the order to create a major fund-raising operation at UNLV. In October 1980 UNLV assistant general counsel and endowment officer Lyle Rivera announced that a new foundation would soon be established to seek contributions as a "supplement," not a substitute, for state funds. At the time, Nevada was experiencing an economic slowdown resulting from the national recession and competition from Atlantic City's casinos. A series of disasters affecting Nevada's casinos made matters worse: The August 1980 bombing of Harvey's Hotel-Casino at Lake Tahoe required the complete rebuilding of that resort; the massive fire at the first MGM Grand (today Bally's) in November 1980 closed that property for nine months; and the Las Vegas Hilton blaze in February 1981 shut down that hotel for several weeks. Also creating a pinch were the conservative spending policies of Republican governor Robert List and his 1981 tax reform, which shifted Nevada's revenue emphasis from the reliable state property tax to the more volatile sales tax. The latter relied more heavily on tourism, which waned during the late 1970s and early 1980s.

In explaining the new foundation's purpose, Rivera noted that a board of trustees composed of eighteen local business leaders "will play a major role in coordinating and encouraging the university's endowment and gift-giving programs."[2] Since only the regents could legally accept gifts for UNLV, the founda-

IRWIN MOLASKY. UNLV FOUNDATION

tion would serve as their administrative arm for this activity, responsible for gift acknowledgment, tax receipts, and accounting services for all contributions.

At its first meeting, in 1981, the foundation's board of trustees elected prominent developer Irwin Molasky as chair. Serving as vice chairs were former governor Grant Sawyer, cofounder of the state's largest law firm and still a behind-the-scenes political power, and Claudine Williams, president of the Holiday Casino (today Harrah's) and cofounder of the American Bank of Commerce (now Nevada Commerce Bank). The foundation's treasurer was Valley Bank chair Ken Sullivan. UNLV vice president for administration Brock Dixon served as secretary, and Rivera was the board's chief advisor.

The board itself was a who's who of prominent Las Vegas business leaders and professionals. It included Marjorie Barrick, attorney and developer Art Ham Jr., developer Ernest Becker, Cadillac-Caterpillar dealer James Cashman Jr., attorney and longtime UNLV supporter George Dickerson, Coast resorts founder Michael Gaughan, and Jerry Herbst of the Terrible Herbst Oil Company (later Terrible's Hotel and Casino and convenience store chain). Also on

ART HAM JR., EARLY 1990S. UNLV FOUNDATION

the board were Southwest Gas president William Laub, Parry Thomas and Jerry Mack of Valley Bank, Nevada Savings and Loan CEO Sherman Miller, R & R Advertising president Sig Rogich, businessman and attorney Louis Wiener, and Tom Wiesner, president of Wiesner Investment Company.

The first board created categories of honor to encourage large donations. Members of the President's Associates, for instance, were those who gave $1,000–$5,000 or more to the campus, or insurance policies, or deferred gifts of $15,000. As one foundation publication explained, "The President's Associates stimulates active interest and participation of alumni and friends in the affairs of the university and forms a group to whom the president can turn for assistance and counsel."[3]

In 1982 Burke "Buck" Deadrich became the foundation's first director. Molasky and his eighteen-member board of locally prominent trustees chose Deadrich, who was at the time the director of the Washington State University Foundation. During the next four years Deadrich helped to mold the organization into a major fund-raising institution.

In the foundation's start-up phase, the board of trustees took the lead in establishing a donor base. Later, it charged Deadrich and the staff with "broadening" that base. The 1983 development campaign plan was "expected to create a new supporting constituency" for the foundation by expanding the board to include representatives "from many of the areas of the Las Vegas community." The trustees recognized the importance of recruiting new blood, as Las Vegas's spiraling growth expanded local elites. Under the new criteria, membership on the board would no longer be offered just to longtime contributors. Instead, the trustees agreed to invite new members, not only to honor them for their substantial gifts but also "according to their ability to attract and provide leadership and funding for the foundation's goals and objectives."[4]

Typical was the case of Thomas T. Beam, a Las Vegas builder and land developer who donated $1 million to endow scholarships in business, hotel administration, and engineering. In 1983, as Frank and Estella Beam Hall prepared to open, the trustees invited Beam to join their board. As one member declared, "Mr. Beam's generosity and concern for UNLV exemplify the spirit that is central to the very nature of our mission."[5] Beam's selection would pay further dividends. Once the builder became part of the effort to establish an engineering

TOM WEISNER AT THE SILVER BOWL. UNLV FOUNDATION

school at UNLV, his enthusiasm grew, and he soon helped to fund the Thomas T. Beam Engineering Building to house the program.

Creating an engineering school, an expensive item by any standard, was one reason why Goodall started the foundation. He intended to use the program's faculty to help Las Vegas attract new industry to the valley. It would, he believed, induce local business to support the foundation. After acknowledging that the early 1980s were "not the best environment for soliciting support," Goodall nevertheless argued that, even if UNLV could not expect to raise much in private donations, "we can be developing plans and identifying needs" for the future when prosperity would again permit generous gift giving. Goodall launched the foundation and then persuaded local business leaders to appoint science, mathematics, and engineering dean David Emerson to the Nevada Development Authority's task force to diversify the metropolitan economy. In a clear demonstration of the university's commitment to Las Vegas's economic development, Goodall sat on the NDA committee that was "coordinating these efforts in Southern Nevada."[6]

The president actively used the information gained from this experience to ask the legislature for money to establish an engineering school on the Las Vegas campus. According to many sources, including executives "of the companies we are trying to attract," Goodall told a gathering of faculty and staff in 1982, "the major stumbling block in inducing high tech companies to move into our area is the lack of an adequately trained high tech manpower pool."[7]

In the 1980s many business and resort executives were drawn to the university because they saw it as the key to liberating Las Vegas from its historic dependence upon gambling. Lyle Rivera often reminded this group that an excellent university was "a major consideration of business" that wished to relocate to Nevada, because it was "a source for a highly-trained work force, continuing education, research, and cultural events."[8] The last was especially vital to a community often criticized for its risqué stage shows and blue comedy acts.

As the 1980s progressed, different business leaders guided the foundation. In 1983 Tom Wiesner succeeded Molasky as chair of the foundation's board of trustees. Wiesner, a real estate developer and owner of the Las Vegas Racquet Club, was a longtime donor to UNLV and its sports programs. Wiesner had been a star athlete at the University of Wisconsin before moving to Las Vegas in the 1960s, where he built a real estate empire that included part of the old Marina Hotel. Wiesner also dabbled in politics. First elected to the Clark County Commission in 1970, he chaired the body from 1974 to 1976. He also chaired the county planning commission, the sanitation district, the airport commission, and the board of Southern Nevada Memorial Hospital (today UMC). In addition, Wiesner was a member of UNLV's President's Associates. In the 1980s, he worked tirelessly for the university, especially in pursuit of an engineering school to attract more industry to the valley. As Wiesner told reporters in 1983, the trustees' goal was "to have the university contribute to the economic diversification of Las Vegas, and an engineering school will be a significant resource in that effort."

As the 1983 fund-raising campaign for engineering began, new faces appeared on the board, including Circus Circus Enterprises chair William Bennett; Fred Lewis, a Summa (Hughes) Corporation vice president; real estate magnate and Boyd Gaming executive Chuck Ruthe; Harry Wald of Caesars Palace; and Frank Scott, chair of Western Financial Holding Company and

CLAUDINE WILLIAMS IN FRONT OF THE RESIDENCE HALL
NAMED FOR HER. UNLV FOUNDATION

co-owner of the Union Plaza. Entertainers Wayne Newton and Frank Sinatra were also added to the board and were expected to raise money for the school. Not only did Sinatra organize two benefit shows for the university in the late 1970s, but the board also charged him with securing network coverage of the Thomas & Mack Center's opening night. In a dramatic departure from recent times, celebrities were brought directly onto the board in the 1980s rather than merely being honored at a fund-raising event.

Those who chaired the foundation's board over the past quarter century came from the top ranks of business, demonstrating UNLV's growing importance to the metropolitan economy. Claudine Williams followed Wiesner and served two one-year terms. Under her leadership, the foundation raised the money to start construction on the Thomas T. Beam Engineering Complex. Williams also spearheaded the initiative to begin major fund-raising efforts.

Women provided strong leadership during the foundation's first decade. Hotel executive Elaine Wynn became the fourth chair in 1985 and served in that capacity for the next six years. Aside from expanding and improving the foundation's business operations and procedures, Wynn began the Annual Foundation Recognition Dinner, which became a crucial vehicle for encouraging even more gift giving in the future. Most important, Wynn's presence enhanced the importance of the foundation. In 1989, when The Mirage opened and immediately became the Strip's signature resort, she symbolized the link between UNLV and her husband, Steve, arguably the most significant figure in the "New Las Vegas." His invention of the megaresort and her popularization of the foundation in the early 1990s paid dividends for the rest of the decade. An increasing number of hotel and business executives affiliated themselves with the organization and its fund-raising activities.

In 1991 longtime attorney and gaming investor Art Ham Jr. finally succeeded

Wynn. Ham's death just four months later led to the selection of John Goolsby, president of the Howard Hughes Corporation, to complete his predecessor's two-year term. Goolsby continued the emphasis on major fund-raising and formalized the Planned Giving Program. Future Nevada governor Kenny Guinn (1993–94) replaced Goolsby before stepping down to serve as interim president of UNLV. Guinn made significant contributions in this office by reforming the procedures governing the president's discretionary fund.

Guinn's successors continued the tradition of dynamic leadership. Tom Hartley (1994–96), president of Colbert Golf Design, began the planning process for the UNLV Foundation's building on campus. Of even greater significance was his help in securing the initial gift from the Lied Foundation Trust that helped build the Lied Library. This episode illustrates the importance of the team effort in fund-raising. While presidents normally receive the credit for major undertakings and accomplishments during their tenure, they would be the first to recognize that it often requires a team effort, with faculty, staff, student leaders, and sometimes others all helping.

TOM HARTLEY, UNLV FOUNDATION

The process for UNLV's obtaining the seed money for the Lied Library spanned the terms of three presidents. Near the end of Maxson's tenure, in 1994, the development committee, a body within the foundation's board of trustees, held a meeting to discuss how UNLV might obtain a new library. As committee chair, Hartley invited Lied Trust executor Christina Hixson to the meeting to hear the discussion. Then dean of libraries Matthew Simon made what was, by all accounts, a convincing presentation that reviewed the present library's weaknesses in light of current trends in the profession and unveiled preliminary sketches detailing how a modern facility could vault UNLV near the top of America's college libraries.

Committee members then agreed that the president could not lobby the 1995 legislature for money unless substantial private donations were pledged. This was the same barrier that Nevada Southern had faced in 1955–56 in its pursuit of state money for a campus and again a decade later in seeking legislative appropriations for a performing arts center. Following the development committee's meeting, Hartley walked Hixson to her car. On the way, she asked him what it would take to make the new library happen. By the time they finished their conversation, she had pledged $10 million for the building, enough to secure the state's share in 1995. During President Harter's administration, Hixson later added another $5 million and, thanks greatly to her generosity, the library opened its doors shortly after the new millennium began.

Hartley's successor as board chair, Don Snyder, was just as effective. Snyder's five-year term (1996–2001) symbolized the continuing relationship between the resort industry and the university. Snyder, president of the Boyd Gaming Corporation, conducted the major fund-raising for the foundation's building and helped to triple total donations during his term. His successors, Mike Maffie (2001–3), former president of Southwest Gas, and Terry Wright (2003–5), board chair of Nevada Title Company, continued to raise record amounts for UNLV by initiating feasibility studies and launching major capital campaigns.

Of course, when President Goodall created the foundation in 1981, another organization already was soliciting donations for the school. Founded in 1965, the UNLV Alumni Association has raised several million dollars for the school. It started awarding academic scholarships in 1982. A decade later, President Greg McKinley and his board voted to establish UNLV's largest scholarship endowment in a collaborative effort between the foundation and the alumni association. By 2004 the association had given more than $1.8 million to students across UNLV's undergraduate and graduate disciplines. By century's end, the organization counted 7,000 alumni and "friends" who responded to its various appeals, including the foundation's annual phonathon.

MICHAEL MAFFIE. UNLV FOUNDATION

In 1983 President Goodall approved director of alumni relations Fred Albrecht's request for a fund-raising campaign to build an alumni center on campus. Thanks to a $1 million gift in cash and property from land developer Richard Tam and help from the UNLV Foundation, construction began on the 23,000-square-foot Richard Tam Alumni Center, which opened in 1991. Although plans originally called for a 10,000-square-foot building, the structure was enlarged to house offices and banquet facilities for the UNLV Foundation, which moved in until its own headquarters opened in 2000.

This temporary arrangement reflected the collaborative relationship be-tween the two organizations, as the foundation helped the alumni association to raise the money it needed to build the Tam Alumni Center. As Buck Deadrich noted in a 1983 update to his board, "Recognizing that the alumni will eventually become the bulk of our donor base, I've been helping the . . . association develop a three- or four-hundred-thousand-dollar capital campaign to erect an alumni building on campus." Deadrich then noted that the campaign had already begun with a $10,000 annual gift from Howard Hughes's Summa Corporation, which "has committed to becoming our first corporate Founder's Society member."[9]

The Tam Alumni Center was not the only project on Deadrich's agenda. He also wanted to press Frank Sinatra into service. Deadrich informed the trustees that he was negotiating with Sinatra for CBS coverage of the Thomas & Mack's opening-night basketball game "that could produce seven figures in TV residual revenue as well as a six-figure gate." Deadrich explained that some of these monies, along with the foundation's "high tech campaign" proceeds of $25,000, would go to UNLV's current priority, the computer science and engineering school. The director was also active on other fronts, asking Wayne Newton "to initiate a UNLV guest artist series named after his former discoverer and mentor, Summa Entertainment Director, Walter Kane."[10] The Walter Kane Memorial Artist Series, Deadrich hoped, would attract popular musicians, singers, and comedians whose benefit performances would periodically net thousands in revenue for UNLV.

After Deadrich left UNLV in 1984, his successors did not follow up on his plans for Newton, and this change in strategy continued into the 1990s and 2000s. In 2004, for example, a benefit to pay tribute to actor Tony Curtis, by then a four-year resident of the Las Vegas area, drew a large crowd of donors and interested residents. However, Curtis was not asked to promote other fund-raising activities, as Sinatra and Newton had been, although Curtis, like Liberace and other earlier entertainers, often visited the campus to share his professional expertise with advanced students in UNLV's fine and performing arts departments.

With the arrival of President Maxson in 1984, the foundation began a period of rapid growth. Maxson was a talented fund-raiser who brought an undeniable energy to gift solicitation. As Elaine Wynn remembered, "In the 1980s, we had the right mood, the right people, and the right personalities that led to the mega-gifts and spectacular new programs." She credited the new president with being the driving force behind the foundation's success: "I don't think we could have done it until he [Maxson] came to campus."[11]

In the 1980s, as corporate gaming and explosive population growth dramatically increased the wealth and size of local elites, the rules changed for naming buildings. No longer were UNLV buildings named for the school's early leaders and beloved professors; the new strategy sought to raise money for buildings by honoring the donors whose contributions helped underwrite their construction. As Elaine Wynn explained, "We have targeted the names of people who have respect in the community. When future buildings and institutions are named, they will match the prestige and contributions of the past."[12]

By 1991 Maxson had raised the bar for donors. For $5,000 the contributor became a member of the President's Inner Circle; a $1,000 donation made one a President's Associate. By the late 1990s, a $1 million to $1.5 million gift put one's name on an endowed chair and $5 million to $20 million meant that the name would be bestowed upon a building. By 2004, as the percentage of state support for total UNLV expenditures continued its downward trend, Carol Harter wanted to raise the bar even higher—perhaps to $20–$25 million for a major building—as she pursued the expensive goal of making UNLV a Doctoral/ Research Extensive University by 2010. For many, having their name appear on a building was the ultimate honor. Indeed, Elaine Wynn once characterized having one's name on a college building as "the noblest form of immortality."[13]

As the Las Vegas economy rapidly expanded and the wealth of prominent business leaders and resort owners increased from the hundreds of thousands to the millions and, in some cases, to the tens of millions, their power and influence over local and state politicians grew apace. Especially after 1990, the advantage of using fund-raising as a tool to strengthen the alliance between the school and local business leaders and power brokers helped UNLV in the state budgetary process. By drawing influential members of the community into the foundation, the trustees, the staff, and the president helped them to recognize the shared interests of the campus and the local economy. This recognition proved to be invaluable in Carson City, as Las Vegas grew into a major metropolitan area. In 1991 Wynn acknowledged how individual lobbying helped UNLV to save several new buildings and programs from the budget-cutting axe. "I think for the first time in the budget process, UNLV this year was in the proper position to bargain with the governor and legislature," she told reporters. "Because of business involvement in the university, personal meetings were possible that kept UNLV's goals in the budget."[14]

Sometimes, as in the case of the law school, private donations were crucial to state funding and authorization. President Harter portrayed the law school as "a collaboration between UNLV, William S. Boyd, and other business leaders" that generated pledges of $7 million. Their donations, she declared, "proved to be the catalyst that helped gain state approval that year." In a 1999 statement she went even further, declaring, "All parts of UNLV's aggressive strategic plan have been heavily influenced by input from UNLV Foundation trustees and other business leaders."[15]

Although Maxson's and Harter's fund-raising strategies had much in common, they differed in one meaningful way. While Maxson encouraged all departments and programs to be entrepreneurial and raise money wherever they could, Harter adopted a different approach. In 1995 she directed that all fund-raising be consolidated under the umbrella of the UNLV Foundation. In 1996–98, this reform helped produce the three best fund-raising years in school history. Supporting her in this effort was John Gallagher, former vice president of university relations at the University of Puget Sound, who came to UNLV in 1995 to be director of the UNLV Foundation. Working with Harter and the trustees, he helped to substantially broaden the university's donor base. For eleven years, Gallagher, who later became vice president for development, organized the events and capital campaigns that contributed to the dramatic surge in donations and pledges to UNLV.

Gallagher, like his predecessors, also helped the administration decide who might be honored at UNLV's graduation. Indeed, besides admitting donors to various honorary groups, presidents have always employed the school's commencement ceremony as another opportunity to pay tribute to major philanthropists and recruit them for future campaigns. In 2002, for example, President Harter used the event to bestow the President's Medal upon Joyce Mack, banking executive Selma Bartlett, contractor and engineer J. A. Tiberti, and hotel executive Claudine Williams, all of whom had been leading donors, as well as Senator Joe Neal, a popular representative of Las Vegas's African American community, who had supported UNLV for years in the state legislature. At the same ceremony, longtime foundation member Tom Wiesner won the Distinguished Nevadan Award, as did MGM-Mirage board chair Terence Lanni. An honorary doctorate of humane letters went to Mandalay Resorts Group

president Glenn Schaeffer for his role in establishing the International Institute
of Modern Letters and bringing UNLV's first Nobel laureate, Wole Soyinka, to
the English department.

Over the decades other presidents also used honorary doctorates to express
the university's appreciation to longtime supporters. President Zorn gave Bob
Hope (1970) and Del Webb (1971) honorary doctorates, hoping they would
return the favor by engaging in fund-raising activities for the campus. President
Baepler did the same when he bestowed upon a windblown Frank Sinatra a
doctorate of humane letters at Sam Boyd Stadium in 1976. President Goodall
awarded doctorates to Wayne Newton (1980), Parry Thomas (1982), and Jerry
Mack (1983), each of whom had served Las Vegas well. Thomas and Mack had
a long history of aiding UNLV with both their money and their expertise; Wayne
Newton was a youthful entertainer who had helped the school earlier but whose
real contributions, Goodall hoped, would be in the future. He doubtless hoped

that the same would be true of Diana Ross, to whom he awarded a doctorate in 1984.

Awards were another way of paying tribute to the school's supporters. Sometimes they were given as a prelude to receiving an honorary degree later for continuing service. Parry Thomas, for instance, received the Distinguished Nevadan Award in 1975, seven years before being awarded the doctorate. Sometimes, as in the case of state senator Joe Neal, the goal was to demonstrate UNLV's appreciation for a lawmaker who had fought for the school's budget during his or her years in the legislature. In 1988 President Maxson presented an honorary doctorate to former state senator Jim Gibson, who was suffering from terminal cancer. It was a touching moment that could have been a testy one. Just a few weeks earlier, on May 4, Gibson's PEPCON factory in Henderson had exploded because of an ammonium chlorate leak. The blast killed an employee and damaged hundreds of homes and businesses in the east valley. The force of the explosion not only rousted everyone out of their classes at UNLV but even lifted sliding glass doors off their tracks across the campus.

At May's commencement, the Thomas & Mack was packed with graduates and their parents (many of whom no doubt had experienced some property damage). But in a masterful introduction, President Maxson recounted virtually every contribution Gibson had ever made to the school and community while carefully omitting any reference to his ownership of PEPCON. The crowd gave the senator a thunderous ovation. Gibson beamed from his wheelchair onstage as he received his award—a fitting last moment of glory for a longtime friend of the school. Ironically, moments later at the same ceremony, Maxson presented a Distinguished Nevadan Award to his successor and Nevada's future governor, Kenny Guinn, in recognition of his fund-raising efforts for the campus.

UNLV employed other approaches to recognize the contributions of corporations. One body created for this purpose was the Academic Corporate Council, which honored the chief executives of its member companies in various ways. For example, in the spring 2003 issue of the foundation's newsletter, *It's Academic,* the publication profiled Steve Petruska, president of Nevada-Arizona operations for Pulte Homes, which had become the largest homebuilder in America when it acquired the Del Webb Corporation in 2001. In his interview Petruska said: "We support UNLV because it's instrumental in building our future workforce in Southern Nevada."[16] Certainly, the school's new master's degree program in construction management in the architecture school contributed to his enthusiasm. In this case, the foundation used Pulte Homes' boosting of UNLV to plant the seeds of enthusiasm with other builders and companies.

In the 1990s UNLV's colleges began to develop their own vehicles for recognizing generous donors to their programs. In 2002 the business college established the Nevada Business Hall of Fame "to honor top business leaders whose visions have made Nevada a booming business center." The original inductees were video poker pioneer Si Redd, a founding investor of International Game Technology, Valley Bank's Parry Thomas, and Steve Wynn. The following year, more than six hundred attended the second induction ceremony, when Irwin Molasky, Claudine Williams, and, posthumously, Howard Hughes joined the select group. Adding to the organization's prestige were not just the accomplishments of the inductees but also the body that selected them, the College of Business Advisory Board, which included "senior Nevada business leaders from a variety of industries." The criteria for admission were also impressive, requiring that recipients "possess a sense of leadership," be strong advocates for the university, exhibit "great leadership skills," and "influence their environment."[17] An unwritten rule would also be that they evidence a proven track record of contributing to UNLV.

The foundation's annual dinner became an event at which UNLV presidents showed their appreciation to hundreds of donors who did not receive special awards. Usually held in one of Las Vegas's more elegant venues and often featuring a speaker of national renown, the dinner reinforced bonds between the foundation and donors. The reception also allowed foundation staff to mingle with gift givers and individually express the school's appreciation while at the same time encouraging further generosity in the future. Of course, an appealing speaker always boosted attendance at the event. For seven years, funding from Wells Fargo Bank helped the foundation to attract high-profile speakers such as astronaut Sally Ride and future secretary of state Colin Powell. In 2002 the foundation brought in Bill Clinton's former secretary of state, Madeleine Albright. A year earlier, former BYU and San Francisco 49ers quarterback Steve Young delivered an inspirational speech on philanthropy.

JOYCE MACK. UNLV FOUNDATION

The event was a convenient occasion for honoring special donors as well, especially those being inducted into the Palladium Society, "a recognition organization for donors who have contributed $1 million or more in lifetime gifts to the university." In April 2002, for instance, E. Parry Thomas, Joyce Mack, Barnes and Noble College Bookstores, and the Andre Agassi Charitable Foundation gained entry to this exclusive society. Thomas and Jerry Mack's widow, Joyce, had clearly earned this recognition, as had Barnes and Noble for its $2 million renovation of the UNLV bookstore. The national retail chain had become a "campus partner" in 1985 and continued to contribute $10,000 annually for student scholarships. The Andre Agassi Charitable Foundation gained admission for its historic support of Child Haven, the Boys and Girls Clubs of Las Vegas, and other community service organizations. Harter also cited the foundation's generous gifts to the Cynthia Bunker Memorial Fellowship Fund.

The UNLV Foundation encouraged even more opportunities by promoting partnerships. Sometimes it involved a member of the board of trustees. In the case of Bill Boyd and the law school, a longtime donor and foundation trustee was crucial to UNLV's obtaining a major professional school. This example illustrates the dynamic nature of the board of trustees. Not only did members contribute their own money and recruit new money, but by the sheer visibility of their position they encouraged partnerships between UNLV and different groups in the Las Vegas business community. As President Harter observed in 1997, "Foundation trustees set an example for other partnerships between the community and campus. New partnership ideas emerge daily, on and off campus. Sometimes those partnerships grow into complete programs in only a few weeks. In other cases, like the physical therapy master's [and doctoral] degree programs, it may take years of patience and persistence to succeed."[18]

In the case of physical therapy, Kitty Rodman's generous donation was crucial. Her contribution made possible the purchase of library materials as well as laboratory and office equipment. Her gift also supported professional development, student scholarships, and program accreditation expenses. In recognition of her contributions, UNLV named the laboratory, library, and office spaces the Kitty Rodman Physical Therapy Teaching Facilities. Today, the program is the only one of its kind in the state that offers a doctorate. Rodman, like Boyd, through her philanthropy and leadership, exemplified the outstanding characteristics that all UNLV presidents looked for in foundation trustees. Both came to the board after forging successful business careers in Las Vegas. While Boyd's achievements lay primarily in the resort industry, Rodman's were in the building industry as a partner in Sierra Construction. UNLV benefited from the business savvy and wealth that Rodman acquired while managing the company that helped build The Mirage, Sands, Riviera, Bally's, Flamingo Hilton, and many other Las Vegas resorts. Her company also contributed to UNLV's physical plant by constructing the science and technology building (today's Lilly Fong Geoscience) in 1960. Through their generous donations, especially to the physical therapy and law programs, Rodman and Boyd epitomized the partnership approach that President Harter championed.

The UNLV Foundation promoted partnerships as a means of raising funds for a range of programs, schools, and other needs. One of the advantages of this approach was that it conditioned donors and prospective donors to think like fund-raisers themselves and devise partnerships of their own. To be sure, not all partnerships were conceived by UNLV. In 2002, for example, William Boyd, whose company owned casinos in Las Vegas and Philadelphia, Mississippi, suggested that UNLV and the University of Mississippi establish a joint hotel management program to train minority students for a career in the hotel-casino industry. As a delighted Stuart Mann, dean of UNLV's hotel college, explained, "The goal of these recruitment programs is to encourage minorities, particularly African Americans and Hispanics, to attend college and consider a career in hospitality and gaming." He went on to observe, "There is a nationwide shortage of qualified minorities to fill management positions in a broad range of hospitality industries. . . . This makes it more difficult for resort corporations . . . to create more diverse management teams."[19]

The UNLV Foundation has also served as a go-between to match donors and programs that may initially seem unrelated, a process that often results in years of mutually beneficial collaboration. Take, for instance, the Wells Fargo Foundation's $100,000 grant in 1998 to the Accelerated Schools Project, a program run nationally by Stanford University and locally by the UNLV College of Education and the Clark County School District. As the program's Las Vegas director, education professor Jane McCarthy, remarked, "By providing the funds needed to help these students learn and succeed, the Wells Fargo Foundation is definitely making an investment in the future of this community."[20] Sometimes the matches were more predictable, such as Weight Watchers founder Jean Nidetch's generous gift to help establish the UNLV Women's Center, or Anchor Gaming founder Stan Fulton's multimillion-dollar pledge to support the building that houses the International Gaming Institute and part of the hotel college.

The foundation and the athletics department also cooperate with donors who give to both academics and athletics. In the mid-1990s, the Conrad Hilton Foundation, which usually contributed to the hotel college or to scholarship endowments, gave $500,000 to build the 328-seat Baron Hilton Auditorium at the Lied Athletic Complex. Over the past two decades, hotel executives who in the past had usually donated to industry-related programs have funded a wider range of UNLV projects. In 1996, for example, Sahara Hotel owner William Bennett pledged $2.7 million for the William G. Bennett Professional Development Center for teachers, next to the Paradise Elementary School, and three years later he provided another $5 million for construction of UNLV's preschool and its early childhood development center, which the university named for his wife, Lynn.

Other donations have simply enhanced academic programs. In the late 1980s, Thomas T. Beam, known for his contributions to the hotel, business, and engineering colleges, gave $100,000 to the history department, which had never before received a major donation. Beam's donation paved the way for significant library acquisitions that in 1991 supported a Ph.D. program in U.S. western history. In 1997 the Tracinda Corporation (the parent company of MGM Mirage) provided a gift of $1.5 million to support initiatives for UNLV's libraries, campus computing, the music program, the new law school, and the alumni program.

EDYTHE KATZ-YARCHEVER, WITH GILBERT YARCHEVER AND
RICHARD MORGAN, DEAN OF THE BOYD SCHOOL OF LAW. UNLV
FOUNDATION

Other individual Las Vegans have also given generously to academic programs and institutions within UNLV. Edythe Katz-Yarchever and her husband,
Judge Gil Yarchever, have supported the school's programs for many years.
Their donations of furniture, antiques, and other gifts to the honors college
ultimately resulted in the college's naming its reading room for Edythe's late
husband, Lloyd. For more than two decades, Edythe has been generous to the
Colleges of Fine Arts, the College of Liberal Arts, the Boyd School of Law, and
the university's libraries.

Mannetta Braunstein and her husband, Michael, made their first gift of
pre-Columbian art to the Marjorie Barrick Museum of Natural History in 1979,
launching the university's now extensive collection of art from that period. Over
the years the couple made further donations, including their substantial book
collection on the subject to accompany the art. Enriched by this collection, in
January 2006 the museum hosted the first Braunstein Symposium on Pre-
Columbian Studies. The Braunsteins have also included UNLV in their estate
planning to ensure that the school will someday receive their entire collection of
five thousand pieces. Like the Yarchevers, the Braunsteins have contributed to

other units within UNLV as well, among them the athletics department and the College of Liberal Arts.

In marked contrast to other state universities, the largest individual donor to UNLV has been the system chancellor. Attorney and television executive James Rogers, along with his wife, Beverly, have personally and through their companies generously supported numerous academic and athletic programs at UNLV. The most notable gift is their $20 million pledge through their estate on behalf of the Boyd School of Law, supplemented by $11 million in additional gifts and pledges for operation of the Law School. In addition, the couple also pledged $1 million to establish the Louis Wiener Law Library and another $200,000 to create the Rogers Program in Law, Philosophy, and Social Inquiry. They also made a $25 million "challenge" pledge for the naming of the UNLV College of Business. The university has been encouraged to use the challenge in efforts to cultivate other prospective donors who might be interested in this naming opportunity. To do that, however, their gift would have to exceed the

MANNETTA AND MICHAEL BRAUNSTEIN. UNLV FOUNDATION
IMAGE NO. D64636-25

pledge of the chancellor and his wife. Besides the law and business schools, the couple has also donated to other UNLV activities, including $500,000 to help build the women's softball stadium, $100,000 to the Coaches Continuity Fund, and lesser amounts to the Black Mountain Institute and other academic and athletic programs.

For the past half century, fund-raising has been crucial to UNLV's rise to prominence, but in the future it will be the key to achieving President Harter's goal of making the school a Doctoral/Research Extensive University. A major project that will help UNLV realize this goal is the science, engineering, and technology building. In 2002 its construction became a leading priority of the foundation, much like the old computer science and engineering school of the early 1980s. After receiving $8.8 million from the 2001 legislature to plan the project, UNLV had to persuade the Las Vegas business community to help finance it.

President Harter and the foundation offered a series of compelling arguments in the organization's quarterly publication, *It's Academic*. The first addressed the issue of economic diversification—always an appealing subject for a business community concerned about Las Vegas's perilous dependence upon gambling and tourism. "The project will help to diversify Nevada's economy by providing research products for development locally and by providing critical research support for high tech companies that require significant university support," the newsletter declared. And, aside from attracting "the highest quality science and engineering researchers and educators in the world," the complex "will educate a large number of students in high-demand technical fields that support workforce development in the state." Finally, the newsletter assured its readers that the project would "provide a state-of-the-art analytical and computing center to support research and development within Nevada and meet the growing demands for high quality research facilities from Nevada's corporations and entities."[21]

In remarks emphasizing the importance of the new UNLV Cancer Research Institute at the Shadow Lane campus, President Harter clearly drew the connection between gift giving, research, and profitability, all of which the science, engineering, and technology building embodies. As she pointed out, "Artists, scientists, and other educators may not often sit around and think of innovative ways to turn a profit with their creations, but Silicon Valley is living proof that it works."[22]

Though mentioned fleetingly in some of the presidential chapters, the beneficence of major donors will be viewed in a broader fund-raising context here. Many of the donors who contributed to the science, engineering, and technology building and other current UNLV projects have been giving to the university for years. Marjorie Barrick, for instance, has been a longtime supporter of the UNLV library and the College of Fine and Performing Arts. In 1951 she and her husband, Edward, came to Las Vegas from Omaha. Over the next quarter century, the two made a fortune in gaming and land development projects. Although she had already earned a business degree from Creighton University, Marjorie Barrick took classes in a variety of subjects at NSU/UNLV over a fifteen-year period, and she recognized the school's growing value to the developing metropolis. In 1978 the couple donated more than $200,000 worth of downtown real estate to the business college. Two years later, after Edward's death, Marjorie established a $1.2 million endowment in his memory to underwrite the Barrick Lecture Series and various faculty and student awards.

Sometimes, as in the case of Marjorie Barrick and Verna Harrah, the surviving spouse is a major donor, but the families of deceased philanthropists also give. Following the death of Thomas T. Beam, his family continued to help UNLV, providing initial funding for the new music building. After Jimma Lee and Donna Lee Beam offered an additional $4 million in 2001, President Harter named the building the Lee and Thomas Beam Music Center. But this was not all that Beam and his family did for the arts. Earlier, they funded the remodeling and expansion of UNLV's fine arts gallery, which today bears the name of his daughter Donna. In a similar vein, Robert T. and Diane Bigelow focused on science. In 1992 they gave $1.5 million to the School of Health and Human Sciences and pledged another $1 million to support the physics program.

Of course, many hotel owners understandably emphasized the William F. Harrah College of Hotel Administration. Although Sam Boyd initially helped renovate the Silver Bowl, he primarily supported the hotel college, giving more than $1 million in his lifetime. In fact, the college's dining room is named for Sam and his wife, Mary. Boyd's son, William, continued the tradition by endowing a hotel college chair and a distinguished professorship in his parents' name

WING FONG (CENTER) AND LILLY FONG, 1982. AT LEFT IS HAU
PEI-JEN. AN INTERNATIONALLY KNOWN ARTIST, SIX OF HIS
PAINTINGS HANG IN ARTEMUS HAM HALL. THEY WERE
PURCHASED UNDER TERMS OF A GRANT FROM THE FONGS.
SPECIAL COLLECTIONS, UNLV LIBRARIES 0062-0969

as well as the Boyd Dining Hall. But the younger Boyd also gave generously to residence programs, in recognition of which UNLV named the multi-winged William S. Boyd Hall near Tropicana Avenue. In the 1990s he donated another $1 million to renovate the Sam Boyd Stadium again. Finally, Boyd's $5 million gift to UNLV's law school in 1996 helped it to open in the face of less-than-expected state funding, and in 2005 he added $25 million more for scholarships and programs.

Women hotel executives also contributed valuable support to the university. Former Frontier Hotel owner Margaret Elardi served on the foundation's board of trustees, and her efforts to bring "the best and the brightest" to UNLV were noteworthy. In 1984 she donated $1 million to establish the Margaret Elardi Nevada Valedictorian Scholarship Program, which awarded a scholarship for up to four years to every valedictorian from an accredited Nevada high school. The program continued until 1991. In 1992–93, 115 valedictorians were enrolled at UNLV through this program.

Women executives have also inspired large donations to the campus. This

PHILANTHROPIST HAROLD STOCKER, WHOSE WIFE, MAYME,
RECEIVED THE FIRST GAMING LICENSE ON FREMONT STREET IN
1931 FOLLOWING NEVADA'S RELEGALIZATION OF CASINO
GAMBLING, WITH U.S. SENATOR HOWARD CANNON AT THE
OPENING OF THE DICKINSON LIBRARY ADDITION, 1981. SPECIAL
COLLECTIONS, UNLV LIBRARIES 0062-0539

was the case with the Judy Bayley Theatre, which required almost $500,000 in private gifts before the state would allocate its share to build the facilty. Judy Bayley, who died in January 1972, personally gave $65,000 to help the fund-raising campaign chaired by Las Vegas developer Wing Fong. Later, the Fleischman Foundation provided $500,000 to equip the theater. Another hotel owner, Claudine Williams of the old Holiday Casino (now Harrah's) on the Strip, made generous contributions to numerous university programs from scholarships to athletics to the natural history museum. In the early to mid-1990s, she gave $500,000 to enhance student life on campus, and in recognition of her generosity UNLV named one of the new residence halls for her.

In the case of Stations Casino chain founder Frank Fertitta Jr. and his wife, Vicki, their primary interest at UNLV has been sports. In 1985 he offered $1 million to build the Frank and Vicki Fertitta Tennis Complex. They later contributed another $500,000 for a variety of projects, including the Lied Athletic Complex in 1994.

Through the years, casino owners, new and old, have supported UNLV. Steve and Elaine Wynn made generous gifts to the school. In the 1990s they pledged $2 million for the Elaine Wynn Valedictorian Scholarship Fund. At the same time, the city's earliest hotel owners helped the school through their trusts. Mayme Stocker, for example, acquired the first gaming license on Fremont Street following Nevada's re-legalization of casino gambling in 1931. In the 1990s, the Harold and Mayme Stocker Trust received Palladium Society status for its donations to the Harold J. and Mayme Stocker Scholarship program, which has benefited numerous students majoring in chemistry, engineering, and medicine. Since 1984 the trust has contributed $3.1 million to that scholarship fund.

While the Wynns and others gave to student scholarships, some donors chose to support student associations. Richard Tam, who enjoyed a distinguished career in Las Vegas real estate and gaming, contributed $500,000 toward construction of what became the Richard Tam Alumni Center. He also offered two pieces of property of equal value, whose later sale provided additional financial support for the alumni association.

Like Tam, builder J. A. Tiberti also contributed to the alumni center. In fact, his company constructed several major buildings on campus, including Carlson Education, Flora Dungan Humanities, and the Moyer Student Union. As a foundation board trustee, Tiberti understood UNLV's needs. Aside from his donations to the Tam Alumni Center, Tiberti also gave hundreds of thousands to the library, the engineering program, and its building. In recognition of this and his generous support of teaching and research programs in the engineering school, UNLV named the large showcase laboratory in the building for him.

Michael Gaughan represents another outstanding example of a resort developer who gave his time and money to help the university. With help from his father, Jackie, another UNLV supporter who made his fortune on Fremont Street, Michael constructed the Barbary Coast, which quickly became a gold mine at the corner of Flamingo and the Strip. With profits from that hotel, he built a chain of casino-hotels around the valley before merging with the Boyd Gaming Corporation in 2004. A founding member of the UNLV Foundation and a board trustee, Gaughan contributed heavily to the Lied Athletic Complex and the UNLV rodeo team, along with other men's and women's sports programs. Because his membership on the foundation board apprised him of the school's many needs, Gaughan also gave to academics, including the William S. Boyd School of Law.

Like Gaughan, developer Michael Saltman has also served as a foundation trustee and contributed to UNLV's Law School and numerous other academic and athletic programs. Michael and Sonja Saltman's $1 million gift established the Saltman Center for Conflict Resolution Program. As has so often been the case, these donations have not been isolated events, but rather continuing efforts to improve the university on multiple fronts. In 2004 Saltman lent his time, expertise, and money to help President Harter begin the initial planning for Midtown UNLV, an ambitious effort to create a university district of cafes, galleries, and other bohemian-like institutions along the eastern margins of the campus.

Some prominent Las Vegans have donated their time and money to NSU and UNLV for decades. Bankers E. Parry Thomas and Jerome Mack not only served on President Moyer's land foundation board but also made frequent financial contributions to UNLV programs, especially in the business school. In 1983 President Goodall rewarded their invaluable service to the school by naming

SONJA AND MICHAEL SALTMAN WITH FORMER ASTRONAUT
SALLY RIDE, 2004. UNLV FOUNDATION IMAGE NO. D64157-45

the Thomas & Mack Center for them. Their families have maintained the tradition. In 2001, for instance, they donated a combined gift of $2 million to the
Law School for the Thomas and Mack Legal Clinic. Four years later, they gave
another $3 million to construct the 6,000-square-foot Thomas and Mack Moot
Court Complex at the school.

Alumni have also played key roles in building up UNLV. While many alumni
have been loyal donors through the years and some, like former regent and
congressman James Bilbray and regent and congresswoman Shelley Berkley,
have helped the school through elective office, others, like Ken Knauss, have
supported the campus's development with significant financial contributions.
Knauss, a 1978 graduate with a B.S. in accounting, and his wife, Tracy, made
their first donation to the College of Business that year. Over the next three
decades, they gave generously to alumni scholarship endowment funds for
students in both the college and the university. Then in 2004 they decided to
endow a chair in the accounting department to bring a nationally recognized

scholar to UNLV. "The education I received from the College of Business has played a major role in my success in this community," Knauss observed. "This is my way of saying thank you." In response, a grateful Dean Richard Flaherty noted: "Having the best faculty is critical to the success of the University. More importantly, is having alumni like Ken engaged with the college in a direct and meaningful way."[23] But Knauss also helped the university in another meaningful way, becoming a trustee of the UNLV Foundation and bringing his business expertise to the board's finance committee. And like the Beam family and so many of the other first-generation donors, the second generation has also demonstrated an interest in the school. In the case of the Knauss family, daughter Nicolette attended UNLV and graduated with a marketing degree in 2004.

In addition to individuals, trusts and estates have also been significant givers. The Stockers are just one example; Andre Agassi is another. In the 1990s the Andre Agassi Charitable Foundation established the Cynthia Bunker Scholarship Fund in the College of Fine and Performing Arts with more than $1 million in gifts. As one might expect, Agassi Enterprises has also been a strong supporter of UNLV athletics by donating thousands to the Athletic Scholarship Donor/RAC Rebel Athletic Fund (RAF) programs.

During his lifetime, William "Si" Redd, a pioneer developer of the video poker machine, was a generous contributor to UNLV athletics. An avid fan of Jerry Tarkanian's Runnin' Rebels, Redd gave generously to upgrade the Thomas & Mack Center with a 1992 grant to establish the Si Redd Room for conferences and small receptions. He received Palladium Society status in the mid-1990s when he contributed $1.5 million to establish the Marilyn and Si Redd Sports Medicine Complex. Along with his late wife, Marilyn, Redd, even after his death, continued to donate generously to the school's athletic programs through his namesake foundation.

The same was true of Donrey Media owner Donald Reynolds, whose company published numerous city newspapers, including the *Las Vegas Review-Journal*. Like local archrival Hank Greenspun, Reynolds established a foundation to earmark part of his immense fortune for charities like the university. At UNLV, the Reynolds Foundation emphasized student services. In 1991 it provided $4 million to fund construction of the Donald W. Reynolds Student Services Building.

But no trust or foundation has been more generous than that of Las Vegas land developer Ernest
Lied. Thanks to the support of the executor, UNLV
Foundation trustee Christina Hixson, the university
has received well over $20 million, including $15
million toward the construction of the Lied Library,
the new centerpiece of the campus. Hixson also approved $1.7 million for the Lied Real Estate Endow-
ment and Real Estate Studies program in the College
of Business, as well as money for science laboratories
and other academic programs. The foundation also
benefited UNLV's sports teams, providing roughly
half of the funding for the $8.5 million Lied Athletic
Complex.

Aside from foundations, many trusts, like the
Stockers,' have earned Palladium Society status at
UNLV with contributions of $1 million or more. For
example, the Hazel Mae Wilson Trust, under the
direction of co-trustees Mel Wolzinger (her husband
Earl's longtime business partner) and Jay Brown,
has given almost $7 million to the university since

MEL WOLZINGER. UNLV FOUNDATION

the 1980s. Students have benefited from this generosity in a variety of ways.
The most visible manifestation of these gifts is the $1.3 million Earl E. Wilson
Baseball Stadium, but another $313,000 went for the Wilson Baseball Scholar-
ship Endowment for student athletes, as well as $261,000 for the UNLV Golf
Foundation. The trust also donated generously to other programs that most stu-
dents would recognize. Another $250,000 helped establish the Wilson Advising
Center in the College of Liberal Arts and $365,000 expanded programs in the
Reynolds Student Services Building. Another $300,000 created the Earl E. and
Hazel Wilson Public Education Initiative Scholarship Endowment for the College of Education. Finally, the trust provided more than $2 million for student
scholarships as part of the Earl E. and Hazel Wilson Scholarship Endowment.
The remaining $2 million helped transform the old 1960 Gym into the Marjo-
rie Barrick Museum of Natural History and the Harry Reid Center for Environ-

mental Studies. In accepting the contribution, President Maxson described the gift as "the best type because it's spread throughout the university. It bridges the gaps between academics and research, [and] between scholarships, athletics, and facilities."[24]

The Greenspun Family Foundation has also been a major supporter of UNLV. The late publisher's wife, Barbara, served as a foundation trustee and, along with her family, has given $3.2 million to support the Greenspun School of Journalism and Media Communications and the Greenspun College of Urban Affairs. The Greenspun Foundation has also pledged another $25 million to pay 40 percent of the costs for constructing a building to house that college and support some of its programs.

Similarly, the estate of a less famous but still significant donor, Mary V. Hughes, has quietly contributed more than $1 million to the endowment for UNLV's honors college, and additional gifts have enhanced student life on campus with a residence hall named for Mitzi (Mary's nickname) and Johnny Hughes. Finally, another $1 million from the estate has enriched the Alumni Association Scholarship Fund, which annually supports talented undergraduates in colleges across the campus.

Sometimes a donor, while still alive, gives money to complete a facilty begun by another donor, but the estate later contributes to something else. This was the case with Franklin Koch, a Las Vegan for more than forty years who amassed a fortune in houseware sales and stock investments and gave $1.3 million to finish work on the Beam Music Center. To recognize Koch's extraordinary generosity, UNLV named the auditorium in today's Harter Classroom Complex for him. Following Koch's death, his estate donated another $3.7 million for the Frank Koch Scholarship Endowment Fund. This gift was particularly significant; if UNLV is to become a Carnegie Doctoral/Research Extensive University, it must expand and strengthen its entire graduate curriculum, recruit academically talented students, and support their research and training.

FACING PAGE:

TOP: HANK AND BARBARA GREENSPUN, CA. 1960. UNLV FOUNDATION

BOTTOM: BRIAN GREENSPUN. UNLV FOUNDATION

Aside from individuals, foundations, and estates, corporations also promoted UNLV's development. The list of corporate donors is substantial and includes such financial titans as Wells Fargo and the Bank of America. The latter absorbed Thomas and Mack's Valley Bank in 1993 but continued the tradition of generosity to UNLV, especially to the College of Business. Wells Fargo, which took over First Interstate Bank in 1996, gave more than $1 million, $600,000 of which established the First Interstate Bank Institute for Business Leadership. The remaining $400,000 went for business scholarships. Wells Fargo continued its commitment by funding the Wells Fargo First Generation Scholarship for academically gifted high school students, majoring in any discipline, who are the first in their family to attend college.

The Howard Hughes (formerly Summa) Corporation has been a major benefactor to UNLV since the 1980s. Hughes, himself a college-educated engineer, recognized the symbiotic relationship between higher education and Nevada's development. He gave the seed money to begin the state's community college system in the late 1960s, and his generous pledges started UNR's medical school, now the University of Nevada School of Medicine. After the eccentric billionaire's death in 1976, his corporation allied with Del Webb to build Las Vegas's first Sun City retirement community and started work on what became the sprawling master-planned development of Summerlin. Both corporations also continued to support the local university. The Hughes Corporation gave $2 million to the Howard R. Hughes School of Engineering as well as many other university programs to earn membership in the Palladium Society. Following its merger with the Del Webb Corporation in 2002, Pulte Homes took over the Del Webb tradition of giving to the campus.

Local utilities have also been generous to UNLV, especially Southwest Gas, which has a long history of helping the school. For years, under William Laub and his successors, the company funded scholarships in economics, but in later years expanded its giving to include minority engineers, the Women's Research Institute, the science bowl, law scholarships, and UNLV's distinguished artist series. In the 1980s and 1990s, Southwest Gas CEO Kenny Guinn gave freely of his time and money to support Rebel athletics and the business college, even serving as UNLV Foundation board chair in 1994. Another CEO, Mike Maffie, not only served as a UNLV Foundation trustee, but also chaired the University Research Foundation in its start-up phase.

Las Vegas's other utilities have also been active. Besides its generous support of UNLV-TV and other programs, Cox Communications pledged $5 million in 1999 to help build the Cox Pavilion. The Las Vegas Valley Water District took a different approach, providing research grants to fund UNLV studies of water quality, capacity, and other subjects of interest to a booming metropolis in a drought-plagued region. Nevada Power's support of the university dates from the Goodall administration. In 1984 the company pledged $1.5 million "to help launch a first-class Engineering and Computer Science School at UNLV" and create the Nevada Power Chair in the college.[25] Over the years, the electric company has also supported various programs in the College of Sciences and throughout the university.

The same can be said of Sierra Health Services. Often, the corporate contacts of a foundation trustee helped generate contributions. In this case, Dr. Anthony Marlon of Sierra Health, a UNLV Foundation trustee, proved to be a vital conduit between the company and the school. Under his leadership, the health care provider gave to many university programs, including a combined gift of $1.35 million in 2003 from Sierra Health and its subsidiary, Health Plan of Nevada, for the science, engineering, and technology building. As UNLV moves closer to its goal of becoming a Doctoral/Research Extensive University, corporate donors will become even more important, because they have the resources that it will take to supplement state revenues enough to make President Harter's vision a reality.

Thanks to the dedication of the university's current and past presidents and foundation trustees, as the twenty-first century began, UNLV had assembled enough of a critical mass of individual and corporate donors to attempt the kind of fund-raising effort normally undertaken by only the largest and most prestigious institutions of higher learning. With the goal of making UNLV a Doctoral/Research Extensive University clearly on everyone's mind, President Harter and her advisors decided that the moment had come to embark upon a major fund-raising drive. The process began in 2001 with a feasibility study and meetings with the foundation's board of trustees as well as conversations with many long-

DON SNYDER, UNLV FOUNDATION

time supporters, alumni, and community leaders. Once Harter and the trustees agreed to initiate the campaign, planning began in earnest. During her State of the University address in 2005, the president officially announced that UNLV would conduct the school's first comprehensive campaign, called Invent the Future, to raise $500 million in gifts and pledges by December 2008.

The overall purpose of the campaign was to raise UNLV to the next level, a goal clearly reflected in the stated priorities, which included new buildings, endowment funds to support new faculty positions, and scholarship and fellowship support for students, equipment, and research. The public phase of this capital campaign included a concerted public relations effort in the media and the community at large. While campaign organizers lined up several extremely large contributions, many of the university's traditional donors, along with alumni and members of the campus community, also participated. Chairing the campaign was UNLV Foundation trustee and former board chair Don Snyder. Snyder's selection, along with the willingness of Bill Boyd and Joyce Mack to serve as honorary co-chairs, underscored the significance of the effort. The presence of William Paulos '69, Ralph Piercy '74, William Wortman '71, and James Zeiter '87 on the Campaign Leadership Committee, along with Dan Van Epp and Terry Wright, symbolized the larger role that UNLV alumni now played in the school's fund-raising efforts. By July 2006, the committee, along with President Harter, had raised almost $335 million.

This campaign, as well as the major donations that UNLV attracted from wealthy individuals and corporations in the last few decades of the twentieth century, contrasts sharply with the philanthrophic history of the school's early years. Indeed, much smaller gifts helped launch Nevada Southern with the Campus Building Fund of 1955. During Nevada Southern's two decades, it was mostly ordinary Las Vegans who bought the books for the school's fledgling library and laid the early foundation for a performing arts center. In the mid-1960s, the resort industry accepted Donald Moyer's invitation to fund a hotel college, and after the legalization of corporate gaming in 1969, companies of all types began giving more to the newly named UNLV. In the 1980s and 1990s, as the metropolitan area grew larger and wealthier, the business community's generosity to the school reached unprecedented levels. These donations and pledges supplemented the smaller gifts of residents and the school's growing core of alumni to fill the university's coffers with the millions needed to build dozens of new buildings and establish a law school. Over the past century, local philanthropy has also financed doctoral programs in the sciences and humanities, as well as scholarships and endowed scholarship programs for advanced student and faculty research. As a whole, these donors have played a major role in transforming the old desert campus of the 1960s into the modern university that is the UNLV of today.

CHAPTER ELEVEN

Sports

W hile new degree programs, buildings, presidents, faculty, and student activists all contributed to the development of Nevada Southern and UNLV, so did athletics. Shortly after the little campus on Maryland Parkway opened in 1957, sports began to play a greater role in the school's life. At first the play was mostly informal, much like the occasional baseball game or tennis match between students when the program was still based at Las Vegas High. The 1957–58 student yearbook mentions archery, golf, swimming, and "body mechanics" (gymnastics) as activities that students engaged in on an individual basis or as a club sport. But according to the yearbook, "the college's first athletic organization" in 1957 was the bowling team, which met every Thursday at 9 P.M. at local alleys.[1]

Intercollegiate sports competition at the Maryland Parkway campus did not formally begin until fall 1958. It all started with the arrival of the athletics program's legendary founder, Michael "Chub" Drakulich, who left his job as basketball coach at Rancho High to start a team at Nevada Southern. At the time, Nevada Southern had a total of 805 full-time and part-time students. Drakulich did most of his initial recruiting from this group, which included a

BOWLING, ONE OF NEVADA SOUTHERN'S FIRST TEAMS. 1958
EPILOGUE, 1958

few former high school players who enrolled at his urging. Basketball was the only sports program on campus until Drakulich started the baseball program in 1960. He coached both teams and served as athletics director.

Helping him was Alice Mason, who came to campus in 1957 and later assisted Drakulich by coaching and teaching classes in various sports, primarily for female students. Mason offered classes in archery, horseback riding, golf, tennis, square dancing, and skiing. In addition, she coached the bowling team whenever Drakulich could not attend a match. Mason and her husband also helped Drakulich with basketball games, serving as ticket sellers, ushering, and handling game-related expenses, even to the point of paying the referees.

Mason was an invaluable asset to Nevada Southern's infant athletics program, helping to launch many of the so-called minor sports. For instance, she coached the school's tennis club, which consisted only of male players, because, she noted, "I couldn't get any girls interested."[2] The club, a precursor of the

later tennis program, played the Boulder City men's club, hotel teams, and other local competition. In 1960 future congressman James Bilbray played for her. In the early 1960s Mason started horseback riding and skiing as club sports. She even tried to get land on campus for a horse-riding ring, but failed. Instead, student members practiced at Edna Gray's Riding Stables on the edge of town. The ski club was so popular that for years Nevada Southern competed with a variety of colleges in the sport.

In the 1950s and 1960s Mason was instrumental in laying the foundation for women's sports at the school, eventually coaching women's tennis, volleyball, and basketball. While she taught classes in tennis and volleyball, the women's teams were not just extensions of these classes. Although Mason could not interest female students in the school's tennis club during the late 1950s, the situation changed in the 1960s. "The girls came to me and asked for teams," she noted in a 2005 reminiscence. They practiced in the Gym, but "the only time we had was at lunch time and [we] had to share the Gym with the men and faculty who wanted that time only." All Mason could do was persevere. As she recalled, "the women's programs really took a back seat to the men's program." The challenge was "very time-consuming," as it was for Drakulich, who struggled also in the early days, trying to build a men's program with virtually no staff.[3]

Mason's work was crucial, because it allowed Drakulich to devote more time to program development and coaching. He launched men's golf and tennis in the late 1960s. After assigning the golf program to a series of assistant basketball coaches in an effort to save money, Drakulich, an avid golfer, finally took it over himself and stayed with it until his retirement in 1987. He also added other sports, hiring Robert Comeau to coach men's track and field and cross-country in 1965 (discontinued in the 1980s) before convincing President Moyer to begin a football program in 1967. Drakulich knew that football, even more than basketball—at least in those early days—was the major sport that would raise Nevada Southern's visibility in the region. On May 12, 1967, he hired fellow White Pine High School graduate Bill Ireland to recruit a team. Ireland had

FACING PAGE:

TOP: ALICE MASON TEACHING TENNIS, 1958. *EPILOGUE*, 1958

BOTTOM: ALICE MASON TEACHING SKIING, 1958. *EPILOGUE*, 1958

MICHAEL "CHUB" DRAKULICH STARTED A FORMAL SPORTS
PROGRAM AT NEVADA SOUTHERN. SPECIAL COLLECTIONS, UNLV
LIBRARIES 0062-1163

been a successful coach in northern Nevada, leading four Fernley High School teams to state championships and nine others to conference championships before becoming freshman football and baseball coach at the University of Nevada in Reno. Drakulich, too, had coached at the main campus, and his former colleagues on the staff there urged him to hire Ireland. It was a good move. Ireland went on to post a winning record at Nevada Southern–UNLV over the next five seasons.

In 1973, when Drakulich decided to resign as athletics director, a job whose pressures had grown with the campus, President Zorn tapped Ireland to replace him. Ireland spent seven years in the position and proved to be a capable administrator. After all, as NSU's football coach, Ireland worked closely with the Las Vegas Convention and Visitors Authority to build the Las Vegas Stadium (later the Sam Boyd Silver Bowl) in 1970, and he presided over its later expansion to 32,000 seats. Ireland stayed until 1980. By 1979 UNLV's two-year probation from the NCAA for recruiting violations, the department's spiraling debt, and a host of problems involving the Rebel Boosters eventually got to him. Worse still, the Los Angeles Lakers were actively courting Jerry Tarkanian to be their next coach. A Tarkanian departure threatened to cut the revenues produced by UNLV's most profitable program—money that helped carry football and other sports. Ireland also fretted over enforcement of Title IX, especially in the wake of having to cut $300,000 from the budgets of swimming, tennis, and other so-called minor sports that produced little or no revenue. While Ireland hoped to stay long enough to ease UNLV's entry into the Western Athletic Conference (WAC), that did not come to pass. A variety of factors conspired to delay the change until 1996. UNLV instead joined the Big West in 1982. Ireland retired, but later agreed to serve as executive director of the UNLV Hall of Fame.

Following Ireland's departure, Charles Bucher and Al Negratti each put in a one-year stint as athletics director until UNLV hired Dr. Bradley Rothermel, who restored stability to the job. Rothermel, with a master's and a doctorate from the University of Illinois, was the first UNLV athletics director with significant national experience. He held athletics posts with Kansas State, George Williams College, and the University of Illinois before serving as associate director of athletics at West Virginia University. A former player in the Milwaukee Braves organization, he had therefore been an athlete, a coach, and an administrator before arriving at UNLV in January 1981.

He came to Las Vegas determined to improve the program. While donations to UNLV's teams, inspired greatly by the success of Tarkanian, football coach Tony Knap, and baseball coach Fred Dallimore, gave Rothermel cause for optimism, the deficit lingered. Between 1981 and December 1990, when he resigned his position and joined UNLV's kinesiology department, Rothermel presided over a program that won thirty-three conference championships in the Big West Conference and the Pacific Coast Athletic Association. Under his direction UNLV participated in fourteen intercollegiate sports. Despite inheriting a deficit, Rothermel balanced his budget every year.

This achievement came at a price: too little money to fund enough scholarships, construct the facilities, and build the programs that would allow UNLV to compete with the major schools in numerous sports. The exception was basketball, where Rothermel spent the money to keep Jerry Tarkanian as coach and offered the scholarships that top recruits expected. Rothermel also worked to make sure that the Thomas & Mack Center, which opened in 1983, would be a first-class venue for basketball. This meant courting fans and major donors like Si and Marilyn Redd, who provided the funds to properly outfit interior spaces at the arena.

But, as Rothermel later explained, aside from basketball, "we were never able to fund any of our other programs at what you would call a top NCAA level. We were always scrambling for dollars. Not funding all of our programs at the top level was probably my biggest disappointment."[4] UNLV's budget grew from $2.75 million in Rothermel's first year to $10 million in 1990. Of that, the state subsidy was about 10 percent. Fortunately, the basketball team annually generated up to $6 million from TV revenues, ticket sales, memorabilia, apparel licensing, and other sources of income. But during the program's free fall in the years after Tarkanian's departure, that figure bottomed out at $527,000 in the 1994–95 season.

In a 1995 interview Rothermel said, "If you look back at the history of the success of the 14 intercollegiate programs we sponsored, . . . virtually all of them had their greatest success" between 1981 and 1990. He credited excellent coaches and no NCAA postseason sanctions to hamper recruiting. Rothermel firmly believed that UNLV athletes could have been more successful if the money had been there. "Las Vegas has proven that it will not support UNLV [sports] unless [they are] successful at the national level because there are so many entertainment alternatives in the city."[5] Therefore he felt it was important to spend the money and make football, baseball, and the other sports more competitive.

In his view, a major barrier to achieving that goal was the lack of support from President Maxson. "To be successful in any program," Rothermel declared, "you have to have certain people aligned. It needs to be regential, presidential, with administrative officials and athletic personnel." Rothermel recalled that he made numerous suggestions to Maxson about how to generate more support for athletic programs. These included transferring surpluses from the Sam Boyd Silver Bowl and Thomas & Mack Center to the Athletics Department and convincing state legislators to allow fee waivers for athletes. "He wouldn't do any of those things for me," Rothermel noted somewhat bitterly, but Maxson did support the reforms for Rothermel's successors, Dennis Finfrock and Jim Weaver.[6]

Conflicts with Maxson clouded Rothermel's last six years. The trouble started in 1986 when the two clashed over the firing of football coach Harvey Hyde. Rothermel saw Hyde as the innocent victim who recognized the embarrassments caused by player arrests and took firm steps to impose strict discipline for players on and off the field. But Maxson saw the continuing incidents as a growing crisis that could threaten the public's perception of the school, its athletes, and his effectiveness as a leader. So he acted to replace Hyde, who, although popular, was no Jerry Tarkanian.

Rothermel and Maxson also clashed over Tarkanian. Rothermel saw the nationally prominent Runnin' Rebels as the linchpin that held all of his programs together. Men's basketball was the financial juggernaut that generated the television revenues, fan enthusiasm, and well-heeled donors that UNLV athletics so desperately needed in order to grow in quality. But Maxson's increasing displeasure with Tarkanian over his program's repeated bouts with the NCAA and the negative national publicity they triggered strained the president's relationship with his athletics director. Although Maxson did not fire Rothermel, their problems did little to win the presidential favor that athletics so desperately needed.

Convinced that Maxson was determined to oust Tarkanian, Rothermel left in December 1990. A series of short-term directors of athletics followed. Rothermel's interim replacement was former coach Dennis Finfrock, who in 1976 had launched UNLV's wrestling program, which Rothermel later discontinued. Finfrock ultimately pressured Tarkanian into resigning after the infamous hot tub incident. Finfrock's role in this episode eventually dashed his own chances of becoming permanent athletics director. That job went to Jim Weaver, who stayed from 1992 to 1994. Weaver also was caught up in the bitter aftermath of Tarkanian's ouster, unfortunately presiding during Rollie Massimino's two mediocre seasons as coach of the Runnin' Rebels. As revenues derived from athletics shrank and UNLV's new interim president, Kenny Guinn, ordered an end to Maxson's Thomas & Mack-Silver Bowl subsidies to athletics, the frustrated Weaver decided to leave.

After a year's search and a commendable performance as interim director by former tennis coach Fred Albrecht, President Harter appointed Charles Cavagnaro in 1995. Cavagnaro came to UNLV from Memphis State, where the revenues he helped generate from that school's nationally prominent basketball program attracted the attention of UNLV officials who were looking for an athletics director with proven ability.

Aside from Title IX and other problems, Cavagnaro faced a formidable challenge in guiding UNLV's transition into the WAC. Once again, the problem was money. As Rothermel observed, "I really believe [UNLV's joining the WAC] was a move forward in basketball, but [it was] a quantum leap in football." He explained, "You have to ask now whether the commitment has been made institutionally as well as financially. Has the commitment been made philosophically, or are you happy just to be in the WAC and go 3–8 or 2–8 in football and be .500 every basketball season."[7]

That question was never fully answered, because Harter and Cavagnaro joined seven other schools to form a new conference, the Mountain West, which began in July 1999. Fortunately, Cavagnaro was a talented builder who worked hard to raise private money for the Lied Athletic Complex, which was perhaps his greatest accomplishment. He also attempted to revive UNLV football by recruiting former USC and Los Angeles Rams head coach John Robinson, who soon restored the stature of UNLV's once respectable program. With basketball, Cavagnaro was less successful, as Bill Bayno failed to rekindle Las Vegas's enthusiasm for Rebel basketball. Cavagnaro finally decided to retire in 2001.

After John Robinson's brief stint as athletics director (2002–03), UNLV hired Mike Hamrick, a talented administrator and proven fund-raiser. President Harter, appreciating Hamrick's value, took matters into her own hands and politely rejected suggestions from boosters and department insiders in support of other candidates. Determined to restore UNLV's winning tradition in major sports, and recognizing the vital role that money played in the process, Harter saw Hamrick as the obvious choice. He got off to an apparent fast start in spring 2004 by hiring the respected Lon Kruger to replace Charles Spoonhour as the Runnin' Rebels coach and by persuading a highly touted Utah assistant, Mike Sanford, to succeed John Robinson.

While directors of athletics were certainly crucial to administering and developing the school's sports programs, the memorable performances of coaches and student athletes created the sense of pride that bound UNLV, its students, and Las Vegans closer together. But who were the young men and women who contributed to the great sports tradition at the school? Over the past five decades, student athletes in both individual and team sports have been responsible for some of the greatest moments in school history. Some of the teams have brought national and even international recognition to the campus. To be sure, it has been not just academic progress but also athletic achievements that have contributed to the school's growing reputation for excellence.

One of the greatest athletes came from the track and field program. Las Vegas native Sheila Tarr was UNLV's first-ever national champion, winning the 1984 NCAA heptathlon title. The next year, she finished second at the NCAA championships and eleventh at the Olympic trials. Tarr won back-to-back Pacific Coast Athletic Association Athlete of the Year awards. In 1997 she was inducted into the UNLV Athletic Hall of Fame, along with Randall Cunningham and Matt Williams. After graduation, Tarr-Smith (now married) became a member of the Clark County Fire Department, where she had many opportunities to use her athletic skills. She died of a rare neurological disease in 1998 at the age of thirty-four. In a lasting memorial to her athletic accomplishments, service to the community, and heroic fight against a terminal disease, the Clark County School District named the Sheila Tarr Elementary School for her.

UNLV also honored her in a variety of ways, most notably by naming its new athletic field for her. In April 1998 the university opened Myron Partridge Stadium and Sheila Tarr-Smith Field for track and field events. With construction of the new Paradise Elementary School on the site of the old track, it became necessary in the late 1990s to build a new track and stadium on the east side of Swenson Street. Since UNLV dedicated its original track in 1981 to Partridge, a respected and beloved southern Nevada sports official, the new stadium also bore his name. But the field belonged to Tarr-Smith. In death, the mingling of Partridge and Tarr-Smith's names at the new venue was fitting, since she gave some of her greatest performances at the old Partridge Stadium.

The new facility, designed by Martin and Martin, included two pole vault pits, two long jump and triple jump lanes, two shot put slabs, and plenty of space for hammer and javelin events—all of which Tarr-Smith excelled in. Partridge Stadium contained seating for 1,000 fans and first-class training facilities. This

MICHELLE SUSZEK, CROSS-COUNTRY TEAM. UNLV ATHLETICS
DEPARTMENT

new venue for track and field finally gave UNLV the opportunity to host national and even international track and field events. Of course, Tarr-Smith was not the only star athlete in women's track and field. Trena Hull won the NCAA 1,000-meter title in 1987 and continues to hold four school records. In 2000 Katie Barto scored the highest finish ever for a Rebel harrier at the NCAA cross-country championship.

Track and field was not the only women's sport to get a new facility. In 2002 UNLV opened the Eller Media Stadium at Jim Rogers Field, built largely by generous donations from Eller Media, future university chancellor Jim Rogers, Jerry and Sue Lykins, and others. The $2.7 million softball venue featured dugouts, bullpens, a second-floor press box equipped for broadcasting, and seating for almost 800 fans. This new ballpark finally provided a respectable home for a women's sport that struggled in its early history but later produced some great athletes for UNLV.

Women's softball began in 1980 under coach Gena Borda. After three subpar seasons, UNLV suspended the sport until 1985, when Frances Cox took over for two more seasons before yielding to Shan McDonald in 1987. McDonald also suffered through two losing seasons before the breakthrough year of 1989, when the team enjoyed its first winning season. The next two years were even better, as the Rebels went 41–27 and 49–17–1, respectively. Part of the reason for the team's success was pitcher Lori Harrigan (1989–92), who set a series of impressive school records, including most career wins (83), complete games (123), shutouts (53), ERA (.77), and no-hitters (6) before going on to win three Olympic gold medals for the United States in softball at the 1996, 2000, and 2004 Games. In 1998 UNLV retired Harrigan's #22 jersey to honor her accomplishments. Even after she left, the softball team continued to prosper, finishing first in the WAC with a

49–14 record in 1995 for the best season in team history. In 1997, however, the sport began a gradual decline.

Although NSU students played informal tennis matches in the early 1960s on the dusty clay surfaces of local schools and tennis clubs, the program did not officially begin until 1969. Records were not systematically kept until 1974, when new coach Fred Albrecht enacted that reform. The early teams played their home matches at the campus's original tennis facility, which consisted of three courts behind Grant Hall on what is today's pedestrian mall fronting the Law School. Unfortunately, they were built incorrectly, facing east and west, which left players with the disadvantage of looking into a low afternoon sun. The situation was not remedied until 1973, two years before the Paul McDermott Physical Education Complex opened, when UNLV unveiled twelve new north-south courts on Harmon Avenue. Although adequate, these courts provided little space for spectators or for major competitions.

That all changed in 1989 when Stations Casinos founder Frank Fertitta Jr. and his wife, Vicki, gave UNLV $1 million to construct the modern tennis complex that is named for them. The twelve-court, $1.5 million stadium and clubhouse opened in 1993 and has served as the home of not only UNLV men's and women's tennis but also numerous youth and community tournaments. The facility has hosted NCAA regional finals and the U.S. Tennis Association's Men's Challenger pro event as well. As UNLV director of tennis Larry Easley described the Fertitta family's contribution, "They saw that for UNLV Tennis to grow it needed to have a first-class facility and that's certainly what we have now. Rebel Tennis is becoming a national collegiate program, and that wouldn't be possible without this stadium."[8]

Women's tennis began in the mid-1960s as a physical education class and then a competitive sport with Alice Mason, who coached until Val Pate took over the team in 1975. Mason, Pate (1975–77), and Tina Kunzer-Murphy (1978–81) were the principal coaches until UNLV dropped women's tennis in the early 1980s. Brad Rothermel secured enough funding to resume the sport in 1986, and new coach Craig Witcher got the program off to a promising start with a 112–89 record over six seasons. He was followed in 1992 by York Strother, whose 18–5 record gave him the highest winning percentage of any coach. Ola Malmquist (1993–98) and Kevin Cory (2000–present) boosted the program further, as both compiled winning percentages over .600. In fact, under Cory the women finished first in the Mountain West in 2000 and 2002. Of course, the WAC had more teams and its championship was harder to win, but the women distinguished themselves with respectable finishes in 1988 (second), 1993 (third), 1994 and 1996 (second). While many fine women athletes have played tennis for UNLV, Witcher had the honor of coaching one of the best. Jolene Watanabe still leads all others in career doubles victories and is second in singles wins.

The men's program is much older, dating back to 1969. But there have been only three major coaches. Fred Albrecht took over in 1974 and compiled a respectable 230–80 record over nine seasons. Craig Witcher's winning percentage was .488, but because of budget constraints he was forced to coach both men's and women's tennis, which restricted his ability to devote enough time to the men. Larry Easley, who became the men's coach in 1992, was able to concentrate on just that team, and his 141–120 record through 2003 reflected that investment of time. While Albrecht had the advantage of coaching Andre's brother, Phil Agassi, whose 25–2 record in 1983 remains the highest single-season winning percentage in school history, as well as standouts Greg Henderson, Matt McDougall, Mike Morgan (UNLV's first Academic All-American Honorable Mention in tennis), and Scott Hunter, Easley has benefited from great athletes, too. Roger Pettersson (most season victories) and 2002 singles All-American Thomas Schneiter helped lift the program. Then in 1997, Australian Luke Smith surprised the sports world by capturing the NCAA singles title before teaming with fellow countryman Tim Blenkiron to win the NCAA doubles title, too. In 1995 and 1996, UNLV won the conference title with the help of these talented Aussies. Ironically, one of UNLV's greatest players, season and career victory leader Scott Warner, played under four different coaches in four years. Albrecht, Witcher, and two one-year coaches all guided Warner, who won the NCAA singles title in his senior year.

Basketball's Lady Rebels began their first season in 1974–75, going 8–7 under coach Barbara Quinn, who stayed only one season. Dan Ayala took over in 1975 and led the team to an impressive 109–23 record over five seasons, including a 23–2 mark in 1977–78. Sheila Strike took the reins in the 1980–81 season and was later joined by Jim Bolla. After two subpar seasons, she and

Bolla (who were briefly married) reeled off six consecutive 20-win seasons. Strike left after 1988, but Bolla continued on with a successful streak. From 1982 until his departure in 1996, Bolla compiled a 300–120 record for a .714 winning percentage.

Victories were harder to come by in the late 1990s, as several coaches came and went before Regina Miller arrived in 1998 to restore the winning tradition. Miller, the first African American head basketball coach at UNLV, came to Las Vegas after spending six seasons as head coach at Western Illinois University, whose team she took to the NCAA tournament in 1995. The North Carolina native wasted no time in revitalizing the Lady Rebels. In 1998–2000, Miller led UNLV to back-to-back 17-win seasons after inheriting a group that had won only 12 games overall in the previous three seasons. She then guided the 2000–1 team to a 19–10 record and an appearance in the WNIT. In 2001–2, she took the Lady Rebels to the NCAA tournament after they compiled a 23–8 record.

Miller, Strike, Bolla, and Ayala all benefited from the presence of talented athletes like Pauline Jordan (1987–90), who still holds the school record for most blocks in a career (286) and most rebounds in a game (27); Misty Thomas (1982–86), the former all-time scoring leader; and Linda Frohlich (1998–2002), the current all-time scoring leader, as well as Penny Welch, Gwynn Hobbs, Karen Hull, Linda Staley, and other great players from the past.

Of course, the most prominent sports program of them all remains men's basketball. This was Nevada Southern's first real intercollegiate sport, beginning on December 5, 1958, with a game against the College of Southern Utah. The first coach was the school's first athletics director, Chub Drakulich, who in five seasons compiled a respectable 68–45 record. The Runnin' Rebels went only 5–13 in their initial year against such competition as Snow College, Dixie Junior College, Antelope Valley Junior College, Nevada-Reno's freshman team, Southern Utah State, and Nellis Air Force Base. In those days, with almost no budget, Drakulich and the coaches had to drive the athletes to out-of-town games, which limited the schedule of all Nevada Southern sports. Despite the hardships, Drakulich took his ragtag group of local basketball players and made them into a team. The next five years were winning seasons, capped off by a 21–4 record in 1962–63. Drakulich coached the school's first Little All-American, Silas Stepp, in 1963 and created the annual Las Vegas Holiday Classic in 1961. The sport's popularity on campus even allowed Drakulich to form a junior varsity squad by 1960.

In the 1950s Nevada Southern played its games at Rancho High and later the city's recreation center, while practicing at Fremont Junior High on St. Louis Avenue. When Fremont was unavailable, they practiced on an asphalt surface behind Grant Hall. In 1960, however, the Gym (today's Marjorie Barrick Museum of Natural History) opened, and the team played the 1961–62 season in that facility, which accommodated 2,000 for basketball. In the next year, the team's growing popularity forced school officials to move home games into the 6,200-seat Rotunda of the Las Vegas Convention Center, where the Rebels played until the Thomas & Mack Center opened in 1983.

Drakulich, who also coached baseball and other sports in addition to running the athletics program (which became a department in 1965), eventually handed off the basketball job to Ed Gregory. In two seasons (1963–65) Gregory posted an impressive .727 winning percentage, with 40 wins and only 15 losses. He was the first coach to take the Rebels to the NCAA regional tournament, where they lost to Fresno State and San Francisco State. Then came Rolland Todd, who led the team to even greater heights. In five seasons (1965–70), the Rebels went 96–40, making the NCAA play-offs for three consecutive years. Drakulich, Gregory, and Todd all contributed to the little school's rise from obscurity to some measure of prominence. An accurate measure of that prominence was the NBA Portland Trailblazers' decision in 1970 to hire Todd as their new head coach.

John Bayer replaced Todd for the next three seasons (1970–73), and while he had a winning record (44–36), Bayer did not replicate Todd's success. Rebel fans, especially the Boosters, wanted a coach who could build upon the successful foundation laid by Bayer's predecessors. The Rebel Boosters, led by Sig Rogich, Bill Morris, Tom Wiesner, and others, had their eye on Jerry Tarkanian. In particular, they were impressed by his 147–23 record at Riverside City College and his 122–20 mark at Long Beach State, a four-year school that faced stiffer competition.

For his part, Tarkanian was interested in doubling his $27,000-a-year salary at Long Beach. But it was not only about money. Tarkanian realized that no matter how much he won in Southern California, he would always stand in the shadow of UCLA's legendary coach, John Wooden. Moving to Las Vegas would allow Tarkanian to operate in a different state, but still be close enough to recruit some of California's best players and compete against some of the Golden State's best teams. Of course, Tarkanian had not yet abandoned his very controlled zone offense in favor of the run-and-gun offense and full-court-press defense that would contribute so much to the Runnin' Rebels' popularity with fans and prospects alike. That would not occur until the late 1970s, but Rogich and the others felt that "Tark" would provide the spark that UNLV and the program both needed.

The new coach far exceeded everyone's expectations. His success at UNLV is a legendary chapter in American basketball lore. Ironically, he lost his first-ever

RUNNIN' REBEL

W 23   L 9

"The N.I.T. Final Four"

JERRY TARKANIAN AND THE RUNNIN' REBELS WITH STAFF IN
FRONT OF THEIR HOME AT THE TIME, THE LAS VEGAS
CONVENTION CENTER, 1980. SPECIAL COLLECTIONS, UNLV
LIBRARIES 0062-0269

UNLV RUNNIN' REBELS NATIONAL CHAMPIONSHIP TEAM, 1990.
UNLV ATHLETICS DEPARTMENT

game at UNLV to Texas Tech 82–76, but he reeled off nine straight wins after that en route to a 20–6 season. Tarkanian never had a losing season in nineteen years. In fact, his winning percentage of .829 ranks with the greatest coaches of all time in any sport, college or professional. He led the Runnin' Rebels to postseason play fourteen times, with nine consecutive appearances (1983–91) and three Final Fours, including two in a row. Capping this achievement was the national championship team of 1989–90 that destroyed Duke 103–73 in the most lopsided championship game in history.

That game, and indeed the whole season, brought UNLV and its city together as never before. By midseason, CSUN unfurled a banner along the Maryland Parkway facade of the student union that proudly declared: "We're No. 1." Reinforcing the message was a giant index finger pointing upward to signal the school's top-ranked position. The banner hung there for most of the year. All of the restaurants and stores along the thoroughfare mounted signs and banners in support of the team as it entered the NCAA postseason tournament. Moments after UNLV's victory on April 2, 1990, thousands of students and residents poured onto Maryland Parkway in front of the humanities building for an impromptu celebration that forced closure of the road between Flamingo and Tropicana for several hours.

Tarkanian had finally done it; he had led the Runnin' Rebels to the pinnacle of collegiate basketball. The coach would be the first to admit that whether it be winning the national championship or accomplishing any of the other great feats of his career, he could never have done it alone. Indeed, he had the help of talented athletes who could have played for anyone but chose to play at UNLV and for him. Tarkanian was as good a recruiter as he was a coach, and these talents complemented one another. Players like Eddie Owens, Reggie Theus, Sidney Green, and others helped lure Armon Gilliam, Gerald Paddio, Greg Anthony, Stacey Augmon, and Larry Johnson to Las Vegas. But Tarkanian's run-and-gun style captured the eye of the television camera and drew them all to the school, creating the magic that put UNLV on the national map. On November-

UNLV BASKETBALL COACH JERRY TARKANIAN BITING ON HIS TRADEMARK TOWEL DURING A GAME, 1985. SPECIAL COLLECTIONS, UNLV LIBRARIES 0062-1808

ber 26, 2005, Tarkanian was formally honored when, at President Harter's behest, the school named its basketball court for him—a lasting tribute to UNLV's winningest coach and the man who helped build the Thomas & Mack Center.

Tarkanian's successors never approached his records. Rollie Massimino became the school's sixth head coach on April 1, 1992. His credentials were impressive: nineteen quality seasons at Villanova, including the 1985 national championship. His two years at UNLV, for all their controversy in the aftermath of Tarkanian's forced departure, were winning seasons (36–21), but the team lacked the fire that had vaulted it to the heights of college basketball. Interim president Kenny Guinn tried to restore some of the old glory by hiring former assistant coach and Tarkanian protégé Tim Grgurich in 1994, but health problems forced his resignation after just seven games. Guinn then tapped young Massachusetts assistant coach Bill Bayno to revive the program's declining fortunes, but he failed after five (94–64) good, but not good enough, years in which the team won two conference championships and made four postseason appearances before losing in the early rounds.

Bayno and the others also coached great players. Eddie Owens (1973–77) continues to be UNLV's all-time career scoring leader with 2,221 points, and Elburt Miller's (1966–68) 55 points in a 1967 game is still the school record, as are his season and career scoring averages of 31.9 and 29.1, respectively. Keon Clark and Dalron Johnson remain the school leaders in blocked shots for a season (112 in 1996–97) and career (194 during 1999–2003). Of course, Tarkanian's players set records, too. Larry Johnson's (1989–91) season and career field goal percentages (.662 and .643), Mark Wade's (1986–87) season and Greg Anthony's career (1988–91) assist records (406 and 838), and Freddie Banks's (1986–87) game (10), and season (152) marks, along with Anderson Hunt's career (1988–91) three-point baskets (283) were just a few.

By any measure, the Runnin' Rebels have been UNLV's most popular and successful team throughout the school's history. Tarkanian's Rebels filled the 18,500-seat Thomas & Mack Center for almost a decade. On December 29, 1986, at the annual Holiday Festival, the Rebels set a home attendance record of 20,321. But they also were a popular attraction on the road, drawing 64,949 in 1987 against Bobby Knight's Indiana Hoosiers. There were undoubtedly many nights during Tarkanian's reign when the Rebels could have filled Yankee Stadium or the Rose Bowl. They were that good; they were that well respected nationally; and they were that beloved by local fans and others around the nation.

When measured by the number of players drafted by the NBA, the quality of UNLV basketball is even more striking. Ricky Sobers (1975), Reggie Theus (1978), Sidney Green (1983), Anthony Jones (1986), Armon Gilliam and Freddie Banks (1987), Larry Johnson (UNLV's only number one pick), Stacey Augmon, Greg Anthony, and George Ackles (all 1991), Elmore Spencer (1992), J. R. Rider (1993), Keon Clark (1998), Shawn Marion (1999), Marcus Banks (2003), and many others got the attention of NBA coaches and scouts.

For years, revenue from the Runnin' Rebels helped fund many of UNLV's other sports programs. Golf, however, had its own fund-raising arm. The Rebel Golf Foundation began in the 1986–87 school year. The organizers' goal was to help create a golf program "with a national reputation for academic excellence, scholarship, and personal achievement." A related goal was to raise enough money "to completely endow the program" so that it would "be able to compete at the highest level for many years to come."[9]

The traditionally close connection between golf and Las Vegas resorts, coupled with the love that many illustrious businessmen felt for the game, helped the foundation attract numerous members. Moreover, the annual PGA Las Vegas Invitational brought them together once a year as a small community to play as amateurs or help run the tournament. During the 1980s and into the 1990s, the three major professional tours, the LPGA, PGA, and the Senior (now Champions) Tour, came to town, which was good for tourism and good for the UNLV teams, which got to play with some of the world's best golfers.

Some of Las Vegas's most esteemed residents have supported the Golf Foundation. By 2003 its more than 220 members included Steve Wynn, Walt Casey, Frank Fertitta Jr., James Rogers, Sig Rogich, Ted Wiens, and Tom Wiesner. Even though UNLV women's golf did not begin until 2001, prominent women have always been members of the foundation. These include former Las Vegas mayor Jan Jones, Lied Foundation trustee Christina Hixson, Kitty Rodman, Kathy Rogich, and others.

Since 1987 the foundation has raised hundreds of thousands of dollars for Rebel golf. In the 1990s, Rebel Golf Day became an important annual event for bringing the Las Vegas golf community together. As UNLV coach Dwaine Knight explained, "It gives the players a chance to play a few holes with the people who support them year in and year out, and offers them an opportunity to get to know them on a more personal basis."[10]

In addition, each year the Golf Foundation, much like the UNLV Foundation, honored members who contributed substantial amounts of time and money to the program. The foundation designated an annual "honored member" for special recognition. The list includes such Las Vegas luminaries as developer Ernie Becker Jr., Tom Wiesner, Christina Hixson, and Steve Wynn.

Of course, the school's golf team debuted long before the foundation was formed. Chub Drakulich launched the men's program and served as its coach for nineteen years. During that time, he worked with Rebel Boosters and golf supporters in the Las Vegas community to lay the groundwork for the foundation. In 1987 Drakulich turned the golf team over to Dwaine Knight, whose arrival and support got the foundation off to a fast start. Knight proved to be a worthy successor. Under the new coach, NCAA tournament invitations and a national ranking became commonplace. Knight's success and his relationship with the local golf community, while just a microcosm of Jerry Tarkanian's romance with the city as a whole, similarly attracted larger donations to support his program. In 1991, for example, International Game Technolgy (IGT) contributed stock worth $500,000 to the golf scholarship fund. Two years later, the Earl E. Wilson estate added another $250,000 to the endowment fund created by the foundation at Knight's behest, and Christina Hixson has also been a generous donor.

With a great coach, plenty of scholarship money, and a warm, sunny, and prominent city to play in, it is no wonder that top college prospects came to UNLV. As a result, men's golf became one of the most consistently successful programs in the athletics department. In 1998 the top-ranked Rebels won the NCAA national championship, only the second team to do so (Jerry Tarkanian's 1989–90 Runnin' Rebels were the other) in the school's history.

In the twenty-first century, Ryan Moore set even more records for Rebel golf. In 2003–04 alone, the eventual four-time all-American won the U.S. Amateur Championship, the U.S. Amateur Public Links Championship, the Western Amateur Championship, the Players Championship, and became only the second UNLV golfer to win the NCAA championship. Moore is the only amateur in history to win these five titles in a single year. Then, in the 2005 Masters Golf Tournament, the UNLV senior shot a one-under-par at Augusta National, earning him a tie for thirteenth place, the best finish of any amateur in more than a quarter century. Later that year, before turning pro, he won the prestigious Ben Hogan Award, given annually to the nation's best college golfer.

Over the years, Knight, with help from Drakulich, recruited and developed a number of players who went on to successful careers in professional golf. Warren Schutte, who won the individual NCAA golf title in 1991, played on both the PGA and Canadian professional tours. Jeremy Anderson (1996–2000), who added his name to the UNLV record books for lowest round, lowest score for a 54-hole tournament, and best single-season and career stroke average, made the PGA tour in 2001. Chad Campbell (1995–96) joined the tour in 1998, and by 2002 he had pro career winnings of almost $1 million. Edward Fryatt (1991–94) had more than $1.4 million in PGA earnings by 2002. Skip Kendall (1982–86), who played for Drakulich, exceeded $4.6 million, and stars Chris Riley (1992–96) and Adam Scott (1998–99) have each surpassed $5 million.

Women's golf is a relatively new program at UNLV. Thanks partly to donations by Donrey Media (now Eller Media), James Rogers, Jerry and Sue Lykins, and the Las Vegas Founders Club, the women's golf program began in 2001 with support from a generous scholarship endowment.

In January 2001 UNLV hired Kelley Hester as the first coach. Just three weeks after practice began, the team played its first match and finished a distant fourteenth, 100 strokes over par. But only six weeks later, in February 2002, UNLV freshman Hwanhee Lee won the Lady Aztec International and paced the Rebels to a sixth-place finish, their best ever up to that point. Two months later the team claimed fifth place at the Mountain West Conference championship, a respectable finish for an inaugural season.

UNLV GOLFER RYAN MOORE HITS A SHOT FROM THE FAIRWAY. UNLV ATHLETICS DEPARTMENT

In May 2003 Hester shocked the team by resigning to accept the head coaching job at the University of Arkansas. Her successor, Missy Ringler, picked up where Hester had left off, guiding the team to the 2003 BYU Dixie Classic and standout golfers Sunny Oh and Hwanhee Lee to medalist honors. Later, Oh and Lee helped lead the women's golf team to the 2004 Mountain West Conference title in just the third year of the program's existence. In fact, Oh became the program's first All-American Honorable Mention. Undoubtedly, as women's golf continues to grow, some of its talented graduates will go on to profitable careers on the LPGA tour.

Unlike women's golf, women's volleyball had a long tradition at UNLV. The program formally began in 1978 under head coach Matti Smith, who, despite a 10–7 inaugural season, left during the following year. Her replacement, Gena

Borda, also enjoyed success until UNLV suspended the sport in 1980 because of budgetary problems. Women's volleyball returned in 1984 under Karen Lamb, who experienced a winning season and a losing one before deficits and the priority of other sports again suspended the program.

Reestablished in 1996 under new coach Deitre Collins, women's volleyball sputtered after a successful 23–8 season in 1998. Still, the program has produced a number of talented players, including career "kills" and "digs" leader Leiana Oswald (1,350 and 812) and career assist leaders Meri-de Boyer (1,566) and Nicki King (3,197), as well as career service ace leader Christel Eves (116).

UNLV soccer also dates from the 1970s. Begun in 1974 under coach Tom Khamis, the men's program enjoyed several good seasons (Vince Hart replaced Khamis after two years) before fading into mediocrity in the late 1970s and early 1980s. Barry Barto's arrival in 1982 reversed the downward trend, as he immediately, in his first season, led the Rebels to a winning record (10–4–3).

UNLV SOCCER PLAYER ALEX HERNANDEZ. UNLV ATHLETICS DEPARTMENT

For the next quarter century, Barto built a nationally recognized program, taking the Rebels to five NCAA tournament appearances while compiling an overall mark of 298–197–43 for a respectable .549 winning percentage. The native Philadelphian, a two-time all-American midfielder, was an original draft choice of the North American Soccer League and captained the U.S. National Team in 1974 and 1975. With a degree in business management, Barto drifted back and forth between soccer and business. In the early 1970s he served as a fullback and business manager for the Philadelphia Atoms, and he concluded his professional career in 1977 as a defender for the NASL Fort Lauderdale Strikers.

Barto came to UNLV after six seasons of coaching at his alma mater, Philadelphia Textile. At UNLV his expertise in business and management proved almost as valuable as his soccer skills. Although UNLV soccer began in 1974, the team never had a home field of its own. When Barto took over in

1982, he worked with athletics director Brad Rothermel to construct a facility. After President Goodall approved plans to build the soccer complex on the site of the old softball field, work began to finance the project. With the help of longtime real estate investor and soccer fan Kenneth Johann and his wife, Alice, who not only established a soccer scholarship fund but also donated heavily to the new facility (named for their late son), construction began. Hundreds of community workers also gave their time and money. Building progressed quickly, and Peter Johann Memorial Field opened in time for the 1983 season. Since its debut, the complex has hosted numerous international matches as well as the 1983 ISAA Senior Bowl All-Star Game, and more than 300 home games for UNLV's men's and women's soccer teams.

Of course, Barto and his predecessors relied on the skills of many talented athletes who played for UNLV over the years. Among these are a number of record holders, including Robbie Ryerson (1982–85) and David Cohen (1977–81), who remain first and second in team history for the most career points (159 and 147, respectively) and the most goals (67 and 66). Ryerson is also second in assists (25) to school leader Daniel Barber (1989–92), whose total of 26 still leads all players.

Women's soccer is a much more recent sport at UNLV. It began in 1998 under coach Staci Hendershott, who established the program that Danny Abdalla took over in 2000. A four-year letter winner and starting goalie (1994–97) for the men's team, Abdalla returned to UNLV after a two-year professional playing career with the Orange County Zodiac, a minor league affiliate of the Major League Soccer's Los Angeles Galaxy. Appointed coach in February 2000, Abdalla compiled a 42–33–6 record in his four years at the helm.

In contrast to women's soccer, the baseball program is almost as old as the campus, beginning in 1960 as Nevada Southern's second intercollegiate sport, with Chub Drakulich as the skipper. After six seasons (game records for these early years are incomplete), Drakulich handed the job over to Bob Doering, who compiled a respectable .554 percentage (158–127–3) between 1967 and 1973.

Doering's successor was his assistant coach for four seasons (1969–73), Fred Dallimore, who coached the Hustlin' Rebels for the next twenty-three seasons and won 794 games. When he retired in 1996, Dallimore (794–558–2) ranked thirty-first on the NCAA list of all-time winningiest coaches. During his tenure

Dallimore led UNLV to the NCAA tournament seven times, including a 1996 appearance in the NCAA South II Regional. That year the Rebels won the Big West tournament championship, defeating nationally ranked UC–Santa Barbara, Cal State Fullerton, and Long Beach State. In 1980 the Rebels finished second in the NCAA Midwest Regional, just one victory away from advancing to the College World Series. For its achievement, this squad won induction into the UNLV Athletic Hall of Fame in 1994.

Dallimore's career at UNLV was impressive. He guided the club to nineteen .500 or better winning seasons and more than nineteen 30-win or better seasons while coaching more than forty major league draft picks. In recognition of his achievements, UNLV retired Dallimore's #13 jersey in 1997, along with that of baseball great Matt Williams, in a ceremony at Wilson Stadium before the season home opener against UCLA. Dallimore (#13) and Jerry Tarkanian (#2) are the only coaches in school history to have their numbers retired.

After Dallimore's retirement, the team went through a series of leadership changes, from Rick Soesbe (1997–2001) to Jim Schlossnagle (2002–3) to Buddy Gouldsmith, a former assistant who assumed the head coaching position in 2004. The program clearly missed Dallimore, but it was time to move on. Even though Schlossnagle stayed for only a short time, he began restoring the Hustlin' Rebels' winning tradition, compiling a respectable 77–47 record.

Through the years many fine athletes played for the team. Ralph Garcia (1967–70) remains the school's all-time strikeout leader with 462 over 363 innings. Garcia is one of only five pitchers in school history to win 30 games in a career. In 1969 he set UNLV's single-season strikeout record with 144, which stood until 1995, when Nate Yeskie fanned 147. Garcia's success continued into the minor leagues and eventually into the majors, where he played for the San Diego Padres. Rivaling Garcia on the mound was Herb Pryor (1971–73 and 1978), UNLV's all-time ERA leader (2.54), innings pitched (453), and complete games (40). In addition to winning 35 games in his career, Pryor threw UNLV's first no-hitter and only perfect game, in March 1971.

UNLV has also produced its share of stars in the field and at the plate. One of the greatest was Matt Williams (1984–86). The Carson City native was a 1986 consensus first-team all-American of *Baseball America, Sporting News,* and *Collegiate Baseball.* In the 1986 major league draft, he was the third overall pick of the San Francisco Giants. Williams enjoyed a distinguished career in the majors, winning four Golden Glove awards as a third baseman. A feared hitter, he was the major leagues' home run king in 1994, with 43 during a strike-shortened season in which he could have made a run at Babe Ruth's home run record years before Mark McGwire, Sammy Sosa, and Barry Bonds. Williams played in the All-Star Game four times. In 1997 he became the only Rebels baseball player to have his jersey number retired.

In the team's early years, the Hustlin' Rebels played at local high school fields until Nevada Southern built a playing field on campus. The site of today's Earl E. Wilson Baseball Stadium was the location of its predecessor, "Hustlin' Rebel Field," which the school dedicated on April 1, 1973, before 1,500 fans at the UNLV-USC game. In 1980 UNLV renamed the venue Roger Barnson Field to honor the school's assistant football coach and assistant athletic director, who had died in an automobile crash that March. Night baseball came to the ballpark two years later when the school erected eight light standards. In September 1984 the Young Electric Sign Company installed a $155,000 scoreboard after Dallimore negotiated a lease-purchase agreement with the company.

Although a comfortable home for the Hustlin' Rebels, Barnson Field was still not a first-rate facility by college standards. That changed in the early 1990s when the estate of Earl and Hazel Wilson donated $1.2 million to build what became the 3,000-seat Earl E. Wilson Baseball Stadium at Roger Barnson Field. The stadium, featuring 2,500 theater-type seats and 500 bleacher-back seats, an enclosed press box, paved parking for 400 cars, and other amenities, opened in January 1994. As estate co-trustee Mel Wolzinger explained, Wilson, a major executive at the Golden Nugget for many years, had played semipro ball in Oregon during his youth. "Earl was a big baseball fan," Wolzinger told reporters on opening day. "Baseball was one of his great loves."[11]

Not all sports had their own separate facilities as baseball did. Completion of the Paul McDermott Physical Education Complex in 1975 established several facilities that allowed UNLV to add new collegiate sports to its athletics program. The opening of the 50-meter indoor pool, renamed in 1980 the Buchanan Natatorium for former regent and swimming enthusiast James "Bucky" Buchanan II, gave UNLV a modern place to train its team.

Over the past three decades, natatorium audiences have witnessed great

athletic performances. In collegiate swimming, school records are usually set by more recent athletes. This was true at UNLV, with freestyle record holders Jonathan Hugo (2002–3), Piotr Krzyskow (2000–1), Jacint Simon (1999–2001), and Erik Scalise (1996–97), as well as with backstroke and breaststroke leaders Tomasz Piotrowski (1996–98) and Patrick Adams (2001–3). On the women's side, Lorena Diaconescu (1999–2002) and Sheri Thiesen (1995–97) dominated the school's freestyle records and Raluca Udroiu (2001–3) and Shayna Burns (2002–03) also starred.

In swimming, however, holding current records is not the only measure of greatness. Past champions were the record holders of their eras, and many great athletes swam for UNLV. Mike Mintenko's (1995–98) relay team twice finished fifth at the 2000 Olympics, Bart Pippenger (1986–90), a four-time all-American, captured the gold medal for the 200-meter butterfly at the 1990 world championships. Vaune Kadlubek (1977–80) helped establish the women's program with quality performances in the late 1970s and served the university for many years after graduation as a coach and student advisor. In 2004 she won induction into the USA Water Polo Hall of Fame, a major honor in that sport. Juliet Mroziak-Santiago and UNLV's top distance swimmer from 1992 to 1996, Melissa Meacham, have also stayed on in various positions in the school's athletics department. These athletes, along with past UNLV champions like Wendy Hoffman-Meyers, Sally Fleisher, Andrew Livingston, Bob Smale, and others have brought recognition to UNLV.

Some of the best student athletes at UNLV have been the swimmers. Many excelled in the classroom and went on to careers outside the sport, using the intense training habits required to succeed in their sport to succeed in life. The examples are legion: NCAA qualifier and Big West Scholar-Athlete of the Year Colin Dircks (1989–93) became a physician; freestyle relay specialist Kristin Lynch became a lawyer; and the list goes on.

The school's football program began in May 1967 when President Donald Moyer appointed McGill native Bill Ireland to be the first coach. It took Ireland a year to recruit and train a team to play in the 1968 season, but he got Rebel football off to a fast start, going 8–0 before losing the last game of the season. Before Las Vegas Stadium (today's Sam Boyd Stadium) opened in 1971, the Rebels played their home games at the old Cashman Field, which seated 8,000. Of course, the competition was mediocre by today's standards; their opponents included Westminster, Azusa, Pacific, and Cal Lutheran. The school's first game against a major college opponent took place in November 1972, when UNLV lost to the University of Miami at the Orange Bowl. Ireland coached for five years, with a .530 winning percentage, before replacing Chub Drakulich as athletics director in 1973.

Ron Meyer replaced Ireland on the gridiron. A successful coach in Texas,

UNLV FOOTBALL COACH RON MEYER, WHO LATER COACHED IN THE NFL, 1973. SPECIAL COLLECTIONS, UNLV LIBRARIES 0062-0767

Meyer came just weeks before Jerry Tarkanian's appointment, and both men ignited fan enthusiasm with their confident outlook and past success. The football team had struggled through a dismal 1–10 season in 1972, but Meyer made the squad winners again. The team was 8–3 in 1973 and 27–8 overall during Meyer's three seasons, for a .771 mark, the best winning percentage of any Rebel football coach in history. In 1974 Meyer led the Rebels to an NCAA Division II play-off after an undefeated season. There was no way the small university could retain Meyer, who left for SMU in 1976. He later coached in the NFL at New England and Indianapolis before spending a season each with the CFL's Las Vegas Posse (1994) and Chicago's XFL franchise (2001).

Meyer's successor was just as talented. Tony Knap came to UNLV from a successful Boise State program, and he picked up where Meyer left off. In six seasons, Knap compiled a 47–20–2 record, for a .695 winning percentage. He led the Rebels to an NCAA Division II play-off appearance in his first year with quarterback Glenn Carano, who went on to the Dallas Cowboys, where he won a Super Bowl ring as a backup to Roger Staubach. Knap presided over the team's graduation to the Division I level in 1978. Three years later, the coach capped off his UNLV career with a shocking road upset of eighth-ranked Brigham Young University and its star-studded team. It was one of the great moments in Rebel football history.

After the 1981 season, Knap retired to his apple orchard in Walla Walla, replaced by Harvey Hyde, who had coached at various California community colleges. In 1982 UNLV became a playing member of the Pacific Coast Athletic Association, later renamed the Big West. After a rough first season, when the Rebels went just 3–8 (1–5 in conference games), Hyde turned the program around dramatically, going 7–4 in 1983 and 11–2 (7–0 in the Big West) the fol-

lowing year. The team, featuring standout quarterback and future NFL star Randall Cunningham, went on to win the California Bowl, routing Toledo 30–13.
Unfortunately, the discipline that players showed on the field did not extend for
some into their private lives. A series of incidents resulted in several arrests,
lots of embarrassing publicity, and Hyde's ouster in 1986.

After Hyde's departure, UNLV football was never the same. A series of
coaches came and went. The selection of former Rebel player Wayne Nunnely
was popular on campus. But Nunnely's 19–25 record was not good enough,
nor was former Notre Dame assistant coach Jim Strong's 17–27 mark, nor Jeff
Horton's 13–44 effort. Horton, however, did manage a 7–5 season in his first
year and a 52–24 victory over Central Michigan at
the Las Vegas Bowl before his team began a steep
decline.

The hiring in 1999 of former USC coaching
great John Robinson promised to inject a new
sense of enthusiasm into the program, and it did.
Las Vegas's proximity to Southern California only
added to fan interest in a coach who had led the
Los Angeles Rams to several winning seasons,
including the NFL play-offs, and USC to the national
championship. Robinson's best year at UNLV was
2000, when the team went 8–5 and beat Arkansas
handily 31–14 in the Las Vegas Bowl. Robinson
had, for him, mediocre seasons after that, and he
finally departed in 2004. Even though his glory
days were over, Robinson reinvigorated the program. He drew national attention, including ESPN
coverage, and raised the program's stature enough
to attract the interest of Utah's talented offensive
coordinator Mike Sanford, who became the head
coach in 2005.

While UNLV football featured some great
coaches over the years, it also fielded some great

UNLV DEFENSIVE BACK JAMAAL BRIMMER IN ACTION. UNLV
ATHLETICS DEPARTMENT

players. By 2004, more than seventy Rebels had played in the NFL, including such stars as quarterback Randall Cunningham (Philadelphia Eagles), running backs Ickey Woods (Cincinnati Bengals) and Mike Thomas (Washington Redskins), and wide receiver Keenan McCardell, who played on the Buccaneers' 2003 Super Bowl team. There have been many others as well: Glenn Carano (Dallas Cowboys), Nate Turner (Saints, Chargers), Henry Bailey (Steelers, Jets, Bills), Talance Sawyer (Vikings), David Hollis (Seahawks, Chiefs), and Jerry Reynolds (Giants, Cowboys, Bengals) are just a few members of this distinguished group.

Over the years, football has been both a blessing and a curse to the UNLV athletics department. Nothing brings a campus community closer together than a winning football season. This was especially important at UNLV. In the Tarkanian years, the basketball team carried the school's banner nationally in the spring, but it was always exciting when a Ron Meyer, Tony Knap, Harvey Hyde, or John Robinson team could carry the campus in the fall. Football, however, was much more expensive to operate than basketball or any other sports program. Moreover, football required reserving many scholarships for only male athletes. This created problems after Congress passed the Education Amendments Act of 1972, whose Title IX mandated the appropriation of equal amounts of money for men's and women's sports. For several reasons, UNLV lacked the revenue to rectify the situation. The Rebel Booster Club's disassociation from UNLV in 1982 and the national recession of that period did little to help. At the time, the athletics departments at both UNLV and UNR experienced significant revenue shortfalls. Much of UNLV's problem stemmed from Rebel football, which had never been highly profitable. As noted earlier, in the 1980s and early 1990s President Maxson eased the cash-flow problem in athletics temporarily by allowing the Thomas & Mack Center and the Sam Boyd Silver Bowl to supplement departmental shortfalls with their surpluses—a process halted by interim president Guinn in 1994.

The Department of Athletics faced a perennial budget deficit, which football did little to ease. For example, despite winning the Big West Conference championship in 1994, the program lost almost $1.4 million. This occurred after cuts reduced football's 1993 budget from $2.6 million to $1.9 million in the following year. With further cuts anticipated, UNLV obviously would be unable to compete with the big California schools and other campuses in the region for talented prospects. Losing seasons in the mid- to late 1990s did little to increase television exposure and fan loyalty. Compounding the problem was the decline of the Runnin' Rebels after Tarkanian's forced resignation in 1991 and the loss of millions of dollars in TV revenues and other sources of income.

Lack of revenue and Title IX obligations forced athletics directors from Bill Ireland to Mike Hamrick to limit the expansion of men's sports and divert more money to women's programs. Men's gymnastics, originally coached by Jan Van Tuyl, was an early casualty of the Title IX and budgetary problems. In its place, Ireland added women's basketball in 1974, volleyball in 1978 (discontinued in 1980), and swimming in 1978. Brad Rothermel began women's softball (1980) and resumed volleyball for two years (1984–85). His various successors started soccer (1998) and golf (2001) and resumed volleyball again in 1996. To accommodate the requirements imposed by both Title IX and limited revenues, the department eliminated men's track and after initiating wrestling in 1976, dropped it seven years later.

These problems continued into the twenty-first century. Three decades after Congress approved Title IX, UNLV was still not in compliance. It was not just the disparity in coaches' salaries and other gender-equity issues but the number of athletes themselves. In the 1996–97 school year, UNLV's full-time student enrollment was 52 percent female and 48 percent male (by fall 2004 it was 54 percent to 46 percent). Even though Title IX required the gender distribution of student athletes to match this percentage, the 1997 figure was 63 percent male and 37 percent female. The gap was embarrassing, especially to Carol Harter, the school's first woman president. Determined to correct the situation, Harter and athletics director Charles Cavagnaro announced a five-year plan to comply with the law to avoid possible NCAA sanctions and lawsuits from women's groups.

UNLV's Gender Equity Committee submitted an initial report in 1996 detailing the school's progress. But the reforms were painful for football and other men's sports. The plan called for men, by 2001, to lose thirty-four roster positions, including ten in football, eight in baseball, three more in basketball and tennis, and five more in swimming. With additional funding under the plan, women gained approximately forty-one roster positions. While still far from the goal of 52–48 percent dominance over men, women were pleased with the progress, especially in scholarships. In 1998, when UNLV began women's soccer, the team had a full roster of twenty-five spots supported by twelve scholarships.

Like other colleges in the NCAA, UNLV struggled to achieve gender equity primarily because of football. In 1997 critics pointed out that if UNLV dropped the sport, its 115 players, and their numerous scholarships, the school would immediately have 13 more female athletes than male. The shift in scholarships would then be even more dramatic—43 for the men compared to 91 for the women.

But there has been little sentiment for dropping football. Even though San Francisco State, Sonoma State, University of the Pacific, the University of Vermont, and Boston University abolished the sport, few on the UNLV campus favored killing what Cavagnaro called "an 85-scholarship gorilla."[12] President Harter also voiced her support for keeping the sport. Cavagnaro faced a daunting task in raising enough revenue to save football and continue progress on Title IX, especially after the Thomas & Mack and Silver Bowl subsidies to his department ended in the mid-1990s. After Cavagnaro's departure in 2001 and John Robinson's brief (2002–3) tenure, Mike Hamrick's job was to generate the millions necessary to supplement limited state appropriations, keep the department solvent, save football, and achieve gender equity.

Besides addressing gender issues and financial problems in an effort to strengthen its sports programs, the school also created a number of institutions and programs to honor and assist its student athletes. Creation of the UNLV Hall of Fame in 1987 helped realize the first goal. All of the great names from the past are there: Randall Cunningham, Elbert "Ickey" Woods, Sheila Tarr, Ricky Sobers, Reggie Theus, Misty Thomas, and Matt Williams, to name a few. In 2002 the Hall of Fame admitted one of its most distinguished classes when Rebel greats Larry Johnson, Greg Anthony, Stacey Augmon, and three-time Olympic gold medalist Lori Harrigan joined the exclusive club. Teams were also eligible, and the school honored a number of squads, allowing in players who may not have entered as individual standouts. Among the inductees in this category were the 1980 baseball team, the 1968, 1974, and 1978 football teams,

Nevada Southern's inaugural basketball team, its 1990 championship squad, and four others.

The UNLV Hall of Fame also honored great coaches and prominent athletics directors: Jerry Tarkanian, Tony Knap, Bill Ireland, Chub Drakulich, and Brad Rothermel. Leading staff members and support personnel have also been selected, among them Dr. Thomas Armour, Dave Pearl, and longtime team physician Dr. Gerald Higgins. UNLV has also used admission as a means of recognizing donors who contributed significantly to athletics programs, scholarship endowments, and facilities. Christina Hixson, Ernie Becker Sr., Bill "Wildcat" Morris, Tom Wiesner, Marilyn Redd, and others make up this group.

The Hall of Fame was not the only sports-related institution for UNLV student athletes. The growing presence of women's sports on campus and their dedicated supporters in the community encouraged the creation of the Women's Sports Foundation in 1989. This organization's purpose was to recognize and encourage excellence by women athletes in sports and the classroom. As associate athletics director Lisa Kelleher noted, the foundation's mission was "to raise funds for areas that may not fit into each sport's budget—such as post-eligibility scholarships, conference champion awards and sometimes even equipment" to help each student athlete achieve "the best possible results."[13] The foundation's efforts have been critical, considering that women now compete in the largest number of sports in school history.

But with so much interest and fund-raising still directed at men's sports, the women struggled to get support for their programs. The WSF came to the rescue on numerous occasions by supplementing regular budgets. With more than seventy-five members drawn from the community, alumni, and faculty, the WSF sponsored various events and fund-raising activities throughout the year, including a dinner that honored the Sportswoman of the Year. Past winners included such notables as Lori Harrigan, Linda Frohlich, Lorena Diaconescu, and Sunny Oh.

Of course, the obligations of student athletes to devote long hours to their sport and maintain good grades create problems not faced by other students. In an effort to help its athletes maintain high academic standards and graduate, UNLV established an academic support system in the 1980s that has been

(FROM LEFT): LANDRA REID, SI REDD, SENATOR HARRY REID, AND
MARILYN REDD AT THE DEDICATION OF THE MARILYN AND SI REDD
BASKETBALL OFFICES AT UNLV, 1993. UNLV ATHLETICS
DEPARTMENT

steadily improved. In 1994 the six athletics advisors housed in UNLV's Newmont Student Development Center moved into the new Donald W. Reynolds
Student Services Building. As the number of intercollegiate sports at UNLV
grew, the athletics department pumped more money into the hiring of tutors
and other support staff to help athletes excel in the classroom.

Student athletes are also more likely than the average student to be injured.
While a nurse and doctor have always been on campus or nearby since the
school's earliest days, the Claude I. Howard Student Health Center did not open
until 1988. Although UNLV's athletes had access to orthopedic surgeons as well
as other specialists, there was no on-campus facility for preventive medicine.
The debut of the Marilyn and Si Redd Sports Medicine Complex in 1996 was
another major advance for UNLV. Funded by a $5 million gift from the Redds,
the 8,500-square-foot facility offered athletes a range of equipment from sta-

tionary bicycles and treadmills to stair machines. Treatment tables for padding, taping, and bracing benefited many. The complex's aquatic room contained three aboveground whirlpools surrounding a ten-foot-deep pool for rehabilitative exercises, all designed to help athletes recover from injuries and prevent future ones.

Aside from safeguarding the athletes' health, offering scholarships, and honoring standout performers, UNLV has also emphasized education and service to prepare graduates for the challenges of life. In 1995 the university launched the CHAMPS (Challenging Athletes' Minds for Personal Success) program, which consisted of five major components. Two of the most important were the Commitment to Academic Excellence and the Commitment to Service. School officials designed the former to develop "an appreciation for learning" and ensure that student athletes earned their degree before leaving UNLV. This component emphasized the role of the athletics department's academic advisors and tutorial services, highlighted by the Academic Top Ten Program to honor athletes with high grade point averages.

The Commitment to Service proved to be almost as important. This initiative emphasized community outreach and encouraged student athletes to visit schools, hospitals, and other civic organizations. Recognizing that many younger students in the Las Vegas area regarded UNLV's high-profile male and female athletes as heroes, the Commitment to Service taught the athletes to view themselves as role models and to appreciate the importance of serving their community. Over the years, Rebel players participated in Nevada Reading Week, d.a.r.e. graduation activities, Toys for Tots, and other events. Working in conjunction with the athletics department's expanded community relations office, Rebel athletes became involved in a steadily growing number of events, including holiday food drives, the Santa Clothes Program for impoverished families run by the Las Vegas Rotary, and the Reading, Writing & Rebels program in local schools.

Clearly, over the last half century, NSU and UNLV athletes brought the campus and the community closer together. Whether through their service to the community's schools and hospitals or through the memorable moments they created on the court, the gridiron, the diamond, the track, the field, the golf course, and in the pool, student athletes and their coaches have done much to enhance the significance and prestige of UNLV. Their thrilling accomplishments sparked an enthusiasm for the school that helped its presidents raise millions to fund programs, buildings, and scholarships.

At the same time, athletics contributed dramatically to UNLV's heritage. The pioneering dedication of Chub Drakulich and Alice Mason, the amazing records of Jerry Tarkanian, the dominance of Lori Harrigan, the achievements and courage of Sheila Tarr-Smith, combined with the dazzling play of Reggie Theus, Larry Johnson, Randall Cunningham, and all the other greats have added a significant measure of glory to UNLV's legacy.

Epilogue

In 2006, as UNLV began preparing to commemorate the campus's 50th anniversary, it greeted a new president, David B. Ashley. Following the announcement of Carol Harter's resignation on January 27, regents moved quickly to have a new president on board by her departure on June 30. While there was debate on campus about the speed of the selection process, there was little doubt that, given the complexity of UNLV's operations and with a legislative session just seven months away, it was vital to give the new president a chance to use July and August to settle in and prepare for the school year. To be sure, the selection process was not without controversy: Faculty senate leaders complained about the composition of the search committee, the length of time faculty were given to question the finalists, and the weight that regents on the committee gave to faculty and student concerns. Tensions came to a head when regents on the committee voted to recommend Lieutenant General William Lennox Jr., the superintendent of the United States Military Academy at West Point. Most faculty on the committee, in the senate, and at public meetings had supported Ashley or Marvin Krislov, vice president and general counsel of the University of Michigan. But regents, citing the need to hire a president who would best serve the system's needs, preferred Lennox. With just a week or so until the entire board of regents voted on the proposal, faculty, along with some student leaders and staff, conducted a spirited campaign of resistance that soon convinced Lennox to withdraw. The issues were myriad and will not be revisited here. Suffice it to say that the general's lack of experience with graduate programs and other academic operations was a major obstacle to securing faculty support.

Regents then moved quickly to offer the position to Ashley, who was considered by many faculty to be the best qualified of the three. Ashley's academic credentials were impressive: After earning bachelor's and master's degrees in civil engineering and project management, respectively, from the Massachusetts Institute of Technology and another master's degree and a Ph.D. from Stanford, he went on to a distinguished career as a teacher and scholar, serving as a professor of civil engineering at MIT, the University of Texas–Austin, and later at the University of California, Berkeley before leaving in 1997 to become dean of Ohio State's College of Engineering. In 2001, he became executive vice chancellor and provost of the new University of California, Merced, where he played a key role in building and developing that school's infant campus. In choosing UNLV's eighth president, the regents picked someone who had experience at leading universities in all four major regions of the country. On July 1, 2006, Ashley took the helm at UNLV when it was well on its way to becoming a respected research university but still faced many challenging problems. Indeed, despite the two-decade emphasis on research and excellence, UNLV's enrollment-driven budget still required the university to admit many average students from the local school district and out of state. Raising admissions standards led to shrinking enrollments in 2006 and then budget cuts that temporarily slowed the march to excellence. At the same time, the need for another large classroom building and more parking garages, especially on the campus's south end, a cheating scandal in the dental school, growing problems in the orthodontics program and the Institute for Security Studies, and a host of other issues all required attention.

Dr. Ashley's presidency may well be a turning point in UNLV's traditional relationship with its parent institution. Within weeks of taking over, Ashley made it clear that, in contrast to the prevalence of conflict that had ofen marked

NEW PRESIDENT DAVE ASHLEY

relations between UNLV and UNR, he preferred to work in collaboration with UNR's new president, Milton Glick, and emphasize consensus in the policy-making process.

Despite all the challenges, the UNLV presidency was still an attractive position for Ashley. He knew that budget reform and increased funding would eventually solve most of these problems. He also recognized that the campus had come a long way since the 1950s and 1960s when Carlson, Moyer, Zorn, and Baepler struggled to raise enough money to construct essential buildings and provide barely adequate services.

Since its earliest days, the school's success has been tied to that of Las Vegas. In many ways, the rise of UNLV and Las Vegas are inextricably linked. Nevada Southern came into being once Las Vegans realized how gambling and resort tourism could boost their city. After the wartime boom in the 1940s, when the Strip was born and Fremont Street entertained thousands of troops and defense workers, Las Vegas's potential as a tourist mecca became obvious. As jobs multiplied and plans for new resorts appeared on drafting boards, population growth led the town to demand a college of its own.

Tax-conscious regents and northern legislators reluctantly agreed to establish an extension program and later a small campus to accommodate the few hundred high school graduates and teachers who wanted to live at home as long as possible while pursuing their degree. No one, not even the most starry-eyed booster, could have imagined what the next half century would bring for the city and its college at the south end of town. In the 1960s, Las Vegas grew into a city of 200,000 people on its way to becoming a metropolitan area of nearly 1.5 million by century's end. And the tiny desert campus grew with it. What regents and even local residents had expected to be little more than a junior college soon became an independent college, then a small university, and by the 1980s, a highly respected urban university with pretensions to greatness.

It never should have happened. After all, Las Vegas had no ocean, no river, no lake, no bayfront, and it claimed only one railroad. But a combination of factors made it the nation's fastest-growing metropolitan area from 1986 into the twenty-first century, and a series of college presidents tapped the power and wealth that accompanied the city's growth and fame to transform their dusty little campus into a substantial institution of higher learning. Unlike New York,

San Francisco, and other great cities, Las Vegas lacks the traditional temples of stone housing the famous museums, opera houses, and government palaces that stand as monuments to a city's glory. Here, in contrast, the Strip, with its Disneyfied architecture and maze of lights surrounded by endless suburbs of red-tiled roofs, symbolizes the city's accomplishments over the past half century. But the modern university that has grown up on Maryland Parkway is fast becoming another testament to Las Vegas's triumph. From a single building in 1957 the school has mushroomed into an impressive complex of more than a hundred buildings that is spawning new campuses around the valley.

Unlike so many new colleges whose aspirations went unfulfilled in their first half century of life, Nevada Southern exceeded all expectations. In 2007 residents have much to celebrate. Not only has Las Vegas surpassed the dreams of its most optimistic pioneer, but the town's little college in the desert is now on the verge of joining a select group of research universities. The credit for this unlikely event lies with the school's dedicated leaders, its faculty, its students, and, most of all, the people of southern Nevada.

The prophetic words of regent Silas Ross on that memorable St. Patrick's Day in 1957 when Nevada's Masons laid the cornerstone for Maude Frazier Hall ring louder today than ever before: "Our purpose is charted and, if we steer an even course the university will continue to grow in strength, value, and influence."[1] Of course, the university that Ross was referring to was the one based in Reno. Little did Ross and his audience realize that the fledgling college on Maryland Parkway would eventually become its own university and that the child would someday more than rival its parent.

CHAPTER ONE | THE BIRTH OF "NEVADA SOUTHERN"

1. *Las Vegas Review-Journal,* August 27, 1951, 3.

2. Ibid., December 27, 1951, 3.

3. Ibid., January 25, 1952, 7.

4. Ibid., July 14, 1954, 3.

5. Ibid.

6. Ibid., August 3, 1954, 2.

7. Ibid., August 15, 1954, 3.

8. Ibid., February 15, 1955, 3.

9. Ibid., January 30, 1956, 1.

CHAPTER TWO | DEVELOPING A CAMPUS

1. *Las Vegas Review-Journal,* February 2, 1975, "The Nevadan," passim.

2. Ibid., February 24, 1960, 4.

3. Ibid., May 20, 1962, 38.

4. Ibid.

5. Ibid., October 29, 1962, 17.

6. Skidmore, Owings, and Merrill, Architectural Planners, *Master Plan*

Report, Las Vegas Campus, University of Nevada, Prepared for the State of Nevada Planning Board and the University of Nevada (San Francisco, February 1963), 17.

7. William Carlson, "Academic Development, the Early Years," UNLV vertical file, Special Collections, Lied Library, 1.

8. Ibid.

9. Ibid., 2.

10. Ibid.

11. Ibid., 3–4.

12. Ibid.

13. Ibid., 5–6.

14. Ibid., 4.

15. Ibid., 3–4.

16. Ibid.

17. Robert W. Davenport, unpublished manuscript on the history of UNLV; see section titled "Under Reno's Thumb."

18. Carlson, "Academic Development, the Early Years," 5–6.

19. Ibid., 6–7.

20. *Las Vegas Review-Journal,* June 4, 1964, 3.

21. Charles Adams to author, telephone conversation, November 14, 2005.

22. Davenport manuscript; see section titled "The Moyer Years." See also James Deacon's April 23, 1997, interview with Davenport in the UNLV vertical file, Special Collections, Lied Library.

23. *Las Vegas Review-Journal,* April 12, 1965, 1.

24. Ibid.

25. Ibid., April 13, 1965, 5.

CHAPTER THREE | THE STRUGGLE FOR AUTONOMY

1. *Las Vegas Review-Journal,* December 20, 1964, 1.

2. Ibid., December 23, 1964.

3. *Las Vegas Sun,* August 10, 1966, 1.

4. "History of the Land Foundation," unpublished manuscript, UNLV Foundation Archives; see also *Statutes of Nevada,* 11, 1967, 1342–43.

5. The source for both maps is Skidmore, Owings, and Merrill, Architectural Planners, *Master Plan Report, Las Vegas Campus, University of Nevada, prepared for the State of Nevada Planning Board and the University of Nevada* (San Francisco, February 1963).

6. *Las Vegas Review-Journal,* May 9, 1965, 1.

7. Ibid., January 19, 1965, 2, 30.

8. Ibid., May 9, 1965, 1.

9. Jerry Crawford to author, letter and telephone conversation, March 7, 2005.

10. *Las Vegas Review-Journal,* May 9, 1965, 1.

11. Ibid., January 16, 1966, 1–2.

12. Ibid.

13. Ibid., January 17, 1966, 26.

14. Ibid., July 29, 1966, 13, 6.

15. Davis, McConnell, Ralston, Inc., *Development Plan, 1968–1978, Nevada Southern University* (Palo Alto, Calif., 1967), 33.

16. Ibid., 18.

17. Ibid., 20.

18. Ibid., 17.

19. Ibid., i.

20. *Las Vegas Review-Journal,* May 1, 1968, 25.

21. *Rebel Yell,* March 15, 1968, 1.

22. *Las Vegas Review-Journal,* April 15, 2002, 1B.

CHAPTER FOUR | THE END OF "TUMBLEWEED TECH"

1. *Rebel Yell,* February 14, 1969, 1, 4.

2. Ibid.

3. Ibid., March 14, 1969, 5.

4. Ibid., September 24, 1969, 1.

5. Ibid., 3.

6. *The Yell,* January 24, 1973, 1.

7. Ibid.

8. *Evaluational Committee Report of the Commission of Higher Schools of the Northwest Association of Higher and Secondary Schools, University of Nevada, Las Vegas,* May 19–21, 1970, 10.

9. Ibid.

10. Ibid.

11. *The Yell,* January 12, 1971, 1.

12. Ibid.

13. Ibid., December 21, 1971, 1.

14. Ibid., March 10, 1971, 1.

15. *Los Angeles Herald-Examiner,* May 2, 1973, 1; see also *Las Vegas Sun,* May 20, 1973, 1; *Las Vegas Review-Journal,* May 20, 1973, 1, and May 23, 1973, 17.

16. Roman Zorn interview with Robert Davenport, August 1995.

17. Donald Baepler telephone conversation with author, August 3, 2004.

18. *Las Vegas Review-Journal,* May 23, 1973, 17.

19. Baepler to author, conversation, February 10, 2005.

20. Richard O. Davies, *The Maverick State: Building the New Nevada* (Reno: University of Nevada Press, 1999), 252.

21. Ibid.

22. *Las Vegas Review-Journal,* July 4, 1982, 5B.

23. *The Yell,* November 20, 1973, 3.

24. Roman Zorn interview with Robert Davenport, August 1995.

25. *Las Vegas Review-Journal,* December 31, 1975, 13.

26. Ibid., February 8, 1976, 3.

27. Ibid., December 31, 1975, 13.

28. *The Yell,* February 27, 1974, 2.

29. *Las Vegas Review-Journal,* May 19, 1980, 12A.

30. *Las Vegas Sun,* February 7, 1979, 2.

31. Ibid., March 16, 1979, 1, 4.

32. Brock Dixon, "Remarks to the President's Cabinet," September 9, 1983, 1.

CHAPTER FIVE | LAYING A FOUNDATION FOR THE FUTURE

1. *Las Vegas Sun,* July 20, 1979, 11.

2. *Las Vegas Review-Journal,* July 20, 1979, B1.

3. Ibid.

4. *Las Vegas Sun,* August 29, 1979, 14.

5. Ibid., July 20, 1979, 11.

6. *Las Vegas Review-Journal,* August 27, 1980, B1.

7. www.unlv.edu, Barrick Scholarship Award.

8. *Las Vegas Sun,* August 27, 1980, B1.

9. *Las Vegas Review-Journal,* May 29, 1984, 4A.

10. Ibid.

11. Ibid., September 9, 1984, B1.

12. Ibid., December 4, 1988, 4B.

13. Ibid.

14. Ibid., August 26, 1981, B1.

15. *Las Vegas Sun,* March 22, 1982, A1.

16. *Las Vegas Review-Journal,* February 19, 1983, C1.

17. Ibid., January 18, 1983, 2B.

18. Ibid., January 20, 1983, 1F.

19. Ibid., April 16, 1983, 1B.

20. Ibid., July 21, 1983, A1.

1. *Las Vegas Review-Journal,* September 9, 1984, A1.

2. Ibid., September 5, 1986, B1.

3. Ibid., March 5, 1986, B5.

4. Ibid., May 13, 1986, B3.

5. Ibid., September 8, 1987, B3.

6. Ibid., January 12, 1990, 6C.

7. Ibid., July 25, 1985, 1D.

8. Ibid., April 6, 1985, 12A.

9. Ibid., October 5, 1989, B1; May 13, 1990, 3B.

10. Ibid., May 13, 1990, 3B.

11. Ibid., December 12, 1989, 10E.

12. Ibid., July 8, 1991, 1B.

13. Ibid.

14. Ibid., September 14, 1990, 6B.

15. Ibid.

16. *Las Vegas Sun,* October 3, 1990, 3A.

17. Ibid.

18. *Las Vegas Review-Journal,* November 30, 1990, 8B.

19. Ibid., January 9, 1990, 2B.

20. Ibid., November 26, 1987, 8B.

21. Ibid., July 18, 1989, B1.

22. Ibid., November 29, 1990, 6B.

23. *Las Vegas Sun,* November 20, 1990, B3.

24. *Las Vegas Review-Journal,* October 10, 1991, 1B.

25. Ibid., February 27, 1991, 1B.

26. Ibid.

27. Ibid., March 8, 1991, 3C.

28. Ibid.

29. Ibid., January 28, 1989, B2.

30. Ibid., March 2, 1989, 2C.

31. Ibid., June 22, 1990, 4A.

32. Ibid., December 29, 1991, 1A.

33. Ibid.

34. Ibid., September 23, 1986, 1D, 4D.

35. Richard O. Davies, *The Maverick State: Building the New Nevada* (Reno: University of Nevada Press, 1999), 266–67.

36. *Las Vegas Review-Journal,* May 15, 1994, 1B.

37. Ibid.

38. Ibid.

39. Ibid.

40. Ibid.

41. Carol Harter interview with author, September 1, 2004.

42. Ibid.

CHAPTER SEVEN | TURBULENCE AND REFORM

1. *Las Vegas Review-Journal,* July 6, 1994, 1B.

2. Ibid.

3. Ibid., June 24, 1994, 4E.

4. Ibid., June 23, 1994, 1B.

5. Ibid.

6. Ibid., August 18, 1994, 1A.

7. Ibid., August 18, 1994, 1A.

8. Ibid., October 11, 1994, 1B.

9. Ibid., October 23, 1994, 1B.

10. Ibid.

11. Ibid.

12. Ibid., November 7, 1994, 1B.

13. Ibid., May 16, 1995, 2B.

14. Ibid.

CHAPTER EIGHT | THE MARCH TO EXCELLENCE

1. *Las Vegas Review-Journal,* September 13, 1995, 3B.

2. Ibid., July 21, 1996, 1B.

3. Ibid.

4. Ibid., May 15, 1996, 4B.

5. Ibid.

6. Ibid., July 21, 1996, 1B.

7. Ibid.

8. Ibid., June 9, 1997, 1B.

9. Ibid., August 17, 2003, 1E.

10. Ibid., February 8, 2001, 1A.

11. Ibid., February 26, 1997, 1B.

12. Ibid., June 15, 1999, 1B.

13. Ibid., October 10, 2003, 5B.

14. Ibid., August 3, 1999, 8AA.

15. Ibid., August 28, 1999, 2AA.

16. Ibid., November 27, 1997, 2B.

17. Ibid., April 9, 1997, 1E.

18. Ibid., June 10, 1998, 3AA.

19. *Las Vegas Sun,* August 8, 2004, 3D.

20. See "Goals" on the WRIN Web site, http://www.unlv.edu/institutes/wrinunlv/.

21. *Las Vegas Review-Journal,* July 14, 1999, 4AA.

22. Ibid.

23. Ibid., July 30, 2003, 7D.

24. Ibid., July 1, 2001, 36A.

25. Ibid., August 15, 1997, 1B.

26. Ibid., July 23, 1996, 1E.

27. Ibid., March 29, 2001, 5C.

28. Ibid.

29. Ibid., May 1, 1996, 7B.

30. Ibid., December 27, 1996, 1B.

31. Ibid., January 5, 2000, 4AA.

32. Ibid., January 30, 2000, 6B.

33. Ibid., August 12, 1997, 2B.

34. Ibid., June 8, 2001, 1B.

35. Ibid., September 21, 2001, 2B.

36. Ibid., September 18, 2002, 1B.

37. Ibid., September 10, 2003, 2B.

38. Ibid., October 1, 1999, 1B.

39. Ibid., December 20, 2003, 1B.

40. UNLV *Magazine,* June 2004, 2, 28.

41. UNLV Planning Council, *The University of Nevada, Las Vegas, The Engaged Research University: Extending the Agenda, 2002–2007* (Las Vegas, 2002), 11.

42. Carol Harter interview with author, September 1, 2004.

43. Ibid.

CHAPTER NINE | STUDENT LIFE

1. NEVSO *News,* October 11, 1954, 1–3.

2. *Rebel Yell,* November 14, 1956, 2.

3. Ibid., October 9, 1958, 1.

4. Jerry Crawford to author, telephone conversation, February 10, 2005.

5. *Rebel Yell,* March 13, 1963, 1.

6. Ibid., September 13, 1960, 1.

7. *Epilogue* (1958), 73; *Rebel Yell,* November 13, 1963, 2.

8. *Rebel Yell,* November 17, 1966, 3.

9. Ibid., May 6, 1970, 1.

10. Ibid., April 14, 1965, 1.

11. *Las Vegas Review-Journal,* May 9, 1965, 1.

12. *Rebel Yell,* February 4, 1965, 2.

13. Ibid., March 10, 1965, 1.

14. Ibid., May 5, 1965, 8.

15. *Las Vegas Review-Journal,* October 16, 1966, 10.

16. *Rebel Yell,* May 5, 1965, 1.

17. Ibid., February 28, 1967, 3.

18. Ibid.

19. Ibid., January 12, 1967, 1

20. Ibid.

21. Ibid., December 17, 1968, 1.

22. Ibid., February 29, 1968, 2.

23. Ibid., February 27, 1969, 1.

24. Ibid.

25. Ibid., 3.

26. Ibid., September 22, 1966, 1.

27. *The Yell,* January 19, 1972, 2.

28. *Rebel Yell,* November 16, 1970, 1.

29. Ibid.

30. *The Yell,* April 20, 1971, 1.

31. *The Yell,* September 4, 1973, 1.

32. Ibid., March 21, 1973, 3.

33. Ibid., April 20, 1971, 7.

CHAPTER TEN | DONORS AND FOUNDATIONS

1. Leonard Goodall, "State of the University Address," August 31, 1982, n.p.

2. *Las Vegas Review-Journal,* October 5, 1980, 5c.

3. "The Early History of the UNLV Foundation," July 15, 1982, n.p., UNLV Foundation Archives.

4. "Report and Recommendations of the UNLV Foundation Development Committee," (1983), n.p., UNLV Foundation Archives.

5. Ibid.

6. Leonard Goodall, "State of the University Address," August 31, 1982, n.p.

7. Ibid.

8. "A+ Bang for Your Bucks on Campus," *Nevada Business Journal,* July/August 1991, 18.

9. Buck Deadrich, General Update (memo) to UNLV Foundation Board of Directors (1983).

10. Ibid.

11. "A+ Bang for Your Bucks on Campus," 17–18.

12. Ibid.

13. Ibid., 17.

14. Ibid., 20.

15. UNLV Foundation, *Annual Report, 1998–99,* 4–5, UNLV Foundation Archives.

16. *It's Academic* (Spring 2003).

17. Ibid.

18. UNLV Foundation, *Annual Report, 1996–97,* 5, UNLV Foundation Archives.

19. *It's Academic* (April 2002).

20. Ibid. (Spring 1998).

21. Ibid. (August 2002).

22. Ibid. (January 2000).

23. Ken Knauss and Richard Flaherty, written comments to UNLV Foundation, November 18, 2005.

24. *Las Vegas Review-Journal,* November 24, 1992, 1B.

25. UNLV Foundation, "Palladium Society Members" report to author.

CHAPTER ELEVEN | SPORTS

1. Confederated Students of Nevada Southern, *Epilogue 1958* (Las Vegas, 1958), 78.

2. Alice Mason e-mail to author, March 9, 2005.

3. Ibid.

4. *Las Vegas Review-Journal,* July 30, 1995, 1E.

5. Ibid.

6. Ibid.

7. Ibid.

8. UNLV *Rebel Tennis 2004* (Las Vegas: UNLV Athletics Department, 2004), 15.

9. UNLV: *2002–2003 Men's Golf* (Las Vegas: UNLV Athletics Department, 2003), 16.

10. Ibid., 18.

11. *2004 UNLV Basketball Guide* (Las Vegas: UNLV Athletics Department, 2004), 96.

12. *Las Vegas Review-Journal,* December 21, 1997, 1A.

13. *Rebel Softball: 2004 UNLV Softball Guide* (Las Vegas: UNLV Athletics Department, 2004), 42.

EPILOGUE

1. *Rebel Yell,* March 29, 1957, 1.

While any number of college histories served as guides for this study, the key reference work for anyone seeking background information about the state university's development is James W. Hulse, *The University of Nevada: A Centennial History* (Reno: University of Nevada Press, 1974), and Hulse with Leonard E. Goodall and Jackie Allen, *Reinventing the System: Higher Education in Nevada, 1968–2001* (Reno and Las Vegas: University of Nevada Press, 2002); especially see Goodall's chapter on UNLV. Also helpful was Robert W. Davenport's unpublished 65-page manuscript covering Nevada Southern's development up to 1968, particularly the sections on the 1950s. John R. Goodwin's *Diamond in the Desert: The University of Nevada, Las Vegas and William F. Harrah College of Hotel Administration* (Las Vegas: Sundance Publishing, 1992) is best for its coverage of the hotel college. But an even better source is Jerome and Florence Vallen, *The Right Place* (Las Vegas: Stephens Press, 2005). Several short papers also provided some perspective. Of these, the most insightful was William D. Carlson's 1981 memoir, "Academic Development: The Early Days."

A number of articles also shed light on different aspects of the school's history. English professor Felicia Campbell, who joined the faculty in 1962, penned a short remembrance, "A Toast to Times Gone By," *Inside Out* 7, no. 1 (December 1985): 12. Alumnus and now communications professor Laurie Fruth provided a useful overview of student life in "Oh, the Things We Did," *UNLV Maga-zine* (1997), 10–13, 16–17. Aside from the student newspaper, another revealing source for student activism in the sixties is Dona Gearhart, "The 1960s Revolu-tion: *UNLV* Style," *Nevada Historical Society Quarterly* 40 (Summer 1997). I found a lot of useful information in *UNLV* Office of Information Services, *Campus Update* (1971–1979), which became first *Inside Out Update* (September 12, 1979–March 27, 1985) and then *Update* (April 1985–December 2002). *UNLV Magazine* (1992–2005), a biannual publication of the Alumni Association, and *Inside UNLV* (Fall 2001–Fall 2005) also contain many instructive short articles on a wide variety of topics, often written by insiders. See, for instance, Carol Harter, "Shadow Lane's Official Opening Signals New Era for *UNLV*," *Inside UNLV* (November 2004), and "Supporting Health, Education, and Research" (December 2004); John F. Gallagher, "Research Foundation Supports Economic Development," *UNLV Magazine* (Summer 2004); and Diane Russell, "Preschool Comes of Age," *UNLV Magazine* (Spring 2004): 17–18, 29. Especially useful for tracking philanthropy and new program agendas for private giving are the *UNLV* Foundation's newsletters, *Funds for Academic Excellence* (Summer 1983– Summer 1984) and *It's Academic* (Fall 1990–Spring/April 2004). Articles for later years can be found in the *UNLV* Foundation's section in *UNLV Magazine*.

For sports, aside from the minutes of meetings and correspondence within the athletics department, which mostly cover policy issues, the media guides for each sport are the best source for accurate information regarding the records of coaches, teams, and individual athletes. For policies regarding student athletes, see the annual reports of the *UNLV* Inter-Collegiate Athletic Council, 1971– present. A balanced analysis of the Maxson-Tarkanian conflict can be found in Richard O. Davies, ed., *The Maverick Spirit: Building the New Nevada* (Reno: University of Nevada Press, 1999), 248–70; Tarkanian provides an insightful memoir of his career in Dan Wetzel with Jerry Tarkanian, *Runnin' Rebel: Shark Tales of "Extra Benefits," Frank Sinatra, and Winning It All* (Champaign: Sports Publishing, 2005).

A variety of materials enabled me to piece together the chapter on student life. Two publications sponsored by the student government were particularly useful. The student yearbook, *Epilogue,* was helpful for the 1957–71 period. The best source for week-to-week events was the *Rebel Yell*, which, between its inception in April 1955 and the present, underwent several name changes. While the quality of coverage varies with the editor, the newspaper generally provides an accurate picture of student thinking on most issues. The universi-ty's orientation brochures and student handbooks are also worth examining.

Obviously, any university history must focus on leadership and the actions of campus heads. The presidential papers of Malcolm Love, Minard Stout, and Charles Armstrong are in Special Collections at UNR's Getchell Library; the correspondence of James Dickinson and William Carlson and the presidential papers of their successors can be found in Special Collections at UNLV's Lied Library.

Of course, presidential records offer only a glimpse of most stories and are more suited for writing detailed studies of specific topics. More beneficial for a general history of the school are newspaper accounts and interviews in which the presidents and other major spokesmen made specific statements to the press. Newspaper stories and oral interviews allowed me to quote the words of presidents and other participants, which enriched the text immeasurably. The *Las Vegas Review-Journal* and the *Las Vegas Sun* were the most useful, although the *Henderson Home News, Boulder City News, North Las Vegas News,* and *Valley Times* also informed this work. Regarding oral history, I relied on information gained from Robert Davenport's taped interviews with Presidents Moyer (April 1992), Zorn (August 1995), Maxson (May 1991), and William Carlson's widow, Marian (April 1992). I spoke for about an hour with Carol Harter on September 1, 2004, and briefly with numerous people, including Presidents Moyer, Baepler, and Goodall, who were knowledgeable about specific events. The full list appears with acknowledgments in the preface.

Perhaps the most important sources for this book were the hundreds of documents produced by the school and its various entities over the last five decades. Anyone interested in funding, enrollment trends, and other quantifiable data should see Office of Institutional Analysis, *Selected Institutional Characteristics* (1979–2004). For information relating to the UNLV Foundation, I sifted through the early correspondence of directors and trustees, located in the Foundation Building. For the Nevada Southern Land Foundation, I consulted the correspondence files for the years 1968–74, in Special Collections, which also contains the files of the Campus Fund Committee for 1955 and the Nevada Southern Foundation for 1962–68. Also helpful are the files of the Public Relations Office (formerly News and Publications), which contain news clippings, press releases, and other materials relating to virtually every event, building, and significant person in the school's history since 1955.

For more detailed coverage of programmatic and construction planning, see the relevant documents found on Lied Library's open shelves and in Special Collections. Some of the most important sources for these subjects are: Skidmore, Owings, and Merrill, Architectural Planners, *Master Plan Report, Las Vegas Campus, University of Nevada, Prepared for the State of Nevada Planning Board and the University of Nevada* (San Francisco, February 1963); Nevada Southern,

Southern Regional Division, *Self-Evaluation Report to the Northwest Association of Secondary and Higher Schools* (1964); Davies, MacConnell, Ralston, Inc., *Development Plan, 1968–1978, Nevada Southern University* (Palo Alto, Calif., January 1968); Commission on Schools, Northwest Association of Secondary and Higher Schools, *Evaluation Committee Report, University of Nevada, Las Vegas* (May 19–21, 1970, and April 16–18, 1980). Also of value are John Carl Warnecke and Associates and Planning Consultants, *Long Range Development Plan, University of Nevada, Las Vegas* (April 1978); UNLV Long Range Academic Planning Committee, *Twenty-five Years and the Future to Serve: An Academic Master Plan, University of Nevada, Las Vegas* (1982); UNLV Planning Council, *The University of Nevada, Las Vegas Premier Urban University: A Public Agenda for the Decade, 1996–2005* (1996); and *The University of Nevada, Las Vegas, The Engaged Research University: Extending the Agenda, 2002–2007* (2002), *Update to Academic Master Plan, 1998–2003* (1998), and *Comprehensive Master Plan: Executive Summary* (2003).

For Nevada Southern's plan to implement a degree program, see Faculty and Administration of Nevada Southern, *Proposal for Degree Granting Status and Degree Curricula for Nevada Southern, Southern Regional Division, University of Nevada, Las Vegas* (April 22, 1963). In some cases, presidential addresses are insightful about past accomplishments and future agendas; see, for example, Carol Harter's Tenth Annual State of the University address, *Covenant with Community* (September 9, 2004). Commencement day brochures periodically list all of the past recipients of honorary degrees and awards; for example, see UNLV Offices of Information Services, Central Services, and Registrar, *21st Commencement, University of Nevada, Las Vegas* (May 27, 1984) for the list up to 1984.

Other documents are significant for curricula, student services, general policies, and similar topics. See, for instance, the University of Nevada, *General Catalog* and *Graduate Catalog* (1951–66); Nevada Southern University, *General Catalog* (1966–70); and University of Nevada, Las Vegas, *General Catalog* (1970–2005). There are still copies of the UNLV *Schedule of Classes* for many semesters, beginning in 1969, on the open shelves of Lied Library; these provide an accurate glimpse of the range of course offerings for any given period in the university's history. Detailed information regarding services, organizations, clubs, and other student data for UNLV's early years can be found in *General Information Bulletin* (1969–72). There are also informative documents relating to a wide variety of subjects; among the many consulted for this book are: University of Nevada, Las Vegas, *Chicanos at UNLV* (1973); UNLV College of Arts and Letters, *UNLV Year of the Arts, 1986–1987* (1986); UNLV Center for Business and

Economic Research, *The Economic Impact of the Thomas & Mack Center and the Sam Boyd Stadium in the Las Vegas Economy* (June 19, 1997).

Maps of the campus in different eras are scattered in planning documents, Land Foundation correspondence, and even student brochures, class schedules, and faculty/staff telephone directories. The best collections of photographs can be found in the UNLV files in Special Collections, Lied Library, although the Department of Athletics and the Office of Public Affairs also have historical photographs.

The amount of source material relating to UNLV's development is immense compared to the relatively meager body of scholarship on the subject. There are literally hundreds of topics in need of research. It is to be hoped that the size and quality of the secondary literature on UNLV fifty years from now will ease the task of writing the school's centennial history.

Hecht, Chic, 222

Hein, Anne, 202

Helldorado Parade, 215

Hendershott, Staci, 311

Henderson, Greg, 300

Henderson (Nev.): chemical industry in, 9; laboratory facilities at Basic High School, 8; and land for Southern Nevada campus, 11; retirement of, 45; and Sam Boyd Silver Bowl, 130

Hendrix, Holbert, 7

Herbst, Jerry, 254

Herr, Helen, 12

Hester, Kelley, 309

Higgins, Gerald, 321

Higher Education Facilities Act of 1965, 57

high-tech industries, 43, 109, 199, 257, 273

Hillel, 219, 220

Hispanic students, 70, 247–48

Hixson, Christina, 187, *188*, 260, 281, 307, 308, 321

Hobbs, Gwynn, 301

Hoffman-Meyers, Wendy, 315

Holder, Tom, 108

Holiday Casino, 80

Holiday Corporation, 120

Hollingsworth, Howard, 216

Hollis, David, 318

Homecoming, 250

Hoover Dam, 1

Hope, Bob, 265

Hopkins, Jim, 157

horseback riding, 291

Horton, Jeff, *188*, 317

hotel and motel management program: and Beam, 110; and Harter, 182; and Meek, 55–56; and Moyer, 62, 65, 66, 205, 287; and Zorn, 71, 74. *See also* William F. Harrah College of Hotel Administration

Houssels, J. Kell, Jr., 48, *48*

Howard, Linda, 201–2, 211

Howard Hughes Corporation, 284

Howard R. Hughes School of Engineering, 102, 114, 122, 251, 284

Howery, Wes, 222

Hribar, Tom, 226, 227, 229

Hug, Procter, Jr., 48, *48*

Hughes, Howard, 63, 65, 262, 267

Hughes, Mary V., 283

Hugo, Jonathan, 314

Hull, Karen, 301

Hull, Trena, 298

Hulse, James, 233

Humphrey, Neil, *48*, 79, 84, 91, 227, 234, 235

Hunt, Anderson, 306

Hunter, Scott, 300

Huntley, Chet, 225

Hyde, Harvey, 143–44, 146, 295, 316–17, 318

Iacocca, Lee, *188*

Indian Research and Education Center, 207

INNovation Village, 191

Institute for Security Studies, 183, 326

Intercollegiate Athletics Council, 78, 165, 248

Intercollegiate Knights, 216

International Conference on Lasers, 125

International Gaming Institute, 190, 251, 270

International Gaming Technology, 308

International Institute of Modern Letters (IIML), 209, 211, 265

intramural athletics, 223

Invent the Future campaign, 286

Iotta Kappa Phi, 216

Ireland, Bill, *198*; as athletics director, 292–93, 315, 319; and football

program, 66, 82, 291–92, 315; and Rebel name, 247; support for school, 221; and UNLV Hall of Fame, 321

Irsfeld, John, 162, 163, 164

Jacka, Bart, 214

Jackson State College, 242

Jacobsen, Harold, *48*, 81–82

J.A. Tiberti Construction, 76

Jean Nidetch Women's Center, 251, 270

Jewish Federation, 219

Jewish Student Union, 219

Jim Rogers Field, 298

Johann, Alice, 311

Johann, Kenneth, 311

John C. Wright Hall, 45, 89, 240

John Paul II (pope), 220

Johnson, Dalron, 306

Johnson, Larry, 147, 305, 306, 320, 324

Johnson, Lyle, 216

Johnson, Lyndon, 57, 68, 225

Jones, Anthony, 306

Jones, Gary, 112

Jones, Jan, 307

Jordan, Pauline, 301

J. Robert Jennings Company, 107

Juanita Greer White Hall, *86*, 87, 140

Judy Bayley Theatre: bonds sold for construction, 70; and budget, 157; and building construction, 77, *77*, *78*; and Nevada Southern Foundation, 54, 65–66, 77, 99; and Oldenburg sculpture, 80; private donations for, 277; and Romito, 129; student productions, 222; and Zorn, 84

Kadlubek, Vaune, 315

Kane, Walter, 262

Katz-Yarchever, Edythe, 271, *271*

Lynch, Kristin, 315
Lynn Bennett Early Childhood Development Center, *192*, 193, 270

Macintosh, Mrs. Louis, 239
Mack, Jerome: donations of, 103, 179, 278, 279; honorary doctorate of, 265; and land acquisition, 51; and Nevada Southern Land Foundation, 48; photograph of, *104*; and UNLV Foundation, 255. *See also* Thomas & Mack Center
Mack, Joyce, 264, 268, *268*, 286
Mack family, 179, 279
Maffie, Mike, 260, *261*, 284–85
Malcolm, Lydia, 215, 245
Malmquist, Ola, 299
Mann, Stuart, 191, 269
Mardi Gras, 249
Margaret Elardi Nevada Valedictorian Scholarship Program, 118–19, 275
Marilyn and Si Redd Sports Medicine Complex, 280, 322
Marion, Shawn, 306
Marjorie Barrick Museum of Natural History, 88–89, 92, 217, 271, 281
Marlon, Anthony, 285
Marnell Family, 177
Marshall, Art, 218–19
Martin, Tony, 233
mascots, 244, 245, *246*, 247
Mason, Alice, 289, *290*, 291, 299, 324
Massimino, Rollie, 149, 158, 159–61, 165, 295, 305
Master Series, 127, 129
Maude Frazier Hall: in 1958, *23*; addition to, 32; capacity of, 221; Carlson's office in, 70; naming of, 24; rattlesnakes in, 28; and sculpture location, 80; as student gathering place, 223, 240;

under construction, 17–18, *17*, 329
Maxson, Robert: and admission standards, 43, 126–27, 142; and athletics, 143–50, 152, 158, 159–60, 174, 175, 294–95, 318; background of, 115–16; and budget, 157, 158–59, 200; and campus development, 89, 110, 114, 131–40, 205; and Environmental Protection Agency, 63–64; and faculty travel funds, 87; and football stadium, 130, 131; and fundraising, 116–21, 134–35, 150, 152, 204, 283; and Goodall, 113, 114; Harter compared to, 171; and honorary doctorates, 266; and library, 133–34, 196, 260; and operating expenses, 156; photographs of, *116, 128*; and program initiatives, 101, 120, 121–25, 139, 142, 150, 151; and public relations campaign, 143; and research focus, 124, 125, 134, 143, 152; resignation of, 151–52, 153, 162, 211; and scholarship program, 118–20; and science and technology programs, 43; and summer sessions, 35; and Tarkanian, 143, 144–50, 153, 162, 295; and term of service, 210; and UNLV Foundation, 116, 120, 136–38, 150–51, 159, 204, 262, 263; vision of, 47
McBride, Jack, 110, 111
McCardell, Keenan, 318
McCarran Airport, 17
McCarran International Airport, 191
McCarthy, Eugene, 68
McCarthy, Jane, 270
McCullough, Joseph, 169
McDaniel, Al, 144
McDermott, Paul, 77, 83, 235, 243
McDonald, Shan, 298
McDougall, Matt, 300

McFadden, Leo, 216
McKinley, Greg, 261
McLeod, Wayne "Red," 12, 29–30
McNab, Warren, 181
Meacham, Melissa, 315
Mead, Margaret, *224*, 225
media: and Baepler, 85, 87; and basketball program, 82–83, 147, 148, 149, 150; and Carlson, 41; and class shortages, 42, 43; and Dickinson, 20; and *Flashlight,* 107; and Guinn, 158; and Harter, 166, 174, 199; and hotel management school, 56; and Maxson, 137, 151, 152; and Moyers, 46; and Nevada Southern budget, 30–31; and quality of school, 141, 142–43; and student political activism, 228, 230; and University Code, 112; and Zorn, 69, 80–81
Medicaid funds, 179–80
Meek, Howard, 55, 56
Mello, Don, 110
Meyer, Ron, 82, 247, 315–16, *316*, 318
MGM Grand Hotel, 49, 80, 253
MGT of America, 201
Midby, John, 120
Midtown UNLV, 278
Miethe, Terry, 164
Millennium Scholarship Program, 200
Miller, Bob, 138–39, 158–59, 178
Miller, Elburt, 306
Miller, Henry, 226
Miller, Regina, 301
Miller, Sherman, 255
Mills, C. Wright, 226
Mills, Rebecca, 171, 205
minority students: and admission standards, 127, 201; and Baepler, 90; and William S. Boyd, 269; and mascot, 244, 247; and Maxson, 121; and Zorn, 69–70
Mintenko, Mike, 315